SOCIAL RADICALISM IN URDU LITERATURE

Social Radicalism in Urdu Literature

A Study of Gender Issues and Problems, 1930–1960

RAJWANTI MANN

MANOHAR
2011

First published 2011

ISBN 978-81-7304-890-6

Published by
Ajay Kumar Jain *for*
Manohar Publishers & Distributors
4753/23 Ansari Road, Daryaganj
New Delhi 110002

Typeset by
FineCurve Computers,
Meerut City 250002

Printed at
Salasar Imaging Systems
New Delhi 110035

Contents

Tables

Illustrations

Preface

As a student of history, it is natural to explore various sources for a deep understanding of social trends, customs, and practices as they affect the lives of men and women. For the last two decades, literature has been increasingly used as a source by historians and other scholars to throw light on various social issues. Owing to my interest in social history and having a good knowledge of Urdu, I decided to study gender issues and problems through the medium of Urdu literature.

This study is based on the fiction of Urdu writers of the Progressive era. I took the help of translated versions in addition to the original works in Urdu. I acknowledge my debt to all those whose translations from Urdu to English have been used partially or wholly in this book. I am grateful to all other scholars whose writings helped me gain a better understanding of the subject from different angles.

Many individuals have been helpful in the course of this study. First of all, I express my deepest gratitude to my guide, Prof. Kamlesh Mohan, for her guidance, help and encouragement at every stage of this study. Her suggestions and comments enabled me to sharpen my argument.

I am grateful to Prof. Parduman Singh for his valuable suggestions and much needed inspiration. I extend my sincere gratitude to Prof. O.P. Grewal (retd.), Department of English, Kurukshetra University, Kurukshetra for his useful comments.

I am indebted to Prof. Mushirul Hasan for his perceptive comments, which helped me broaden my canvas. I am also grateful to Sh. K.L. Zakir for his constant encouragement and valuable guidance, which I sought time and again. I am obliged to Sh. Gobind Thukral, a senior journalist, and to Sh. V.S. Godara, Regional Director, Ministry of Health and Family Welfare, Government of India for extending their help during my time at IIAS, Shimla.

I am especially thankful to Dr J.S. Dhanki and Dr Surinder Singh of the Department of History, Panjab University, Chandigarh, for their constant encouragement and support.

In the course of my research, I incurred a debt of gratitude to a number of institutions. It is my pleasant duty to acknowledge the cooperation extended to me by the staff of Haryana Urdu Akademi, Panchkula; Indian Institute of Advanced Study, Shimla; National Archives of India, New Delhi; Haryana State Archives, Panchkula; Haryana Civil Secretariat Library, Chandigarh; Central State Library, Chandigarh; Library of Indian Council of Social Science Research, Chandigarh; Panjab University Library and the libraries in History and Urdu departments, Panjab University, Chandigarh. I extend my thanks to the staff of the Nehru Memorial Museum & Library, New Delhi; Ghalib Academy, Delhi; Anjuman-i-Taraqui, Delhi; and Ajoy Bhawan, Delhi.

My heartfelt thanks go to my husband, Sh. M.S. Mann, for his cooperation and help at all stages. I am also thankful to my son, Prayas, and daughter, Shiksha, for their patience and understanding during the time I was immersed in the preparation of this book.

1 December 2009 RAJWANTI MANN

Abbreviations

AIPWA	:	All India Progressive Writers' Association
AIWC	:	All India Women's Conference
CLO	:	Chief Liaison Officer
CRO	:	Central Recovery Office
DIB	:	Director, Intelligence Bureau
DIG	:	Deputy Inspector General
HSA	:	Haryana State Archives
ICA	:	International Council on Archives
ICHR	:	Indian Council of Historical Research
IIAS	:	Indian Institute of Advanced Study
INC	:	Indian National Congress
IPC	:	Indian Penal Code
ITC	:	Isabella Thoburn College
MEO	:	Military Evaluation Organisation
NAI	:	National Archives of India
NMML	:	Nehru Memorial Museum & Library
NWFP	:	North West Frontier Province
NWP	:	North West Provinces
PEN	:	Poets, Playwrights, Editors, Essayists and Novelists (Federation)
PWA	:	Progressive Writers' Association
PWM	:	Progressive Writers' Movement
UP	:	United Provinces
USA	:	United States of America

Glossary

Abbu–Amma	:	Father–Mother
Angare	:	Spark or ember
Anjuman	:	Society or association
Apa	:	Elder sister
Badchalani	:	A woman of loose character
Bahisthi Zevar	:	A book in Urdu by Shaukat Thanavi
Bahu	:	Daughter-in-law
Baithak	:	Outer room of the house, especially for men
Bade	:	Elders
Bhabi	:	Brother's wife, sister-in-law
Biradari	:	Brotherhood
Boski silk	:	A kind of fine cloth
Brahman	:	Hindu Priestly caste
Burqa	:	Veil or covering
Chacha	:	Father's younger brother
Chadar andazi or *Chadar dalna*	:	Putting a sheet on a woman (widow) who was given into a man's protection.
Chait	:	First month of the Hindu lunar calendar
Chapatti or *Roti*	:	Bread
Chaprasi	:	Peon
Chauk	:	Courtyard, also a mark made by a *nain* (barber's wife) depicting planets
Chhatar	:	Umbrella
Choli	:	Blouse, jacket
Churidar pyjama	:	Pair of tight close fitting trousers
Daftar	:	Office
Dai	:	Midwife, who is generally a *dhanak* or sweeper by caste

Darmian	:	In the middle
Devi	:	Goddess
Dharma	:	Duty, obligation
Duppatta	:	Scarf used by women to cover the upper body
Fakir	:	Medicant, saint
Fatwa	:	Order issued by a religious body
Fun	:	Skill
Gandharva	:	A kind of marriage requiring only mutual agreement
Garbhadan	:	To conceive, be pregnant
Ghar	:	House
Ghungat	:	Veil
Got or *Gotra*	:	Clan
Guru Granth Sahib	:	Holy book of the Sikhs
Gur	:	Jaggery
Hartal	:	Strike or work stoppage
Harijan	:	A scheduled caste
Jacha	:	Woman who delivers a child
Jachaghar	:	Room or place where a woman delivers child
Janeo	:	Sacred thread worn by the upper castes
Jati	:	Caste, creed or race
Jhagra	:	Amount of money paid by a man to the husband of the woman with whom he eloped
Joru	:	Wife
Kajal	:	Antimony, lampblack
Kamasutra	:	An ancient Indian classic on love and sexuality
Kanyadan	:	Gift of the virgin
Kanyashulka	:	Bride price
Karao or *Karewa*	:	A form of marriage in which both parties consent to co-habit, and devoid of elaborate ceremonies, practised among tribes that allow widow remariage
Kartik	:	Eighth month of the lunar calendar (October–November)
Khandan	:	Lineage

Khat	:	Clothes, ornaments, and other items supplied by the bride's parents to the bridegroom among Muslims
Khatoon	:	Gentlewoman or lady
Khatri	:	A Hindu caste
Kirars	:	Term used for the Aroras
Klarkni	:	A clerk's wife, also used for a female clerk
Kulta	:	Woman of bad repute
Kumari	:	Virgin
Kurta	:	A shirt
Kusumba	:	Herb used to dye clothes
Lagan	:	A document containing the date and number of baratis expected in marriage agreed upon
Lakshman rekha	:	Line of control, line that is forbidden to cross
Lathi	:	Stick
Lawan	:	Hymns of the fourth Sikh Guru, sung by women during Sikh wedding
Lehanga	:	A long skirt or petticoat
Magh	:	Ninth month of the Hindu lunar calendar (January–February)
Mahabharata	:	Great epic of the Bharata dynasty
Mahila	:	Woman
Manjhale	:	Between older and younger
Malida	:	A cake made of milk and sugar
Mardana	:	Men's area
Masail	:	Issue or concern
Mattar pulao	:	A dish of rice and peas
Maulvi	:	Muslim priest
Mazhabi	:	Sweeper caste among Sikhs
Muklawa	:	Clothes and jewels given to a wife when her husband goes to fetch her from her parent's house after a period of one to three years from the date of marriage
Mullah	:	Muslim religious leader
Naherna	:	Instrument used by a barber to cut nails, etc., or a nail parer

Nawabzadi	:	Daughter of a nawab
Naujawan	:	Young man
Nikah	:	Muslim wedding
Niyoga	:	Custom of marrying a issueless widow to the younger brother of her deceased husband to get a son
Pandal	:	A temporary shelter or shed
Palki	:	Palanquin
Panigrahan	:	To give the bride's hand in the bridegroom's hand to mark their union
Pao	:	One-fourth of a kilogram
Parkarma	:	To go around the *Guru Granth Sahib* four times
Phere	:	Circumambulate the sacred fire during the Hindu rite of marriage
Pili chitthi	:	A notice written on paper smeared with turmeric, announcing the wedding date
Posh	:	Tenth month of the Hindu lunar calendar (December–January)
Parayadhan	:	Wealth belonging to another
Pulao jarda	:	Rice dish
Pundit/purohit	:	A learned man, Brahman
Purdah	:	Veil, covering
Purusha	:	Inner strength of a man
Rahu, Ketu	:	Two planets in Hindu mythology
Rujhanat	:	Attitude
Shadi	:	Marriage
Shakhsiat	:	Personality
Salwar	:	Pair of loose trousers
Sanskar	:	Good values/rituals
Sardar	:	A common prefix to the names of Sikhs
Sati	:	Immolation of a widow on her husband's funeral pyre
Ser	:	Two pounds in weight
Shanti	:	Peace
Shastra	:	Sacred book of Hindus
Shlok	:	Sanskrit verse

Shudra	:	Lowest of the four categories of Hindu society, or labouring caste
Suhagpura	:	Amount of dower fixed in Hoshiarpur, Punjab according to the bridegroom's pecuniary position at the time of the betrothal or wedding
Swadeshi	:	Use of indigenous goods and services
Swaraj	:	Self-government or self-rule
Syed	:	A high caste among Muslims
Triachilatar	:	Male view of a woman's special ability to get her demands accepted
Taraqui/ taraqqui	:	Progress, advancement
Thappa	:	Hand prints made on either side of the outer door on the occasion of a marriage or the birth of a son
Ustani	:	Female teacher
Veshya	:	A woman who sells her body for money, prostitute
Varna	:	Four categories of Hindu society, constituted on the basis of hereditary or traditional occupation or job
Varshulka	:	Bridegroom's price
Zadid adab	:	New literature
Zamindari	:	Land tenancy rights granted to local feudal lords
Zar	:	Wealth
Zamin	:	Land
Zenana	:	Women's area in the house
Zuhr	:	Midday

Introduction

The use of literature to explore and understand the past is not new. The spread of new, radical ideas in the twentieth century was a chief feature of the contemporary world. Mushirul Hasan argues that although literature cannot bring about significant changes, it can nevertheless illuminate aspects of our collective existence often left untouched by political and economic practices.[1] In India, popular awakening and social reform in the twentieth century was based on the dissemination of certain values and attitudes, followed by the establishment of institutions through which these new ideas were propagated further. Contemporary Urdu literature forcefully articulated these radical values and attitudes.

To examine the depiction of society in literature (both poetry and prose) and to adequately assess the progressive element of literature, particularly aspects relating to gender issues, is a difficult task. In India, the progressive trend in poetry started earlier than in fiction. Ghalib may be regarded as a powerful progressive voice, who introduced new vistas of human experience in poetry. Hali raised specific social issues in his poems and made the link between socially relevant ideas and poetry more direct and palpable. Firaq and Josh were vital links connecting society and poetry, and they paved the way for great poets like Iqbal and Faiz. The study of poetry as a form of literature requires considerable time and effort. It is a formidable task. In this book, I have chosen to concentrate on fiction, which I found more manageable because herein society is mirrored more directly and clearly.

The analysis of Urdu fiction requires a lot of hard work. The prose narratives of the writers who participated actively in the socio-political movements of the first half of the twentieth century offer a rich and

1. Mushirul Hasan and M. Asaduddin (eds.), *Image and Representation: Stories of Muslim Lives in India*, New Delhi, 2000, p. 1.

illuminating representation of historical events and the general state of society. Although several studies have been based on literature as a source material, a study devoted to an analysis of the portrayal of society in contemporary Urdu literature has seldom been attempted. A review of the published works shows that the literature available in Urdu has not received the serious attention it deserves. For example, *Social Transformation and Creative Imagination* (1984) edited by Sudhir Chandra has drawn attention to the role of literature in understanding social reality. In his article, 'Literature and Colonial Connection', Sudhir Chandra examines 'colonial consciousness' through an analysis of contemporary literature. *Social Consciousness and Polity* (1987) edited by Iqbal Narain and Lothar Lutze deals with the early nationalist and progressive writings in Maharashtra. Politics and literature in post-colonial India (as seen by some contemporary Hindi writers) included a sharp critique of orthodox Hinduism and a rejection of its irrational elements. This is evident in the writings of Mulk Raj Anand. Sulochana Rangeya Raghav's study, *Sociology of Indian Literature: A Sociological Study of Hindi Novels* (1987), analyses the deep concerns of novelists in examining social problems and challenges. The book covers ten selected Hindi novels of the post-Independence period.

Ralph Russell, in his *The Pursuit of Urdu Literature* (1992), surveys various phases of classical poetry, the literature written as a reaction to British rule in the period 1857–1927, and focuses on the period from the 1920s onwards. The last portion of the book describes the Progressive Writers' Movement (PWM) and the major writers associated with it. Some other works have appeared on this theme in Urdu, but as this language does not enjoy wide readership, they have not reached many serious readers.

Thus a review of the available works shows that there is enough scope for a full-length analytical study of Urdu literature from the 1930s to the 1950s. I found it a worthwhile project because many more new sources that were not earlier accessible are now available to the researcher.

In this book, I have endeavoured to show how literature can be helpful to historians in understanding the portrayal of social issues and problems, though literature cannot be taken in its literal form as a testimony to the existence of social evils. It was only during the twentieth century that literature became a subject as well as a source for historical analysis. Theodore Zeldin, an Oxford historian, argued that truth can be better discovered in 'free history' otherwise known as fiction. Under the impact of Western education and influenced by Marxism, communism, and socialism, some intellectuals challenged the traditional role of literature in India. The young and socially conscious writers diverted their pen from sentimental romanticism and religious matters to an examination of social problems. It has been rightly pointed out that in the earlier period 'Indian literature since the breakdown of classical culture has had the fatal tendency to escape from the actualities of life. It has tried to find a refuge from reality in spiritualism and idealism.'[2]

The progressives argued that literature should be taken out of the priestly cloak and brought into the closest touch with the common people. *Angare*, a collection of ten short stories in Urdu by progressive writers was published in 1932 and created an uproar. This forced the UP government to ban the book. The writers whose stories were included in the volume were influenced by communism and were extremely radical in temperament.

In 1936, an All India Progressive Writers' Association (AIPWA) was established in Lucknow. Munshi Premchand in his presidential address declared:

> The literature that is being produced today is mostly of a stoical, mystical and romantic type, which is doing more harm than good. There is a great need for the evolution of popular literature, which is in close contact with the naked realities of life. . . . It can no longer be considered as mere amusement. . . . We want a literature which may produce in us a movement, change and restlessness.[3]

From among the galaxy of the progressive writers I have selected those who were influential in forming the Progressive Writers'

2. Ralph Russell, *How Not to Write the History of Urdu Literature and Other Essays on Urdu and Islam* (an extract from the manifesto of the Indian Progressive Writers' Association, London, 1935), New Delhi, 1999, p. 1.
3. 'To Protect Literature from Conservatism: Writers Protest Against Repression of Thoughts', *Tribune*, 15 April 1936.

Association (PWA), namely Sajjad Zaheer, Rashid Jahan, Saadat Hasan Manto, Krishan Chander, Ismat Chughtai, and Rajinder Singh Bedi. These writers supported PWA and dealt with the bitter realities of life boldly and sensitively. They focused on social problems, injustice, gender inequality, as well as the relationship between these issues and economic and political exploitation under colonial rule. Among them, Sajjad Zaheer, Rashid Jahan, and Ismat Chughtai belonged to UP, while Saadat Hasan Manto, Krishan Chander, and Rajinder Singh Bedi belonged to Punjab. My focus, thus, remains confined to these two states.

The book has been divided into nine chapters. In the first chapter, an attempt has been made to connect history and literature. In the second chapter, I have discussed the position of women, particularly issues like infanticide, child marriage, and widow remarriage. In the third chapter, I trace the factors leading to the formation of the PWM such as the emergence of progressive ideas in the United States and Europe, the evolution of Marxian ideology, the impact of the Russian Revolution, the awakening among the younger generation and their frank expression of views regarding all social evils, and the formation of various writers' associations.

The fourth chapter discusses the formation of the AIPWA, its aims and objectives, the founder writers of PWA, and their supporters and associates. The biographical sketches of some eminent progressive writers, such as Sajjad Zaheer, Rashid Jahan, Saadat Hasan Manto, Krishan Chander, Rajinder Singh Bedi, and Ismat Chughtai are presented and their writings have also been covered briefly.

In the fifth chapter, the custom of *purdah*, its evolution and influence and the attitude of the progressive writers to this practice have been discussed, as also the rituals, taboos, and superstitions concerning pregnant woman, attitudes towards the female child, infant mortality, conditions and care of pregnant woman, and an analysis of Urdu stories reflecting these issues.

In the sixth chapter, the focus is on the essentiality of marriage, age of marriage among various castes, match-making, various forms of marriage, wedding ceremonies, and dowry. In the second part of the chapter, the proportion of widows in Punjab and UP among different castes is examined and issues like the condition and status of widows and the custom of widow remarriage have also been taken up.

The seventh chapter focuses on the constituents of sexuality, attitudes of males and females towards it, and the radical thoughts of progressive writers as depicted in their short stories.

The eighth chapter describes the agonies of women during Partition (1947), their uprooting, the loss of families, and the incidence of rape and abductions.

In the ninth and last chapter, I evaluate the significance of contemporary literature in providing an intimate glimpse into society in addition to what we can learn from various conventional sources of history.

1

Theoretical Approaches to Literature and History

Words denote something specific and, at the same time, connote something different. They reflect the dialectics of the particular and the universal through which an understanding of reality is sought. Things at one level seem so bound together as to suggest the unity of all phenomena. Infinite particularity appears at another level.[1] These diverse pulls are reflected in words. It is in the understanding of the subtle interplay between the emerging social consciousness of different collectivities and the 'objective' structure dictated by the needs of the state, and the social processes reflected in the contradictory impulses in the political sphere, that a study of literature could be extremely useful.

Before proceeding further, it is essential to know the meaning and significance of the word 'literature'. The Latin word from which it is derived, *littrerae*, was apparently exclusively applied to what we now call *belles lettres*. It would be a good thing if the term today were restricted exclusively to the written or printed word. But for a century or so, this term was applied to various arenas of human activity—to records, to catalogues, and to tendentious works of every kind.[2] One way of dealing with this puzzle is to define literature as everything in print. Edwin Greenlaw has argued that nothing related to the history of civilization is beyond our province. According to Greenlaw's theory and also to the practice of many scholars, literary study has become not merely closely related to the history of civilization but indeed is also identical with it. Such study is literary only in the sense that it

1. Sudhir Chandra, *Social Transformation and the Creative Imagination*, Delhi, 1984, p. 17.
2. Ford Madox Ford, *The March of Literature*, London, 1947, p. 14.

is concerned with printed or written matter, necessarily the primary source of most history. Undoubtedly, nobody should be forbidden to enter any area that he or she likes and there is much to be said in favour of cultivating the history of civilization in the broadest terms. But still the study ceases to be literary. The study of everything connected with the history of civilization crowds out strictly literary studies. All distinctions fall, extraneous criteria are introduced into the study of literature. Consequently literature is judged valuable only insofar it yields results for this or that adjacent discipline. The identification of literature with history is a denial of the specific methods of the field of literary study.[3]

Social and political disturbances throw up many important issues, that demand a close scrutiny and often call for a radical change. Whatever separation may have existed between literature and politics earlier, this distinction is largely demolished in such turbulent and fluid situations. Literature, in its different forms, becomes a key factor in mobilizing the minds of people and in preparing them for change. In such situations, 'literature' definitely becomes an important source for many historians. It is not sufficient to say that history cannot be literature. Sometimes history itself can take on a literary quality. Actually, whether history is considered literature or not depends entirely, on the animation, perspicacity, insight, incisiveness, poetic quality and the personality of the writer. The quality required for the production of literature is simply that of a personality of wide appeal. Art is the highest form of communication. The more attractive the personality making the communication, the wider and deeper will be its appeal. The quality of literature, in short, is the quality of humanity. It is the quality that communicates between man and man the secrets of the human heart and the story of our vicissitudes.[4]

Literature may be defined as the representation of life through the medium of language. The writer tries to communicate his conception of life, the life as he sees it, as he observes it, as he feels

3. Rene Wellek and Austin Warren, *Theory of Literature: A Seminal Study of the Nature and Functions of Literature in all Its Contexts*, n. p., 1948, p. 20.
4. Ford Madox Ford, op. cit., p. 15.

it, and as he deals with it. Indeed, human life is the basic raw material for the creation of literature by the writer. Human hopes and aspirations, human joys and sorrows, human progress and regress, human greatness and degradation, human virtues and vices become the stuff of his writings. Literature not only expresses the culture and feelings of the people but also as a reflection of their hopes and aspirations, anger and resentment, it is possibly the best key to an understanding of resilience and change.[5]

So we can say that literature is a record of what men have seen in life and what they have thought and felt about its different aspects.

The nature of literature emerges most clearly under the referential aspect of the meaning of words. The statements in a novel, in a poem, or in a play are not literally true; they are not logical propositions, but even then they seem to convey information about actual happenings. The same information may appear in a different form in a book of history or sociology. A character in a novel differs from a historical figure or a real-life figure. He is made up only of sentences describing him or those that have been put into his mouth by the author. He has no past, no future, and sometimes no continuity of life. Even an apparently realistic novel—the very 'slice of life'—is constructed according to certain artistic conventions. And yet it does not mean that literature is far from the truth. Literature has to be truth oriented, although this truth may have to be discerned through by a very sensitive, alert, and critical reading of the form in which it is embodied in a literary work. Who will deny the power of the writings of Bankim, Tagore or Premchand in articulating the lived experiences of a whole era or in shaping the social consciousness or the voice of Saadat Hasan Manto in describing the trauma of Partition.[6] His focus on the realities of life is so sharp that a historian will do well to treat his work as an important means for understanding what was really happening during the traumatic days.

To understand the relationship between literature and society is

5. Iqbal Narain and Luther Lutze, *Literature, Social Consciousness and Polity*, Delhi, 1987, p. vii.
6. Ibid.

not an easy task. It calls for an alert awareness of different issues. These issues are not easily tackled.

Outwardly, literature is concerned with beauty, and inwardly it is related to the welfare of the people and focuses on the truth of their experience. Man is a social animal and he is also the creator of literature. A writer cannot avoid society while creating literature. The norms and values of different societies are reflected in their respective literatures, and this can be useful in highlighting regional and geographical differences. However, men and their societies all over the world have some elements in common that help them understand and appreciate the literature of different regions and periods.

The writer is not restricted by the boundaries of countries and ages. His creative imagination can cross every limit. He can portray eternal themes in his writings. And yet literature, first and foremost, is a record of the lived experiences of people belonging to a particular period in a particular region, so it also embodies the specificities of historical circumstances. It is a product of society as it develops through history. 'It is an integral part of the entire culture tied by a tissue of connections with every other element in the culture.'[7]

The social influence of literature is very broad. Every prevailing system of social organization, including the class structure, the economic system, the political system, dominant ideas, beliefs, and emotions, the sense of the past and the present, the myths and aspirations of the people, and the realities of life influence literature. That is why there is a marked difference between the literature of the present and that of a century ago. The earlier literature laid great stress on ethics and morality, but modern literature stresses the realities of life as they are, even if these do not fit into a conventional model of ethics. It has also become more materialistic in approach. It defines human actions as related to economic and social factors. In this context, Syed Fazle Rab's comment is apt:

Literature differs from one nation to another, and from one social system to another. Every society has its own norms of behaviour as well as different problems and anxieties. Each society also sets some kind of goal. A country

7. Syed Fazle Rab, *Sociology of Literature: A Study of Urdu Novels*, New Delhi, 1992, p. 2.

like India, which is based on secular and democratic ideals, provides different themes and content to literature in a comparison to the literature of a communist country like China, where there is no freedom of speech and expression. Thus, literature develops under different social, political, and economic conditions, but the kind and quality of literature depends on the conditions of the society.[8]

Literature is also influenced by scientific developments and inventions. Science provides new thoughts and new directions. Scientific developments have made the world smaller. An incident in one part of the world affects the whole world. Literature reflects all the changes that take place in the arena of culture on account of these scientific developments. It is a symbolic expression of the social reality existing at a particular time. Literature also affects the existing norms and behaviour of people. It changes the attitudes and aptitudes of people and stimulates the masses to revolt against outmoded ideas. It motivates individuals to know themselves as well as others. The writings of Rousseau and Voltaire created a climate of opinion that ultimately led to considerable turmoil, culminating in the French Revolution in France. Marx, Gorky, and Tolstoy prepared the people to overthrow the tsarist regime and brought about a revolution in Russia. Likewise in India, literature played an important role in spreading the nationalist ideology and class consciousness.

The question about the role of literature in transforming society has a long history. In his famous dictum, Aristotle remarked, 'Poetry is more philosophical than history, since history relates things which have happened, poetry such as might happen, the general and probable.' So one may say that literature is more general than history. However, the specific degree of generality shifts from work to work and from period to period.[9] A novelist can teach us more about human nature than a psychologist. Fiction reveals the introspective life of the characters. One might argue that the great novels are source books for many psychologists or that they are case histories (that is, they are illustrative and typical examples). It is sometimes argued that truth in literature should be the same as truth outside of literature, that is,

8. Ibid., p. 3.
9. Wellek and Warren, op. cit., p. 32.

systematic and publicly verifiable knowledge. But among the arts, literature specifically seems to claim truth not so much through the verifiability of the specific details or through their systematic arrangement as through the view of life presented therein. The truth of literature seems to be the truth in literature. The writer is not the discoverer but the persuasive purveyor of the truth.[10] Interfacing creatively with other human disciplines, literature makes space for articulating a variety of experiences and voices and brings to light the interconnections between different strands of life and thought.[11]

Literature is a social institution, using as its medium language that is undoubtedly a social creation. Traditional literary devices are social by their very nature. There are conventions and norms that could have arisen only in society. Literature represents life, and life is in large measure a social reality. The poet or writer himself is a member of society and possesses a specific social status. Literature has, therefore, a social function or use, which is an integral aspect of its very mode of existence.

A writer in giving expression to his experience and projecting his total conception of life would invariably reflect the life and events of his own time. He becomes a representative voice of his age and society. Explaining this point, Rene Wellek has remarked:

> The question, how far literature is actually determined by or dependent on its social setting, on social change and development is one which in one way or another, will enter into all the three divisions of our problems: the sociology of the writer, the social content of the works themselves, and the influence of literature on society. Since every writer is a member of society, he can be studied as a social being.[12]

Munshi Premchand, the master storyteller, and Sarat Chandra Chatterjee, Bengal's outstanding fiction writer, both stressed the social function of art.[13]

History is a record of the past. The English word 'history' has

10. Ibid., p. 95.
11. Mushirul Hasan and M. Asaduddin (eds.), *Image and Representation: Stories of Muslim Lives in India*, New Delhi, 2000, p. 1.
12. Wellek and Warren, op. cit., p. 96.
13. Hasan and Asaduddin, op. cit., p. 2.

almost the same meaning as the Greek word *istoria*; it means 'that which we come to know as a result of an enquiry'. But the German word *Geschichte* has three meanings: the things that have happened; the activity by which we can come to know them; and the narration of what we have come to know.[14] In this way, we can say that history refers to the deed, the story of the deed, and the procedure adopted for telling the story, which makes it possible for the storyteller to recount what has really happened.

Why do we want to know about the past if it is as Gibbon said 'little more than the register of crimes, follies and misfortunes of mankind'. What shall we gain by keeping a record of this kind in any detail or with any accuracy? Why should scholars toil and sweat to recover the details of these follies and deeds ?[15] To these questions we may reply that an accurate and reliable record of the past may provide a clue to what is happening in our own times and may help us in understanding our present problems. There is something to be learnt from history that cannot be learnt from physics or psychology. Therefore, it can be said that we read history for at least three reasons. First, we may find pleasure in knowing what really happened to someone, somewhere, and at some point of time in the past. Second, we may find a useful solution to a complicated issue by studying history. Third, which is, in fact, an extension of the second reason, history may help us know what we should do. History is never more important than when it is a question of how to make the future. We study history, wrote Collingwood, 'in order to see more clearly into the situation in which we are called upon to act'.[16]

History is an expression of a people's pride in the past. Obviously 'there can be no formulae in history, because no formulae apply to human affairs'.[17] Nevertheless, by studying history 'We understand the causes of the religious, moral, political, social and economic environments in which we live and we consider that understanding to be quite as important and quite as educational as training in [the]

14. K.B. Smellie, *Why We Read History* ?, London, 1947, p. 7.
15. Ibid.
16. Ibid., p. 8.
17. A.F. Pollard, *Factors in Modern History*, 3rd edn., n. p., 1948, p. 5.

method of expression or the understanding of men's physical environment.'[18]

History is a continuous process of interaction between the historian and his facts, an unending dialogue between the present and the past. One can view the past and arrive at an understanding of it only through the eyes of the present. The historian is of his own age and is bound to it by the condition of his human existence. The historian belongs not to the past but to the present. Professor Trevor-Roper tells us that the historian 'ought to love the past'.[19] However, the basic function of the historian is neither to love the past nor to emancipate himself from the past, but to master and understand it as the key to the understanding of the present.

History is not only a record of the past but is also progressive. People who struggle, say, to extend civil rights to all or to reform penal practice or to remove the inequalities of race and wealth are consciously seeking to do just these things. They are not consciously seeking 'progress' to realize some historical 'law' or hypothesis of progress. It is the historian who applies his hypothesis of progress to their actions and who interprets the actions as progress.[20] Progress is an abstract term and the concrete ends pursued by mankind arise from time to time out of the concrete course of history. It is the crux of objectivity in history.

'History is ruthless and fiercely objective, it has no idols, no darlings. The only idol of history is truth. For a historian, it is very important that he constantly questions the past. You have to love the past to write history but this love does not have to be blind. True love understands and only relentless questioning can lead to understanding,' remarked V.N. Datta, a noted historian, at a lecture at the Department of History, Panjab University. 'History can never be written with preconceived notions. It has to be a scientific, holistic, independent enquiry into the past. The historian has to cleanse himself of all biases and then undertake the task of writing history',[21] he added.

18. Ibid., p. 11.
19. E.H. Carr, *What is History?*, London, 1961, p. 25.
20. Ibid., p. 117.
21. *The Tribune*, Chandigarh, 11 September 2001.

Gyanendra Pandey maintains that the relationship between history and memory has always been an unstable one—more so perhaps than historians have acknowledged. Modern memory is above all archival, and we speak so much of memory because there is so little of it left. Indeed, Pierre Nora, a French scholar, speaks of a new historical memory based on increasingly institutionalized sites of memory. There is some force in the argument. The face-to-face communities of peasant society may be in decline, and may have disappeared in many places, but other communities of shared and inherited cultures bound by common memories and rituals continue to have a real existence in the form of memory.[22]

With the spread of nationalism and the modern state, new sites of memory have been established. So it is not incorrect to suggest that history itself appears in the form of a memory based on some privileged sites of archives. In other words, the world today is populated not only by the 'historical memory' of various groups dependent on archives, museums, flags, and publicly funded celebrations, but also flooded with the mythical histories of nations and states, histories that are themselves an institutional 'site of memory' locked in a circular and somewhat parasitical relationship with other, more obvious *lieux de memoire*. This 'memory history' is surely one of the distinguishing marks of this age.[23]

Gyanendra Pandey writes, 'There has been a decisive shift from the historical to the psychological, from the social to the individual, from the concrete message to its subjective representation.'[24] Memory has become the discourse for writing new histories, and memory as a commentator on society and societal issues helps in rewriting history. It broadens the basis of history. We find that much of the diversity and specificity of our lives and times is reflected in our contemporary literature. In addition to the traditional sources and facts of history, the use of literature as a source can help us in writing history with much more depth and subtlety of perspective. The domain of history is much bigger than any other subject. It includes the histories of

22. Gyanendra Pandey, *Remembering Partition*, Cambridge, 2001, p. 8.
23. Ibid., p. 9.
24. Ibid., p. 11.

diverse traditions and practices that once shaped people's lives, and these traditions and practices continue to have a significant life of their own. Literature is the best possible means for engaging with and encountering these traditions and practices.

In this age of sophisticated literary theories, the historian has drawn close to literary scholars. The latter have challenged the traditional historian's raw material. A new survey of universal knowledge reveals that the historian carries his inquiries beyond both written and printed matter. For some historians, literature has acquired a preponderance over other modes of history. Lionel Gossman and M. Taylor Pyne, professors of French at Princeton University, have thrown light on the problematical relation between literature and history.[25] These two disciplines are likely to discover new ways in which each can assist the other.

A growing number of historians have realized that fiction writers can contribute substantially to an understanding of the past. Sir Walter Scott who wrote historical novels widened the scope of history. In his novel, *A Passage to India*, E.M. Forster showed a profound sensitivity to the problem of racial division that affected Indo-British relations. V.N. Datta stresses the need for flexibility by striking a balance between narrative and analytical approaches.[26] There are some other sources that can be used as evidence for reconstructing history. Manto's stories on the tragic events of the Partition cannot be overlooked in writing the history of the Partition. Social history is incomplete without considering the fictional works of major contemporary writers.

The institutional boundaries between history and literature can be challenged by showing that the historical discourse is subject to the same kind of analysis as any other discourse. The categories of literature also have a history. Literature as a social institution, and above all as a medium of instruction, provides better representation and is amenable to historical analysis. Literature cannot be considered as constituting an aesthetic realm that is altogether irrelevant to the historian. Theodore Zeldin, an Oxford historian, argues that truth can be discovered only in 'free history', otherwise known as fiction.

25. Shelley Walia, 'History No More Authentic than Fiction', *Tribune*, Chandigarh, 19 March 2000.

26. Ibid.

The past treated as the sum total of actual facts and happenings has now been turned into a text that is needed, interpreted, and analysed. Historians are nowadays more concerned with the contribution that they are making to the shaping of a society in a particular mould and inculcating in the new generation rapidly. The attitudes, loyalties, and opinions appropriate to that society. The horizons of history are rapidly widening.

The need to add various sources to our attempts at (re)figuring history arose when scholars began to question the adequacy of official archival records in representing every facet of social transformation. Various political, social, cultural, and economic changes over the years were not necessarily captured in the official records.[27] In this context, James remarks,

> Community archives and persons in society came in to 'fill the gap' as best they could, though they were often left out of the mainstream. Oral history, which is increasingly being used as a documentary tool since 1940s, literature has come in to its full form in finalizing the shape of complete history. Even those periods of time in which the records appear most complete will usually be found wanting, the documents seldom adequately reflect the considerations that contributed to key decisions and very rarely betray the candid opinions of events and people with whom the principal actors worked.[28]

It is evident that literature is a good source for writing and understanding history. It reveals society sensitively and insightfully. Contemporary society and polity during the period under study will be discussed in the next chapter.

27. Ndyoi Mutiti, 'Re-figuring the Archives', *Comma,* International Council on Archives, Paris, 2002, p. 201.
28. James E. Fogerty, 'Oral History as a Tool in Archival Development', *Comma,* International Council on Archives, Paris, 2002, p. 207.

2

Contemporary Society and Polity

After the disintegration of the Mughal Empire, the socio-political situation in India was favourable for the conquest of the country by a well-organized, united, and economically and militarily more advanced foreign power. The Marathas broke the power of the great Mughals. The Afghans broke Maratha power, and while all were struggling against all, the British rushed in and were enabled by circumstances to subdue them all. A country divided not between Muslim and Hindu but between tribe and tribe, between caste and caste, a society based on an equilibrium resulting from a general repulsion and constitutional exclusiveness between all its members, such a country and such a society were, it can well be surmised, destined for conquest. Although India had been conquered many times, the earlier conquests had led to a change in political regime only. They did not affect the basic economic structure of society in a radical manner.

The British conquest of India was of a different type. It was the conquest by a modern nation that replaced feudalism by a modern bourgeois capitalist society. It was socially, politically, economically, and culturally stronger than a feudal nation. It was imbued with a high sense of patriotism and nationalism. It had a highly integrated social order under one political regime and a single economic system. That is why throughout British history, one hardly comes across Britons who betrayed the interests of the British nation in India in contrast to hundreds of Indians—princes, generals, and merchants—who went over to the British and assisted them in dominating India.[1] The British operated from a position of strength derived from

1. A.R. Desai, *Social Background of Indian Nationalism*, Bombay, 1975, p. 318.

European rationalism and presented themselves as heirs to and offspring of that discourse. So they negotiated from their vantage point with a clarity of purpose and determination that their native opponents could hardly match.[2]

Indian society experienced a qualitative structural transformation during British rule, which led to a different path of development. British rule initiated some basic changes in the social structure of Indian society, although to serve its own interests.[3] The British transformed the social setting in India. The British conquest released forces that kindled a democratic urge among Indians. One of the most remarkable manifestations of this transformation was the changed attitude towards women. The subjection of Indian women in the pre-British period was rooted in the social and economic structure of society. Birth determined the status of an individual in society. The disabilities of a woman arose from the fact that she was born a woman. This inferior social status of women was further cemented by religious beliefs and rituals. The condition of women was, however, not uniform in all parts of the country but was very diverse just as Indian society was highly stratified. Some castes followed the custom of dowry while others followed that of bride price.

Most rural women in Punjab and in the United Provinces[4] (now UP) were constantly and almost exclusively engaged in agricultural tasks and processes.

Table 2.1 shows that nearly 85 per cent of the population lived in rural areas and the bulk of this population was engaged in various agricultural activities. The participation in labour work by the wives of middle and marginal peasants in family-owned farms and wage work by women among the landless lower strata of agricultural society was invisible.[5] They also performed various tasks such as cleaning

2. Indu Banga and Jaidev (eds.), *Cultural Reorientation in Modern India*, Shimla, 1996, p. 36.
3. Desai, op. cit., p. vii.
4. *Gazetteer of India*, Ministry of Information & Broadcasting, Faridabad, vol. 1, 1964 (cited hereafter as *Gazetteer of India*, vol. 1, 1964), p. 525.
5. A.M. Shah, B.S. Baviskar and E.R. Ramaswamy (eds.), *Social Structure and Change: Women in Indian Society*, vol. 2, New Delhi, 1996, p. 14.

TABLE 2.1: PERCENTAGE OF RURAL AND URBAN POPULATION, 1931–61

Year	% of rural population to the total population	Variation	% of urban population to the total population	Variation
1931	88.01	–0.81	11.99	+0.81
1941	86.14	–1.87	13.86	+1.87
1951	82.71	–3.43	17.29	+3.43
1961	82.03	–0.68	17.97	+0.86

and plastering the house, bearing and rearing children, cooking, milking cows and buffaloes, spinning, sewing and mending clothes, agricultural labour, embroidery of clothes and shoes, etc. All these activities, although of the utmost importance, were regarded in the census as 'no work at all', and a very large proportion of women engaged in these activities from down to dusk were treated as 'non-working dependents'. The rule was that the products of economic utility, in the form of commodities sold in the market, alone were to be treated as workers.

The legal and political system in India was based on the principles of individual equality and contractual freedom of the individual. But the wife was not treated as an autonomous individual and was conceived of as the moral and religious half of the husband, who was viewed as her superior. It did not admit in principle all inequalities based on birth, sex, caste, or community, but in practice the denial of autonomy to a woman in accordance with traditional norms persisted. The struggle to get this principle realized progressively in different spheres of life had to be organized. For the large majority of small farmers and landless labourers, agriculture had always been a family-based activity. This presumed the interdependence of the two sexes on terms set by patriarchal norms. The means of ensuring such interdependence was marriage, which was a precondition to successful agriculture. The male preference among rural societies revealed the desire for sons rather than daughters because even if sons were often only of little use, they added permanent women to the households while daughters moved away to their affinal homes.[6]

6. T. Scarlett, Epstein, 'Culture, Women and India's Development, Social Structure and Change', in A.M. Shah, B.S. Baviskar and E.R. Ramaswamy

The neglect of females is best reflected in the sex ratios in Punjab.[7] As Table 2.2 shows, the sex ratio for children in the age group 0–5 was 959 : 1000. The proportion is higher than the proportion of males at birth, which was 894 : 1,000. It shows that either the record of female birth was defective or that males died at a greater rate than females up to the age of 5. The proportion in the next quinquennial drops to 859 per 1,000 males, which shows that female children suffered much during the plague epidemic of 1924. The general mortality rate is also higher among girls mainly because they stayed at home while their brothers spent much time outdoors. Table 2.3 shows the number of females in UP and Punjab in 1951.[8]

TABLE 2.2: PROPORTION OF FEMALES PER 1,000 MALES IN PUNJAB

Age	No. of Female in 1931
0–5	959
5–10	859
10–15	815
15–20	820
20–25	848
25–30	817
30–35	773
35–40	784
40–45	800
45–50	769
50–55	766
60–65	737
65–70	695
70 above	771

TABLE 2.3: NUMBER OF FEMALES PER 1,000 MALES URBAN/RURAL IN 1951

Province	Rural	Urban
UP	820	925
Punjab	812	870

(eds.), *Social Structure and Change: Women in Indian Society*, vol. 2, New Delhi, 1996, p. 37.

7. *Census Report*, Punjab, vol. XVII, Part 1, 1931, Lahore (cited hereafter as *Census Report*, Punjab, 1931), p. 156.
8. *Gazetteer of India*, vol. 1, 1964, p. 528.

Although the number of females in proportion to males was low, their condition was distressing. One cause of the low female sex ratio was that parents killed their girl babies because the marriage of a girl was too expensive for poor parents. The British first discovered female infanticide in 1789 in NWP,[9] but it continued until the nineteenth century. In 1870, the British passed a law to prevent female infanticide. By then, several other measures had started showing results.[10] It was also declared a crime.

The custom of *purdah* was also in vogue in Punjab and UP, not only among Muslims, but also among sections of Hindus. Whether the practice was introduced during the period of Kautilya or the Muslim invasions is not certain but, women were forced to adopt *purdah* due to socio-political reasons. Segregation of women was partially the direct result of Muslim conquest in the later stage. According to B.P. Majumdar, 'This institution was prevalent in northern India before the Muslim invasions.' Scholars like Kapadia and Ojha, on the other hand, argue that the practice of *purdah* among the Hindus was a defensive reaction adopted at the time of the Muslim invasions in order to protect their women.[11] The conquerors used to keep their own women in seclusion to hide them from the eyes of strangers. On the other hand, they were inclined to carry away any girl who caught their fancy and to make her the victim of their lust. So the people had to confine their women within their homes. Patriarchal family organization meant different and specific reasons for confining women within the home. Some feminist writers define patriarchy as a system that sustains male control over woman's productive and reproductive capacities.

The Hindus for whom *purdah* has no religious sanction found it comparatively easier to bring their women out of the home. For the

9. L.S. Vishwanath, 'Towards Conceptual Understandings of Female Infanticide and Neglect in Colonial India', *Proceedings of Indian History Congress*, Delhi, 1995, p. 606.
10. Ibid., 'Female Infanticide and the Position of Women in India', in A.M. Shah, B.S. Baviskar and E.R. Ramaswamy (eds.), *Social Structure and Change*, vol. 2, New Delhi, 1996, p. 181.
11. Quoted in Varsha Joshi, *Polygamy and Purdah: Women and Society Among Rajputs*, New Delhi, 1980, p. 87.

Muslims, it was not, easy. By this time, *purdah* had come to be regarded as obligatory and its observance a sacred duty.[12] The detrimental effects of *purdah* on the body and mind as well as on social progress were underlined by the leaders of women's movements.

Child marriage had been one of the principal evils under which women suffered more than men. Thanks to the efforts of Ishwar Chandra Vidyasagar, the Act of 1860 was passed, raising the age of consent for married and unmarried girls to ten. However, radical women continued criticizing child marriage. In 1929, the Child Marriage Restraint Act, popularly known as the Sarda Act, was passed raising the marriage age for girls to fourteen and for boys to eighteen.[13] Table 2.4 presents the mean age of marriage among various religious groups.[14]

Blunt's observations in the *Census of the United Provinces of Agra and Oudh, 1931* regarding child marriage among Hindus and Muslims is relevant:

> The marriage age is, generally speaking, lower among the lower Hindus but it is evident that there has been an all round increase in infant marriage since 1911 and 1921. This is slight in the case of the higher classes but is very marked among the lower castes. Among Muslims a similar state of affairs prevails. The reason for the lower marriage age, the lower we go in the social scale, is that the lower castes have clung to or have adopted the practice of

TABLE 2.4: MEAN AGE OF MARRIAGE OF MALES AND FEMALES AMONG RELIGIOUS GROUPS IN INDIA, 1891–1931

Religious group	Male	Female
Hindu	12.5	19.7
Jain	13.1	20.5
Muslim	13.2	21.0
Sikh	15.0	22.5
Christian	17.1	23.9

12. Ibid., p. 38.
13. Karin Deutsch Karlekar, 'A Return to Purity of Islam: Muslim Women and Social Reform in India, 1914–38', in *Breaking Out of Invisibility: Women in Indian History*, ed. Aparna Basu and Anup Taneja, New Delhi, 2002, p. 198.
14. *Gazetteer of India*, vol. 1, 1964, p. 540.

infant marriage in an endeavour to raise their social status as in the past the practice has been regarded as a badge of social respectability.[15]

Early marriage was common among the Hindus in eastern Punjab. Wedding were a costly affair. Hindus and Sikhs observed the rules of exogamy, which forbade marriage within the tribe, and that of endogamy, which permitted it only within the caste. A third social rule, which has been called the law of hypergamy, also existed. By this a father bestowed a daughter on a man of a higher social status than his own, although he might seek a bride for his son among a lower ranking group. This law rendered it difficult and costly for the middle classes to find husbands for their daughters or brides for their sons.[16]

The British considered several social customs barbaric and wished to eliminate them. With the cooperation of some Indian intellectuals, they abolished *sati*, the burning of a Hindu widow on her husband's pyre. However, they also realized that the encroachment on Indian social and religious institutions or practices might create resistance and prove dangerous for their rule. So they not only encouraged but also gently prodded those Indians who received their patronage to undertake some limited social reforms.[17]

Women suffered under the barbarous custom of *sati*. Even though *sati* had been abolished, widows were prohibited from remarrying. In 1856, the marriage of widows was legally permitted. There were more widows among the upper classes than among the lower castes. Here one factor was at work, namely, the attitude of the caste concerned towards child marriage and widow remarriage. The lower the marriage age, the more women were likely to become widows. Many agricultural and menial castes allowed the marriage of widows, preferably to the brother of the deceased husband, and it was among them that polygamy was commonest. The ceremonies of remarriage were much

15. *Census Report*, United Provinces of Agra and Oudh, 1931, vol. XVIII, Part I (cited hereafter as *Census Report*, United Provinces of Agra and Oudh, 1931), p. 305.
16. *Imperial Gazetteer of India*, Punjab, vol. I, Calcutta, 1908, p. 45.
17. Jamila Brijbhushan, *Muslim Women: In Purdah and Out of It*, New Delhi, 1980, p. 38.

simpler than those of marriage, and the woman never acquired the status that she had enjoyed in the house of her first husband, although the children of the second marriage were regarded as legitimate.[18] But some castes absolutely forbade widow remarriage. Some castes permitted but discountenanced it, and others accepted it as a rule. Recent movements by certain social reformers to popularize widow remarriage has so far not had any significant effect on the figures.

Childbirth, a very important event in the life of an Indian woman, was surrounded by a number of social rituals, taboos, and practices. In Hindu villages, a different attitude prevailed towards pregnant women. Several taboos were applied to an expectant woman. Until the 1920s, infant and maternal mortality rates in Punjab and UP were high. More female deaths were caused by plague and childbirth. But it is noteworthy that the female mortality rate from fever was always lower than that of males due to the fact that males in the course of their agricultural activities were more exposed to the vagaries of the weather. A very large proportion of women died as a result of the perils and troubles attending childbirth.[19]

The census reports recorded the details about the process of childbirth. Generally, a delivery was effected on the ground. In Hoshiarpur, delivery was said to be effected on the *charpai*. When the pain began, the woman was either made to kneel on all fours and to hold a basket, pillow, or some other article to her breast or she sat in the lap of the *dai*, who was generally a *dhanak* or sweeper by caste.[20] The *dai* pressed the expectant mother's knees against her loins and kneaded her abdomen with her hands. 'It also appears to be most universal in Hindus and Muslims to tell the mother that she has given birth to a one-eyed girl in order that the heat engendered by this ill news may force out the afterbirth quickly and the joy of having given birth to a male child may not retard it.'[21] 'If the infant was a boy, a

18. Ibid., p. 46.
19. *Census Report*, United Provinces of Agra and Oudh, 1931, pp. 242–3.
20. *District Gazetteer*, Gurgaon, vol. IVA, 1910 (cited hereafter as *District Gazetteer*, Gurgaon, 1910), p. 46.
21. H.A. Rose, *A Glossary of Tribes and Castes: Punjab and NWF Province*, vol. I, Lahore, 1919, p. 763.

brass dish (*thali*) was beaten to apprise the neighbours of the fortunate event, while if it was a girl an earthen vessel was broken.'[22] Among Muslims, birth observances included making the mother lie with her head to the north and her feet to the south. She thus faced Mecca and if she died in childbirth, she expired in the posture in which Muslims are buried.[23]

Infant and maternal mortality were high due to improper childbirth practices, unhygienic conditions of *jacha ghar*, lack of sanitation, and widespread infection. The general tendency to care more for the male than the female and the neglect of the female led to increased female mortality amongst Hindus, Muslims, and Sikhs of all castes.[24] According to the official computation, 'Infant mortality was highest under the age of one year than between one and five years. On an average, about one-fifth of the children born died before reaching one year of age, but during 1908 two-fifths of the number born succumbed to death. Malarial fever and bowel complaints due to defective nourishment, specially amongst the poor, were the prevailing causes of infant mortality'.[25]

Some improvements took place with the implementation of various schemes for the expansion of medical relief in the province. Under the programme of one dispensary for every 100 square miles of territory or for every 30,000 of population, 359 dispensaries were opened in Punjab between 1925 and the end of 1930.[26] The Lady Aitchison Hospital in Lahore and the Lady Reading Hospital for Women and Children in Simla gained much popularity. Women in the Women's Christian College in Ludhiana could qualify for appointment as sub-assistant surgeons. During 1920–30, 15 new hospitals for women were opened in various districts of Punjab, including Lahore. The number of hospitals and dispensaries rose from 583 in 1921 to 1,035 on the last day of 1930.[27] In 1931–2, 13

22. *District Gazetteer*, Gurgoan, 1910, p. 46.
23. Rose, op. cit., p. 763.
24. *District Gazetteer*, Amritsar, vol. XXA, Lahore, 1914 (cited hereafter as *District Gazetteer*, Amritsar, 1914), p. 27.
25. *District Gazetteer*, Gurgaon, 1910, p. 45.
26. *Census Report*, Punjab, 1931, p. 27.
27. Ibid.

girls were enrolled in medical colleges. The first few girls were admitted to the Christian Medical College in Ludhiana, since the Women's Christian Medical College was a part of it. The number of girls in medical colleges rose to 353 in 1941–2.[28] In UP, the lower mortality rate in the period 1921–30 can be ascribed to the increasing popularity of Western medicine and to the efforts of the Public Health Department.[29]

From the beginning of the twentieth century, the demand for women's education received wider support and social approval. A more congenial climate was created by writers who raised the woman's question more clearly and openly for a larger readership. This also included women writers and readers. There was a time when the education of girls in India had not only no supporters, but also attracted opponents. Lack of education among women was the main cause of their low status in the family. Female education had gone through all the stages—apathy, ridicule, criticism, and acceptance. The need for the education of girls as much as boys was recognized as an urgent need. Pioneering work began in this area. The growth of women's education in India was reflected in the fact that the number of girls attending schools rose from 1,230,000 in 1917 to 2,890,000 in 1937.[30]

TABLE 2.5: NUMBER OF GIRLS ENROLLED IN PUNJAB IN RECOGNIZED EDUCATIONAL INSTITUTIONS[31]

Recognized Institutions	1921–2	1931–2	1941–2
Art colleges	35	240	906
Professional colleges	33	29	562
High schools	2,966	12,263	17,887
Middle schools	10,982	28,135	55,401

Widespread poverty was a basic social evil. There was heavy indebtedness among agriculturists. The growing percentage of people dependent on agriculture is seen in the following census figures:[32]

28. Karuna Chanana, 'Schooling of Girls in Pre-Partition Punjab', *Indian Journal of Gender Studies*, vol. 4, no. 2, July–December 1997, p. 157.
29. *Census Report*, United Provinces of Agra and Oudh, 1931, p. 57.
30. Desai, op. cit., p. 278.
31. Karuna Chanana, 'Schooling of Girls in Pre-Partition Punjab', p. 156.
32. Desai, op. cit., p. 53.

TABLE 2.6: PERCENTAGE OF POPULATION DEPENDENT ON AGRICULTURE

Year	Percentage
1891	61.1
1901	65.5
1911	72.2
1921	73.0
1931	75.0

The increased dependence on agriculture resulted in the decline of dependence on industry.[33]

TABLE 2.7: PERCENTAGE OF POPULATION DEPENDENT ON INDUSTRY

Year	Percentage
1911	5.5
1921	4.9
1931	4.3
1941	4.2

Regarding Punjab, a relatively thriving agricultural zone, the Royal Commission on Agriculture observed: 'The Punjab figures indicate that 22.5 per cent of the cultivators cultivate 1 acre or less, 15 per cent cultivate between 1 and 2.5 acres, 17.9 per cent between 2.5 to 5 acres and 20.5 per cent between 5 and 10 acres.[34]

Excessive land revenue and commercialization of agriculture under British rule further led to the impoverishment of agriculturists. The British pioneered modern industry in India such as plantations for indigo, tea, and coffee and other industries like cotton, and jute mills in the nineteenth century. Industrialization was recognized as the main remedy for relieving the excessive pressure on agriculture.

Transfer of land from the cultivating owner to the non-cultivating owner, a merchant or a usurer did not result in any improvement in the plight of agriculturists. The economic ruination of millions of artisans and craftsmen accelerated the process of the subdivision of land and fragmentation of landholdings.

The essence of the caste system was the arrangement of hereditary groups in a hierarchy. The popular impression of the hierarchy was a

33. Ibid., p. 54.
34. Ibid.

clear-cut one, derived from the idea of *varna*, with Brahmins at the top and the Harijans at the bottom. But, as a matter of fact, only the two opposite ends of the hierarchy were relatively fixed. In the middle regions there was considerable room for debate. Each caste argued its superiority over the other. The Muslim caste system differed in some respects from the Hindu caste system; there were no ethical or religious ideas justifying the hierarchy or regulating inter-caste relations based on the idea of purity and pollution. There were no *varna* categories. Instead, what we have is a hierarchy formed by several *jatis*.

In UP, some Muslims of foreign descent (Iran, Arabia) were called *shurafa* or Ashraf and enjoyed a high social standing. After them came converts from the higher caste Hindus such as Rajputs. Next were occupational castes such as the weaver (julaha), barber (nai), cotton carder (dhuniya), potter (kumhar), and oilman (teli). Last came the sweepers. Among the Ashrafs, the Syeds ranked the highest.[35]

In Punjab, Sikhism also could not prevent the spread of castes. Sikhs were broadly divided into sardars and mazhabis, the former consisting of the high castes and the latter of sweepers. The sardars included Jat and kamboh (landowners), tarkhan (carpenter), kumhar (potter), mehra (water carrier), and cimba (washerman). The first two castes regarded themselves as superior to the others. The mazhabis not only came from a low caste but also were converted to Sikhism later than the higher caste groups. In some parts of Punjab there were found the sansi (shepherd) who were formerly included among the 'Criminal Tribes', sansi converts to Sikhism ranked even lower than the mazhabis.[36] The hereditary association of a caste with an occupation has been so striking that it has occasionally been argued that caste was nothing more than the systematization of occupational differentiation. But traditionally agriculture was a common occupation of all castes.[37]

In the region under study, we do not find prostitution flourishing to the same extent as in Bengal. But it was in vogue in military

35. *Gazetteer of India*, vol. 1, 1964, pp. 504–5.
36. Ibid., pp. 505–6.
37. Ibid., p. 501.

cantonment areas to fulfil the needs of British officials. In 1931, in Punjab, we find 227 and 1,142 procurers and prostitutes who belonged to the lower castes.[38] In UP, women of the lower castes, for example Kanjar (1,243), Nat (1,072), Bhat (575), Sansiah (1,346), and Shaikh (82) were engaged in prostitution. As per the census report of the United Provinces, 1931, this was their principal occupation.[39]

It seems that the Anti-Prostitution and Suppression of Brothel Act, 1936, adopted on the initiation of Allah Nawaz Khan, Member, Legistative Council, NWFP, had a great impact. Under this Act, living on the earnings of prostitution, procurement of girls or women for prostitution, importing women or girls for prostitution in the NWFP, their detention in brothels, or allowing one's premises to be used as brothel, etc., were made illegal.[40]

British rule generated forces that directly or indirectly weakened the caste system and laid the ground for the emergence of new social classes, strata, and associations and thereby laid the foundation for a modern class system. During the British period, Indian society witnessed the introduction and growth of new and modern means of transport, communication, and education. It should be recognized that all these changes took place to suit the needs of various phases of British capitalism and to serve their basic interests. However, it should not be forgotten that British rule, although acting to advance its self-interest, also inaugurated a qualitative structural transformation, which took Indian society down a new path.[41]

The nineteenth century witnessed the steady growth of a nationalist press and literature, which reflected the growing discontent among the people. The lives of Garibaldi and Mazzini were translated. *Neel Darpan*, a drama in Bengali, portrayed the sufferings and struggles of workers of European-owned indigo plantations.[42] A.O. Hume designed the Congress as a safety valve for the growing political discontent. He said, 'A safety valve for the escape of great and growing

38. *Census Report*, Punjab, 1931, p. 217.
39. *Census Report*, United Provinces of Agra and Oudh, 1931, pp. 438–42.
40. *Home, Police*, No. 24/11/35, NAI.
41. Desai, op. cit., p. viii.
42. Ibid., p. 318.

forces generated by our own action was urgently needed and no more efficacious safety valve than our Congress movement could possibly be devised.'[43]

In spite of its loyalist character, the Indian National Congress incurred the displeasure of the British government soon after its establishment. The government enacted Section 124(A) and 153(A) of Indian Penal Code in 1897 to combat Congress activities. Secret press committees were established in 1898, restricting the freedom of the press. Lord Curzon split Bengal into two provinces and passed the Indian Universities Act, 1904. These steps raised a storm of protest among Indians. In the first decade of the twentieth century, the government added to its armoury a number of weapons such as the Criminal Law (Amendment) Act 1908, the Newspapers Act 1908, and the Indian Press Act 1910. This led to a serious curtailment of civil liberties such as the freedoms of the press, platform, and assembly.[44]

The refusal to meet the political and economic demands by the British government and its repressive measures against the growing national movement shook the faith of an increasing number of Indians in the ideology of liberal nationalism. They began to rally around the militant nationalists.[45] These nationalists tried to infuse national pride and self-respect among them. Non-cooperation in 1920–1 and civil disobedience in 1930 drew some politically conscious women out of their private and domestic spheres. However, the entry of women into politics was but the tip of the iceberg. Nevertheless, it helped to redefine the role of women in various spheres of life.

Another development of this period was the growth of socialist and communist groups and the rise of independent economic and political organizations of the working class. The victory of the socialist revolution and the establishment of a socialist state in Russia aroused interest in socialist and communist doctrines among the radical nationalists in India. A section of those who were dissatisfied with the Gandhian ideology as well as with the Swaraj Party studied and

43. Ibid., p. 319.
44. Ibid., p. 325.
45. Ibid., p. 328.

embraced the socialist ideology. The first socialist weekly in India, *The Socialist*, was started in Bombay in 1923 by S.A. Dange. Dange was arrested and imprisoned for four years.[46]

Socialist ideas began to spread among the radical youths in subsequent years. Workers' and peasants' parties were formed in Bombay, Bengal, and Punjab. They supported the economic and political demands of the workers and peasants and organized them along class lines for voicing their demands. The writers produced a literature of a progressive nature in consequence of these social developments.

The growing political consciousness could not be controlled by the Gandhi–Irwin Pact and the India Act, 1935 that followed. The press and literary writings played an important role in creating an awakening among the masses. A few politically conscious young men started their activities in England itself. They were deeply influenced by the changing scenario all over the world and by the political philosophy of Marxism. Its articulation in Urdu literature assumed the form of the PWM, which shall be discussed in the next chapter.

46. Ibid., p. 356.

3

Dynamics of the Progressive Writers' Movement

Before the formal establishment of the Progressive Writers' Association (PWA) in 1936 in Lucknow, the movement had started in England. Some historians designate the broad spectrum of widespread political and social reform activities in the period from 1900 onwards as the Progressive Movement. This movement was not confined to one city or country; it spread geographically to both Eastern and Western countries. In the United States, the crusade of reform was felt in the farming communities of Iowa and Wisconsin, and in the great urban centres of New York, Cleveland, Chicago, and San Francisco. Its presence was also felt in the southern states like Georgia and in the widely different scenarios found in states like Maine and California.[1] Starting at the local level, the reform crusade made its way upwards in the political structure, finally reaching the national level. The reform crusades led by different leaders at different places were all varied manifestations of the progressive impulse, which had asserted itself in different parts of the world. In the United States, this movement acquired a national character under President Theodore Roosevelt.

Explaining the complex nature of the Progressive Movement, the US historian George E. Mowry writes:

> The immediate ends of the Progressive Movement were as varied as its centers of activity. In the cities, its proximate purposes were the overthrow of more rule through the institution of such new political devices as the direct primary and the non-partisan political ticket, and such new schemes

1. George E. Mowry, *The Progressive Movement, 1900–1920: Recent Ideas and New Literature*, American Historical Association, n.p., 1958, p. 1.

of city government as the city manager plan and the commission form. Its wider aims included the abolition of franchise politics, which under the corrupt bosses had resulted in inefficient, inadequate and costly city utilities, organized prostitution, a lawless liquor trade and general corruption and venality. But an even more comprehensive aim of the municipal movement was to make the twentieth-century American city a decent, healthy and enjoyable place in which to live. This meant the abolition of slums and tenements, the abatement of crime, juvenile delinquency and disease, the creation of parks, playgrounds and efficient social services.[2]

The Progressive Movement in the USA was concerned not only with democratic political devices but also with economic and civic issues such as the regulation of rail-roads, the adjustment of the tax system, the conservation of natural resources, and, most significantly, the protection of women and children both at home and at work. Aiding the historians more directly concerned on progressive politics were a number of scholars working in tangential but closely allied fields. Among the most important of such ancillary works were those produced in the area of what is known generally as intellectual history?[3]

The intellectual background of Progressivism is explained in Morton G. White's *Social Thought in America: The Revolt Against Formalism* (1949). Morton traces the evolution of social thought in the United States through the examination of the ideas of people like Justice Holmes, John Dewey, and Charles Beard. The socialist movement was another important movement of this time. Howard H. Quint's *The Forging of American Socialism: Origins of the Modern Movement* (1953) covers events only up to 1901 but is of interest to the student of progressivism because it argues that American socialism rose more in response to American conditions and thought rather than under the impact of European radical and Marxian doctrines.[4]

In England, the Victorian era nominally closes in 1900, but actually it came to an end in the 1880s. This period, like American progressivism, saw a ferment of new ideas and fresh forces in the literary, social, political, and economic fields. It witnessed a reaction against many

2. Ibid., p. 2.
3. Ibid., p. 5.
4. Ibid., p. 6.

of the old Victorian ideals.[5] The new movement resembled to some extent the Romantic revival, which quickened people's sensibility at the close of the eighteenth century. It was also affected by revolutionary and democratic ideas.

The early twentieth-century tendencies in literature have certain characteristics. First, they reiterated the old revolutionary formula that emphasized the individual. They drew attention to the importance of man as man, irrespective of class distinctions, and their reading of 'equality' and 'fraternity' was a moral and sentimental one. But under these tendencies a new formula also emerged that emphasized collectivism instead of individualism. It was economic, rather than moral or sentimental. It did not express itself in a humanitarian appeal to the influential classes to help their poorer brethren but hit them in a more radical way by aiming at the abolition of class distinctions.[6]

Briefly, the difference between the old revolutionary formula and the new revolutionary formula was that the old was addressed to the community as a whole, while the new was addressed to the state as an organic and collective whole. This revolutionary gospel was not confined to a few isolated figures in prose and poetry, but progressive writers from the middle classes spread it. These progressive writers dealt with issues relating to socialism more systematically and logically, and less sentimentally and didactically. They stressed on equality, liberty, and fraternity.

A notable feature of the writings of progressive writers was the return in fiction to the treatment of a wide range of subjects, to a great number of characters and to action, involving entire families and multiple generations. It became customary to group works into series, to follow out a destiny or theme, through time and space.[7]

Another characteristic of modern progressive writings was the worship of power rather than beauty. In its inception, this characteristic was a wholesome reaction to the narrow ideal of beauty upheld by Victorian ideals. Many Victorians imagined that beauty was

5. Arthur Compton Rickett, *A History of English Literature: From Earlier Times to 1916*, Toronto, 1958, p. 657.
6. Ibid., p. 6.
7. Emile Legous, *History of English Literature*, n.p., n.d., p. 1966.

something merely static. But as soon as it is restricted, it tends to lose its primal inspiration and consequently its vital appeal weakens, artificiality creeps in to make it a source of enervation rather than a stimulus.[8]

But the new generation of writers went further and found an effective way of getting involved in the movement that has been called Realism. This new movement challenged the old moral and social values and questioned older literary forms of describing beauty. Windows must be smashed to let in fresh air. Idols must be overturned to revitalize reverence. So was the case with progressive literature. It grew very quickly and covered a wide range of subjects. Not only was the intellectual restlessness of the time obvious enough in the content of progressive literature but it has influenced its form as well. The worldwide phenomenon was also going through a change.

The period of twenty-five years (1914–39) between the outbreak of the First World War and the beginning of the Second World War offered the safest possible contrast to the official serenity and complacency of the Victorian era. The First World War with its almost overwhelming anxieties, sacrifices, and disasters came as a terrific shock to a society that had felt itself permanently freed from the barbarousness of the wholesale destruction of life and devastation of property.[9]

The end of the First World War created as many problems as it solved. The crusading idealism of the war period gave way to nationalistic self-seeking and aggrandizement. The Peace Treaty signed in Versailles, while it brought to many small nations opportunities for political self-determination hitherto denied to them, was so harshly punitive that it contained within itself, as it is now evident, the noxious germs of an even more frightful world disaster.[10]

At the end of the decade, the economic consequences of the First World War at last made themselves felt with the onset of an economic depression such as the modern world had never experienced. The

8. Rickett, op. cit., p. 658.
9. Fred B. Millett, *A History of English Literature*, New York, 1956, p. 420.
10. Ibid.

five years between 1922 and 1927 saw a retreat on almost all fronts. Industry entered a period of stagnation and even crisis;[11] taxes were increased partially to defray the enormous costs of the conflict, mounted to such an extent that they not only bore heavily on the salaried professional classes but also threatened to wipe out the estates of all save the most favoured of the aristocracy. A large number of rare books appeared on the auction block and found their way across the Atlantic into the great public and private collections of American millionaires. With the onset of the depression came new social burdens and responsibilities.[12] The collapse of the world economy increased unemployment. Further tax burdens had to be imposed in order to maintain hundreds of thousands of families on the dole which sapped their morale and created a permanent pauper class. As a result, the First World War created severe problems for the big empires.

The whole system on which the empire had been haphazardly constructed began to be challenged by new theories of state and society, by communism in Russia after 1917, by fascism in Italy after 1922, and by Nazism in Germany after 1933. All these doctrines influenced the British intelligentsia and further weakened national morale. Hitler's attempt to create a new European order in which Germany, not England, would dominate brought about a resurgence of English patriotism, the repression of critical political elements within, and determination to protect the empire and to put down Hitlerism.[13] These developments in England also mobilized intellectuals and scholars in colonial countries. They too adopted the progressive attitude.

The major dynamic behind the evolution of the Progressive Writers' Movement (PWM) was the impact of Marxist ideas. In 1875, the Manifesto of the Communist Party was published in London for the first time. Marx and Engels were commissioned by the Communist League to draw up a theoretical as well as a practical programme for the party. Marx suggested that in every historical epoch, the prevailing

11. K.N. Pannikar (ed.), *National and Left Movements in India*, Delhi, 1980, p. 228.
12. Millett, op. cit., p. 421.
13. Ibid., p. 21.

mode of economic production and exchange, and the social organization following it, have formed the basis upon which could be explained the whole political and intellectual history of the society. The history of mankind had been a history of class struggle, conflicts between the exploiters and the exploited, and the rulers and the ruled; now a stage had been reached where the exploited and the oppressed class could not attain emancipation from the ruling or exploiting class and at the same time emancipate society at large from all exploitation, oppression, class distinction, and class struggle.[14]

Marx had a highly practical approach and was convinced that all human activities were motivated and governed by the basic needs of food, clothing, and shelter. Societies differ from one another on the basis of their economic situation and are governed by a superstructure. Marx considered ideas the products of the environment, which were at the same time capable of bringing about a change in the social order, but that are otherwise passive accompaniment to economic activity.[15] Marxist ideas had the capacity to liberate millions of people and to give them access to their culture. It provided a programme for building a society. Fighting and scientific techniques for establishing that society.

Marx rejected all existing ideas of class and social differentiation and instead formulated a dichotomous division of social classes, namely the bourgeois and the proletariat. By the bourgeois, he meant the class of modern capitalists, such as the owner of the means of production and the employer of wage labour. By the proletariat, he meant the class of labourers who have no means of production of their own and who are bound to sell their labour and thus constantly remain oppressed workers. The exploitation of the working class or labour by the capitalist or employer arouses dissatisfaction among the oppressed. The workers take steps towards organizing trade unions. At times the conflict between both classes results in sporadic riots. Marx believed that the working class having similar interests allover the world would increase in strength and overthrow the bourgeoisie. These ideas spread throughout the world. Although

14. Syed Fazle Rab, *Sociology of Literature: A Study of Urdu Novels*, New Delhi, 1992, p. 97.
15. Ibid., p. 99.

socialism had emerged in Europe a century ago, in India most people were not acquainted with this ideology before the First World War.

Although the destiny of progressivism is undoubtedly linked with Marxism, in India the very idea of united movement presupposes the presence of different forces working at their own level and within their own sphere. Hindi magazines like *Stree Darpan* whose themes have been critically analysed by Kamlesh Mohan in *Breaking Out of Invisibility*, started discussing gender issues in articles written by women themselves from the beginning of the twentieth century. Urdu journals like *Tahzib-un Niswan* (1898),[16] *Khatoon* (1904),[17] and *Ismat* (1908)[18] also appeared on the scene. But Urdu journals were founded by men and favoured a standardized domesticity. They stressed the need for women to be educated in order to improve their housekeeping and child-rearing skills and their role in enlightening the community.

Munshi Premchand was the first writer in the NWP to focus on social problems in his writings. His first book, a small collection of Urdu short stories titled *Soz-e-Watan*, was published in 1908, it had a patriotic theme. Dubbing it an inflammatory piece, the British burnt all available copies. His second novel, *Prema*, portrayed the unhappy lot of the Hindu widow in Urdu under the title *Hamkhurma-o-Hamsawab* (1907). In *Pratigya*, Premchand focused on the man–woman relation, the problem of Hindu widow, and found a new conscious woman in Sumitra.[19] The name Premchand appeared for the first time on his novel *Seva Sadan* in 1918.[20] In this novel, Premchand focused on the tragic predicament of an innocent wife forced into prostitution.[21] In *Nirmala* (1927)[22] Premchand portrayed a young

16. Gail Minault, *Secluded Scholars: Women's Education and Muslim Social Reform in Colonial India*, New Delhi, 1998, p. 110.
17. Ibid.
18. Ibid., p. 133.
19. Gobind Narain Sharma, *Premchand: Novelist and Thinker*, Delhi, 1999, pp. 111–12.
20. Gordon C. Roadarmel, *The Gift of a Cow*, a translation from the Hindi novel *Godaan*, London, 1968, p. v
21. Nandini Nopany (tr.), *Twenty-Four Stories by Premchand*, New Delhi, 1980, p. 10.
22. Alok Rai (tr.), *Nirmala: Premchand*, New Delhi, 1999, p. x.

woman who is a victim of dowry and an unequal marriage with an old man. Premchand turned from writing in Urdu to Hindi due to a dearth of Urdu publishers. Until about 1916, his stories were written first in Urdu but sharing with Hindi its major proportion of the vocabulary.[23] His many stories depict the themes followed by the progressive writers. In his story 'Nai Bivi' he portrayed the characters of an elderly bania and his young wife, Asha, and a young servant. The servant felt contempt for his old master. Motivated by sexual desire for the young wife and feeling sympathy for her plight, he makes advances to her.[24] In 'Beton Wali Widhwa' (Widow with Sons), Premchand described the hardships of a widow and a mother of four sons. In 'Second Marriage' and 'The Actress', Premchand focused on women's boldness in their marital affairs. Premchand's numerous stories are women oriented. His admiration and idealization of women is so pervasive that one finds women in almost every story. Mothers and daughters, wives and widows, whores and sometimes even the dreaded mother-in-law of Indian folklore are evidence of his compassion towards various societal issues.[25]

Let us briefly examine the history of the spread of these socialist ideas in India. After 1920, some Indians migrated to Kabul and from there they arrived in eastern Russia. They imbibed socialist views.[26] When they returned home, they sowed the seeds of socialism in India. These views spread so rapidly that the British had to recognize their presence and the suspected persons were arrested in the Kanpur Conspiracy Case.[27] Dange and other socialist leaders were arrested.

23. David Rubin (tr.), *Premchand: Deliverance and Other Stories*, New Delhi, 1988, pp. v–vi.
24. Ralph Russell, *The Pursuit of Urdu Literature: A Select Story*, New Delhi, 1992, p. 201.
25. David Rubin (tr.), *Widows, Wives and Other Heroines: Twelve Stories by Premchand*, New Delhi, 2000, pp. ix–x.
26. Mahmuduzzafar, 'Seeds of Socialism in India', *Hindustan* (Urdu daily), 26 March 1939, p. 15.
27. With the advance of the new ideology of the working class or socialism, its ideas began to penetrate among youths and the left. From 1924 onwards, a journal, *The Socialist* began appearing in Bombay under the editorship of S.A. Dange, who become assistant secretary and later

The number of socialists and communists increased. They organized a political association of labourers and peasants with a view to launching a revolutionary movement in India. With major strikes, the movement grew so rapidly that it dominated the trade union session in Nagpur in 1929. Fearing the ill effects of this rising wave of socialism,[28] the British drafted the Meerut Conspiracy Case in 1929 in which 33 communists and socialists were held and tried for two years and jailed for 14 years. The British spent approximately Rs. 15 lakh on curbing these ideas and in handing down severe punishment to violators in the hope that these harsh steps would create panic among the communists. On the contrary, the prisoners clarified their aim more clearly and loudly. Youths in large numbers adopted communist views. The case was brought to the Allahabad High Court, which ruled that being a communist was not a crime but its propaganda was made illegal.[29]

In India, the Russian Revolution had become a model for workers and peasants. Its propagandist literature, brought to India between 1925 and 1929, often hailed the achievements of the Workers' and Peasants' Government in Russia. In the party's training camps, workers were told to build a strong revolutionary party just as the Bolsheviks had done. By and large, the leaders of the Workers' and the Peasants' Party and those of the communist Party, whether in exile or in India, acknowledged the leadership of the Soviet communists in the international communist movement and looked to them for guidance in ideological and strategic matters.[30]

---

president of the Trade Union Congress. The government lost no time to strike. In 1924 (under the Labour Government in England), the Kanpur Conspiracy trial was staged against four communist leaders, S.A. Dange, Shaukat Usmani, Muzaffar Ahmad, and Nalini Gupta. All were sentenced for four years. The Kanpur Conspiracy Trial of 1924 showed the determination of the imperialist government to stamp out the first sign of revolutionary working class politics argues R. Palme Dutt.

28. For the spread of socialism, see Kamlesh Mohan, *Militant Nationalism in Punjab 1919–1935*, New Delhi, 1985.
29. Mahmuduzzafar, op. cit., p. 15.
30. Pannikar, op. cit., p. 84.

The Russian legacy became an object of reverence in India. In the early years of the twentieth century, the prevailing situation in India was conducive for an intellectual and cultural renewal. The development of new thought and culture, deriving inspiration from all sources was nevertheless rooted in India's own traditions and social realities. As a part of the process of intellectual renewal, there was a reawakening of interest in Marxism among the Indian intelligentsia.[31]

Marxism, which was the product of an industrial society, underwent qualitative changes when it was transplanted to societies that were industrially underdeveloped. In Russia, Marxism turned into Stalinism and in China into Maoism. Some aspects of Stalinism represented a gross vulgarization of Marxism. The internal metamorphosis of Marxism brought out the significance of the interaction between forms of consciousness and social existence. If Marxist theory became a force in bringing about a change in social conditions, it was also necessary that the conditions of social existence should, in certain respects, be ripe and favourable for receiving Marxist theory.[32]

In India, Marxism first spread as a political programme, contrary to the situation in developed countries where it emerged as an intellectual force before it gathered strength as a political force. In India, its emergence as a political force preceded its emergence as an intellectual force. Indian Marxism was slow in responding to this intellectual challenge. Some peasant organizations emerged out of the growing Indian left-wing activities based on the theory and practice of Marxian socialism, particularly the Bolshevik model.[33]

The Communist Party's foundation was laid at the Second Congress of the Communist International in Moscow in July–August 1920. M.N. Roy was the leading Indian communist. During this period, a number of intellectuals influenced by communism were engaged in different activities, including forming a group of progressive writers all over the world. They were creating literature of a progressive nature.

In 1928, Jawaharlal Nehru visited Moscow. He was greatly influenced by the October 1917 Revolution and the establishment

31. Ibid., p. 180.
32. Ibid., p. 181.
33. Ibid., p. 80.

of a socialist society in Russia. After returning, Nehru started propagating socialist ideals. Consequently, a progressive class emerged within the Congress. Their views influenced the Congress. As a result, it demanded complete freedom in its Lahore session in 1929. Jawaharlal stressed the need for reaching the common man. He condemned the exploitation of labourers and peasants by capitalists in India and abroad. The socialist movement was gaining momentum. The formation of the PWA was one of the products of these ideas. Many more associations came into being, such as the Labour Party, the Labour Union, and the Congress Socialist Party.[34]

Marx also provided a more specific thesis about the relation of literature and society. According to Marx, the system of production in existence at a given time determines both the content and the style of the literature of a society.[35] The relation of literature and society was of value because it specified the particular aspect of a society and insisted on a continuous dynamic interchange among all parts of that society. Many scholars representing a wide range of intellectual commitments to Marxist sociology have adopted this point of view in studying literature, and their views have been influential.[36]

Prior to the formal set-up of the PWA of India in 1936, the group of progressive intellectuals was engaged in organizing meetings at different places outside India, particularly in England. The PWM was a new and radical phenomenon in the intellectual field, described as a leftist movement by some writers. Even today, some people either deny the existence of this movement or do not like it.[37] Ali Sardar Jafri, a noted progressive writer, wrote, 'Recently a Hindustani poet told a Pakistani newspaper, *Akhtar Jahan* (dated 14 May to 30 May 1984), that actually the Progressive Writers' Movement was a propaganda platform of communism.'[38] But Swami Dev Mahanand, a great nationalist, considers this movement a pioneer of a new social revolution.

34. Mahmuduzzafar, op. cit., p. 15.
35. Rab, op. cit., p. 7.
36. Ibid., pp. 7–8.
37. Ali Sardar Jafri, *Taraqui Pasand Tehreek Ki Nisf Sadi* (Urdu), New Delhi, 1991, p. 17.
38. Ibid., p. 18.

The PWM was the voice of the most conscious group of intellectuals. Their writings expressed the truth and inner voice of their creators. The Communist Party in France admitted a proposal in March 1966 which raised the question: who is a creator? Whether of music, poetry, novel, drama, cinema, architecture, painting or sculpture ? The creator is not a mere manufacturer or arranger. In every work of art, there is a part that is not reducible to a set of given data, and this part is the creative artist himself.[39]

In this connection, Ali Sardar Jafri notes:

> The movement was an expression of the conscious and unconscious wishes and aspirations of the people in a particular period. These organized feelings rose out of the changing moods of the time. These feelings may be progressive, regressive or a combination of both. An organization provides an easy platform for the success of the movement, and creation becomes the total outcome of the movement. At times, creation and movement go side by side, but it is not an easy task. In the words of Luis Ishtrago, when you put ten frogs in each pan of a scale, four can jump out of the second pan and two more can sit in the first one.[40]

So is the case with literary movements because, in contrast to political movements, they have a slow effect. They are always thinly built. The PWM was also of the same nature.

The progressive writers associated themselves with the concerns of the growing numbers of labourers in the cotton textile and jute industries.

> By the end of the First World War, capitalism had started growing. In this period, the level of investment in cotton textiles, produced mainly by nationalist capitalists, grew in relation to the level of investment in jute textiles where there was a great involvement of British capital. As against the pre-war figure of 356, the total number of newly registered companies was 948 in 1919–20 and 1,039 in 1920–21.[41]

The condition of the large number of labourers employed in such companies stirred socialist sentiments. Intellectuals, writers, and leaders highlighted the workers' plight.

39. Ibid., pp. 19–20.
40. Jafri, op. cit., pp. 21–2.
41. Pannikar, op. cit., p. 215.

Fascism, which was also gaining strength in those days, was a setback to the freedom of expression of writers. To protect freedom of thought, a proclamation was brought out under the leadership of Romain Rolland of France, who was a friend of Mahatma Gandhi and Rabindranath Tagore. This proclamation was signed by, among others, Maxim Gorky, Henry Barbouse, Bertrand Russell, Rabindranath Tagore, and A.K. Coomaraswamy. This was a step towards the PWM. In August 1921, an organization of workers was formed in Berlin with Clares Taxon as president. It also included George Bernard Shaw, Henry Barbouse, Martin R. Santaxo, Anatole France, and many others.

In 1923, two workers employed in a mine in Rheinsch Westphalia region of West Germany brought forth commission to act against the dangers of the First World War and fascism. Clares Taxon and Henry Barbouse were deeply involved in this venture. In 1924, a conference of the representatives of several anti-imperial organizations was held in Berlin. Consequently, an international congress was organized in Brussels on 10 February 1927 with the object of constituting a platform against colonial exploitation. Jawaharlal Nehru, Barkatullah Khan, and Birendranath Chattopadhyay participated in this congress.[42] It was also attended by British and Chinese representatives. In 1931, this congress appealed to intellectuals not to associate in disruptive activities. In 1933, a congress of anti-fascist forces was organized in Paris. Communists, socialists, and democratic progressive thinkers attended it. Another international congress was also held in Paris in 1935 against the impending dangers of war and fascism.[43]

An international conference of progressive writers began working for the protection of culture. Maxim Gorky, E.M. Forster, André Malraux, Romain Rolland and, Thomas Mann were some of the members of this conference. Boris Pasternak from the Soviet Union, representatives from Uzbekistan, Kazakhistan, China, Japan, Iran, Turkey and Arabia also attended. From India Sajjad Zaheer and Mulk Raj Anand participated. They were the young writers at the meeting.[44]

42. Jafri, op. cit., p. 26.
43. Ibid., p. 27.
44. Ibid.

Describing the conference, Sajjad Zaheer remarked that the meeting, which was held at Balbalbe in Paris, had great historical and literary significance. It was the first occasion when writers from every civilized country gathered at one place to discuss literature and realized the need to protect literature from old beliefs, conservatism, and the clutches of the priests and the need to organize a forum of progressive writers. It was the only way by which they could help the masses and make progress. They could encourage progressive writing and protect writers from the warlike situation then on the horizon.[45]

This international conference was held for several days in Paris. Thousands of people attended the open gatherings. The hall in which the meetings were organized was overcrowded although entry was by ticket only. Most of the audience consisted of people from workers' organizations. They wanted to show the specific and newly created relationship between writers and the masses. In the capitalist era, intellectuals had moved away from the masses.[46]

Urdu literature of the 1920s and 1930s articulated the growing emotional bond between the writer and the oppressed section of society, especially women. It also demonstrated the rising protest against the foreign yoke and anger at the internal social system based on the convenience of the privileged. In 1932, an anthology of ten stories in Urdu entitled *Angare* was published in Lucknow. The progressive writers showed the power of their pen by criticizing almost all the prevailing social evils.

The publication of *Angare* was the opening salvo in the literary war launched by the Urdu PWM. Two stories in this volume—'Dilli Ki Sair' (A Visit to Delhi) and 'Purde Ke Pichhe' (Behind the Veil)—were contributed by Rashid Jahan (1905–52) a doctor by profession. Five stories were by Sajjad Zaheer (1905–73), an Oxford student, a staunch communist, and a force behind PWM. One story was by Mahmuduzzafar (1903–56), a well-known Oxford-educated journalist. Two stories were by Ahmad Ali (1910–94),[47] who is best known as the author of *Twilight in Delhi*. The stories in *Angare* were considered

45. Ibid., p. 28.
46. Ibid.
47. Minault, op. cit., p. 274.

a challenge to conservative society and orthodox religion. These authors, under the influence of communism, set a new literary trend which turned away from sentimental language, romantic expression, and the glorification of capitalism. It addressed the problems of the middle and lower classes of the exploited labourer and the oppressed women. Sajjad Zaheer's stories 'Nind Nahin Aati' (Sleep doesn't Come) and 'Jannat Ki Basarat' (Vision of Heaven) openly talked about sexual issues, horrifying the conservatives. The book created an uproar and the authors were denounced as rebels. Listening to the outcry of religious leaders, the UP Government banned the book.

It is evident that the growth of progressive ideas was diverse and multi-faceted in different countries. In United States progressivism was concerned with economic and civil issues, while in Europe it gave birth to new ideas in the literary, social, political, and economic fields. In Russia, it was basically concerned with economic issues under the impact of Marxian ideas. In India, various social issues were highlighted by writers protesting foreign rule from the beginning of the twentieth century. The impact of the Russian Revolution and the democratic expression of ideas in Europe inspired the socially conscious group of intellectuals to engage in an organized movement. Consequently, the PWA in India came into being in 1936 thanks to the efforts of Sajjad Zaheer and Rashid Jahan. We shall discuss the activities and objectives of PWA in detail in the next chapter.

4

Progressive Writers' Association: Aims, Objectives, Founders, Associates and Sympathizers

One of the significant events in the history of modern Indian literature is the formation of the PWA. It was an all-India association and included in its ranks writers of the major Indian languages. But in no other language did the PWA exert so great an influence as it did in Urdu. The writers who joined this association or who sympathized with its aims made new contributions of enduring value to Urdu literature. Prior to PWA the only other all-India literary association was the Indian chapter of PEN started by Sophia Wadia (1901–91) in 1934 along with the British playwright Herman Ould (1886–1957), whose one-act play, *The Discovery*, was assigned as a text in many Indian universities for a long time. K.M. Munshi and Kaka Saheb Kalelkar also started an Indian Literary Association[1] in the same year, known as the Bhartiya Sahitya Parishad, but it actually started operations in April 1936.

Before the establishment of PWA, India was experiencing considerable changes. Young self-conscious writers had diverted their pen from sentimental and religious subjects to social problems. PWA was the culmination of efforts and initiatives that had begun in the 1930s, and expressed in *Angare* (Embers). *Angare* was a collection of ten Urdu short-stories by Sajjad Zaheer, Rashid Jahan, Ahmad Ali, and Mahmuduzzafar, and extremely radical in temperament. It was published in Lucknow in December 1932.

Angare was the first ferocious attack in Urdu on contemporary

1. Sisir Kumar Das, *A History of Indian Literature 1911–1956: Struggle for Freedom: Triumph and Tragedy*, New Delhi, 1995, p. 86.

society. It was a declaration of war by the middle-class youth against the prevailing social, political, and religious institutions.[2] All the writers of *Angare* except Ahmad Ali were communists. The publication of this volume raised an uproar. Religious and civil leaders strongly reacted. Newspapers and journals published angry editorials and articles denouncing the book. The *Hindustan Times* of 21 February 1933 carried an article, 'Urdu Pamphlet Denounced: Shias Gravely Upset', quoting a resolution passed by the Central Standing Committee of the All India Conference, Lucknow, which declared that,

> the meeting strongly condemned the filthy pamphlet called *Angare*, which had wounded the feelings of the entire Muslim community by ridiculing God and his Prophets and which was extremely objectionable from the standpoints both of religion and morality. The Committee further strongly urged upon the attention of the UP Government that the book be at once proscribed.[3]

Consequently, the book was banned by the Government of the United Provinces under section 295A of the Indian Penal Code on 15 March 1933. Nearly all the stories in the volume contained accounts of intimate sexual relations, which even today would shock readers. There were satirical attacks not only on religious leaders but also on religion. In one story, God himself was portrayed in scathing and sarcastic terms. Because *Angare* was seen as a challenge to the accepted literary values, its appearance was regarded as a landmark in the history of Urdu literature.[4]

There was widespread anger against the authors. Funds were collected for the prosecution of the authors and punishment sought for them included 'stoning to death' and 'hanging by the neck'. *Maulvis* issued *fatwas* against the book and the authors.[5] But the authors were not at all perturbed or discouraged. In a reply to this widespread resentment, they issued a statement, drafted by Mahmuduzzafar, which

2. Shabana Mahmud, 'Angare and the Founding of the Progressive Writers' Association', *Modern Asian Studies*, vol. 30, part 2, 1996, p. 447.
3. Ibid., p. 448.
4. Ralph Russell, *The Pursuit of Urdu Literature: A Select Story*, New Delhi, 1992, p. 204.
5. Mahmud, op. cit., p. 449.

was published in the *Leader* (Allahabad) on 5 April 1933 under the title 'In Defence of *Angare*, Shall We Submit to Gagging?' It reads:

> Some five months back four young authors, among them a young woman, brought out a collection of short stories in Urdu under the title *Angare*. I happened to be one of the contributors to this collection. This book at once raised a storm in Muslim circles. It was said to be a shameless attack on Islam and everything decent in society. The book has already been proscribed by the UP Government under section 295A of the IPC. It was even said that funds are being collected to start the prosecution of the authors. Shall we submit to such a gagging? That is the question I wish to raise here. Referring to the contents of the book itself, the stories of my friend, Sajjad Zaheer, are concerned chiefly with the criticism and a satire of current Muslim conceptions, life and practices. His attack is directed primarily against the intolerable theological burden that is imposed from childhood on the average Muslim in this country. . . . Ahmad Ali essays into the realms of poverty, material, spiritual and physical, especially the poverty of Muslim women. Imagination and admirable boldness breaks through the veils of convention to expose the stark reality. Rashid Jahan, who is also a doctor of medicine, drawing on her practical experience, also portrays boldly the ghastly plight of women behind the *purdah*. My own single contribution is an attack on the vanity of man, which seeks to find an outlet at the expense of weak and defenceless womanhood. Nobody can deny the truthfulness of those portraits. . . . The authors of the book do not wish to make any apology for it. They leave it to float or sink by itself. They are not afraid of the consequences of having launched it. . . . We hope that others will not be discouraged. Our practical proposal is the formation immediately of a League of Progressive Authors, which should bring forth similar collections from time to time, both in English and [in] the various vernaculars of our country. We appeal to all those who are interested in this idea to get in touch with us.[6]

In this statement, the authors announced the idea of forming a League of Progressive Authors. The publication of *Angare* in 1932 paved the way for the formation of the PWA in 1936.

The practical move towards the formation of PWA was made at

6. *The Leader*, 5 April 1933, Allahabad, p. 9. (The full text is reprinted in Mahmud, 'Angare and the Founding of the Progressive Writers' Association'.)

the Nanking Restaurant, on Denmark Street, in London in November 1935. A number of Indian students and intellectuals of different political views participated. They ranged from adherents of radical socialist nationalism (of which Jawaharlal Nehru was the chief representative) to the communism of Sajjad Zaheer, Jyoti Ghosh, Pramod Ranjan Sen Gupta, and M.D. Tasir.

Sajjad Zaheer returned, with the manifesto of the Indian Progressive Writers' Association, London. Entitled as 'London 1935', it was printed in the *Left Review* of London in February 1936. It reads:

> Radical changes are taking place in Indian society. Fixed ideas and old beliefs and, social and political institutions are being challenged. Out of the present turmoil and conflict a new society is arising. The spirit of reaction, however, though moribund and doomed to ultimate decay, is still operative and making desperate efforts to prolong itself.
>
> It is the duty of Indian writers to give expression to the changes taking place in Indian life and to assist the spirit of progress in the country. Indian literature, since the breakdown of classical culture, has had the fatal tendency to escape from the actualities of life. It has tried to find a refuge from reality in spiritualism and idealism. The result has been that it has produced a rigid formalism and a banal and perverse ideology. Witness the mystical, devotional obsession of our literature, its furtive and sentimental attitude towards sex, its emotional exhibitionism and its almost total lack of rationality. Such literature was produced particularly during the past two centuries, one of the unhappiest periods of our history. A period of disintegrating feudalism and of acute misery and degradation for the Indian people as a whole.
>
> It is the object of our association to rescue literature and other arts from the priestly, academic and decadent classes in whose hands they have degenerated so long; to bring the arts into the closest touch with people and to make them the vital organs which will register the actualities of life, as well as lead us to the future.
>
> While claiming to be the inheritors of the best tradition of Indian civilization, we shall criticize it ruthlessly in all its political, economic and cultural aspects, the spirit of reaction in our country, and we shall foster through interpretive and creative work (with both native and foreign resources) everything that will lead our country to the new life for which it is striving. We believe that the new literature of India must deal with the basic problems of our existence today—the problems of hunger and poverty, social backwardness and political subjugation, so that it may help

us to understand these problems and through such understanding help us to act.[7]

Keeping the above-mentioned aims in view, the following resolutions were passed.

1. The establishment of organizations of writers to correspond to the various linguistic zones of India and coordination among organizations by holding conferences, publishing of magazines, pamphlets, etc.;
2. To cooperate with those literary organizations whose aims do not conflict with the basic aims of the association;
3. To produce and to translate literature of a progressive nature and of high technical standards;
4. To strive for the acceptance of a common language (Hindustani and a common script (Indo-Roman) for India;
5. To protect the interests of authors; to help authors who require and deserve assistance for the publication of their work;
6. To fight for the right of free expression of thoughts and opinions.[8]

The Hindi version of this manifesto was published in the issue of *Hans*, edited by Munshi Premchand, in October 1936.[9]

The responsibility of establishing an organization in limited time with such ambitious aims was discharged primarily by Sajjad Zaheer and a number of his associates. Sajjad Zaheer was a communist at heart. His colleagues too were either already communists or were shortly afterwards to become communists. Their main concern was to promote communist and socialist views in literature through PWA. In 1930, a movement among Muslims influenced by socialist views was started in NWFP; it joined forces with the Indian National Congress (INC). This was known as the Red Shirt Movement because its associates wore red shirts and marched with banners bearing the symbol of a crossed hammer and sickle, with the slogan 'Workers and peasants of the world unite'. Their objectives were to 'win freedom for the country' and 'to feed the hungry and clothe the naked'.[10] Within a couple of weeks, it became evident that remarkably wide support

7. Russell, *The Pursuit of Urdu Literature*, pp. 204-5.
8. Ibid., *How Not to Write the History of Urdu Literature and Other Essays on Urdu and Islam*, New Delhi, 1999, pp. 71–2.
9. Das, *A History of Indian Literature*, p. 87.
10. Mahmud, op. cit., p. 455.

for the aims of the projected association would be forthcoming. In a short span of time, some of the most prominent writers of verse, prose, fiction, and literary criticism declared their sympathies for the movement. They were not only supporters of the left but also Congress supporters of a predominantly Gandhian outlook. People who were sympathetic to nationalist sentiment had held aloof even from the Congress, but they supported the movement with no explicit political views.[11]

A few days before the formation of PWA in India, a large gathering of Indians, including merchants, doctors, lawyers, and students, was organized by the Indian PWA on 11 April in London. The gathering discussed the problems of communalism in India from different points of view. Members from the *majlis* of Oxford and Cambridge had made a special trip to London to take part in that discussion. Although the speakers dealt with different aspects, there was striking unanimity on three major issues, namely that the whole communal problem had at its root economic motives; that the vested interests, including the government, played a considerable role in intensifying the tension to achieve their own ends; and that the only way out of the present impasse was by sterilizing the dangerous virus of communalism by shifting the emphasis from the political to the economic sphere.[12] The speeches of V.K. Krishna Menon, Mulk Raj Anand, Som Nath Chibb, Pramod Ranjan Sen Gupta, and V.J. Rao were lucid and inspiring. All of them belonged to young India—an India that was earnest and sincere.[13]

Owing to the wishes expressed by several speakers, the Secretary of the Indian PWA decided to publish a pamphlet outlining the history and nature of the communal problem in India with a view to placing the issue in its proper perspective. Incidentally, when PWA was set up in India, the association in England published its first booklet, *New Indian Literature*. In not more than 22 pages, the editor gave readers plenty of matter to digest. Written in an admirable style by young

11. Russell, *The Pursuit of Urdu Literature*, p. 205.
12. 'Indian News in London, PWA Meeting', *Tribune*, Lahore, 15 April 1936, p. 6.
13. Ibid.

Indians, it had notes on Urdu literature by M.D. Tasir, a prologue calling for a positive attitude to life by Mulk Raj Anand, and an extract from a novel in progress by Raja Rao. Dr K.S. Shelvankar had in his own inimitable language, in not more than 20 words, given a thought-provoking review of Subhash Bose's *Indian Struggle.*[14]

In India, the formation of PWA gained much sympathy. Pandit Amarnath Jha, then Vice-Chancellor of the University of Allahabad, and Dr Tara Chand, then Secretary of the semi-official Hindustani Academy, expressed their sympathy.[15] Sajjad Zaheer, Rashid Jahan, Mahmuduzzafar, and Ahmad Ali were a great force behind the PWA. Ismat Chughtai, Saadat Hasan Manto, Krishan Chander, Ali Sardar Jafri, Maqdoom Moinuddeen, Razia Sajjad Zaheer, Niaz Hyder, and Kaifi Azmi also supported PWA. They set a new trend of producing powerful and inspiring literature. To produce a complete list of the associated writers is not possible. Rajinder Singh Bedi, Upendra Nath Ashk, Khwaja Ahmad Abbas, Abdul Sattar, Ahmad Nadim Qasmi, and Suhail Azimabadi were actively associated with PWA. Among the poets who were associated with PWA were Faiz Ahmad Faiz, Josh Malihabadi, Firaq, and Sahir Ludhianvi. Hasrat Mohani had already started writing against the foreign government.

On 13 April 1936, a dream of the progressive writers came true. Munshi Premchand presided over the meeting of the All India Progressive Writers' Association at the Rafah-Am Club, Lucknow. Writers from different parts of India came together to discuss progressive view on literature. PWA, which promoted this conference, aimed at establishing organizations of writers corresponding to the linguistic zones of India and fostering closer contact with the writers of the different provinces who held similar views. They also aimed at producing and translating the literature of a progressive nature, and, above all, to fight for the liberty of expression of writers in all parts of the country.

In the midst of a hall hung with banners proclaiming 'Literature must serve the people', 'Freedom of thought and expression', and 'Free education for all', Munshi Premchand delivered his presidential

14. Ibid.
15. Russell, *How Not to Write*, p. 72.

address to the writers present. In the course of his speech, unique both in language and thought, Munshi Premchand said:

Literature is no longer the mere effort to improve language but the expression of a true idea and must have the power of moulding the mind of man. It must be critical of contemporary life and tackle the realities of our day-to-day existence instead of frittering itself away in futile romanticism. If literature talks only of amusement and sex, and strikes only a note of poverty, despair and hopelessness, it reflects the pathological and alarming state of the nation's mind.[16]

In perfect Hindi, Munshi Premchand expressed the view that in the writing of a story the author must be direct, must study the psychology of his protagonists, and create living characters so that the story could be read like a biography of people and not as a series of fantasies. He emphasized that literature was in fact the psychological autobiography of the writer. His definition of beauty as the harmony of elements for which our soul craves, was the central point of the latter part of his speech.

You should try to find the beauty of woman in her hardships, problems and struggles, not in dyed lips and threaded eyebrows. If you don't see beauty in a poor woman who is feeding her child sitting on the farm boundary, then it is the fault of your narrow-sightedness.[17]. . . A true artist who strives after this beauty cannot be affected by the ugliness of social degradation, economic poverty and political slavery in the society around us. The outlook of PWA is influenced by the world around it, so much so that in our lives today, 'Literature can no longer be considered as mere amusement but, according to our present standards, literature must have thought, it must have feelings for liberty, and appreciation of beauty, and an impulse towards social reconstruction, the power to reflect on the hard realities of life. In short, we want a literature that may produce in us movement, change and restlessness.[18]

The literature that is being produced today is mostly of a stoical, mystical and romantic type, which is doing more harm than good. There is a great

16. *Tribune*, 15 April 1936, p. 13.
17. Ali Sardar Jafri, 'Tahreek Jamalyat Aur Siyasat', *Taraqui Pasand Adab* (Urdu), ed. Qamar Rais and Syed Ashoor Kazmi, New Delhi, 1987, pp. 46–7.
18. *Tribune*, 15 April 1936, p. 13.

need for the evolution of popular literature, which is in close contact with the naked realities of life, which is free from the dreamy unreal haze of this pure romanticism, and which stirs in us our dormant energies to action, to a conscious realization of our backwardness, helplessness, and national humiliation.[19]

Thus declared Munshi Premchand, presiding over the first All India PWA Conference held in Rafah-Am Club, Lucknow, where authors, novelists, poets, editors, and journalists from all over India had gathered. Munshi Premchand also stressed that the power of the pen was great and said that it was the duty of all authors not to misuse this power but to rebel against the tyranny of form and the figure of speech of the existing standards of literature and to resurrect our dead literature into something more vibrant, truthful, and inspiring to progress.

After his presidential address, a number of resolutions were adopted. The first among them was for the adoption of a manifesto that laid down the aims and objectives of PWA. Another resolution that was adopted was,

against the restrictions placed by the Government on the freedom of thought and expression by promulgating repressive Press Laws, the Customs Act, and the Criminal Law Amendment Act and in this way arbitrarily suppressing hundreds of journals and magazines, proscribing progressive literature and stopping entry into this country of a large part of radical literature from foreign countries.

This resolution was moved by R.S. Pandit.[20]

This resolution included an assertion concerning the writer's right to freedom of thought and expression. The conference called upon the writers of India to beware of the impending dangers of imperialist war. It requested the Indian university authorities to give liberty of expression to students by way of organizing journals and associations. It protested against the restriction on higher education as contemplated by the Sapru Committee Report.

Mrs Kamla Devi Chattopadhyay also addressd the conference. The veteran nationalist writer Maulana Hasrat Mohani, participated in the

19. Ibid.
20. *Tribune*, 14 April 1936, p. 16.

discussion.[21] Sajjad Zaheer wrote about his experience in *Roshnai* that he was deeply worried because of the shortage of funds with PWA. To avoid expenditure on the boarding and lodging of delegates, arrangements were made with friends and relatives. Munshi Premchand stayed with him. But after its formal formation, he relaxed.[22]

Sajjad Zaheer was appointed general secretary of PWA, and Bisham Dev and Khwaja Ahmad Abbas were appointed joint secretaries. Mama Warerkar was the treasurer. After the formal establishment of PWA, the primary task was to raise funds through membership subscriptions and donations. Any writer who accepted the aims and objectives of the association was eligible for membership. The admission fee was fixed at Re. 1 and subscription for membership was Rs. 2 p. a.[23]

In Punjab, Mian Iftikhar-ud-deen, a wealthy Punjab landlord and prominent progressive who later became popular as the owner of the *Pakistan Times*, was helpful in getting PWA organized. In Aligarh, Mohammad Ashraf, Khwaja Gulam Syaddin, Bashiruddeen, Manjoor Hussain, and Prof. Mohammed Zeb were staunch nationalists and socialists.[24] They were the supporters of the PWA manifesto in Aligarh. A branch of PWA was organized at the Muslim University in 1936, whose first meeting was held at the house of Manjoor Hussain. Dr Mohammad Ashraf was the chief architect. Ali Sardar Jafri read an article, 'Zadeed Adab Aur Naujawanon Ke Rujhanat'. Abdul Alim, who was a lecturer in Arabic, was also present at the meeting. When, in April 1936, the first All India PWA conference was held, Dr Abdul Alim participated on behalf of the Aligarh unit of PWA.[25] Sabat Hasan organized a branch of PWA in Hyderabad with the support of Abdul Gaffar. It was on the pattern of the

21. Ibid., 15 April 1936, p. 13.
22. Ali Sardar Jafri, *Guftgoo: Manifesto of Taraqui Pasand*, Bombay, 1980, pp. 87–8.
23. *Directory of Educational, Scientific, Literary and Cultural Organisations in India*, Compiled from Authoritative Sources, Manager of Publications, Culcutta, 1948, p. 293.
24. Rais and Kazmi, op. cit., p. 237.
25. Ibid., pp. 240–1.

'London manifesto', which was sent to them. Akhtar Hussain Raipuri set up a unit of PWA in Delhi. In Bombay, the progressive writers used to meet at a cafe called the Silver Fish, now converted into a bustling commercial centre.[26]

By 1936, a few Hindi writers apart from Premchand declared their support for PWA, though quite a number of writers had expressed sympathy for the movement. It was among Urdu writers that the most striking headway was made. Mohammad Iqbal was contacted, but his active sympathy could not be gained because of his death (on 20 April 1938). The reason for the widespread support enjoyed by PWA and its rapid expansion was its aim of harnessing literature for the cause of social and political ends. By the 1920s, however, the themes of revolt against imperialism, of nationalism, and of radical social reform had become common in literature. Nevertheless, PWA represented the continuation and development of such themes in a more vibrant way. It sought the support of the great *ghazal* singer, Hasrat Mohani, a committed worker for India's complete Independence, Josh Malihabadi, the self-styled 'poet of Revolution', and Firaq Gorakhpuri, who was equally eminent in Hindi and Urdu literature. In literary criticism, Abdul Haq, secretary of the society for the Advancement of Urdu, Anjuman Taraqui-i-Urdu, supported the new movement.[27]

PWA made the most solid gains in the Hindi- and Urdu-speaking areas where in 1937, 1938, and 1939 it held joint conferences of Hindi and Urdu writers. The earlier aloofness of Hindi writers was overcome to some extent. In 1938, a prominent Hindi poet, Maithili Sharan Gupt, attended the Allahabad Conference and read a poem. Jawaharlal Nehru also attended the Allahabad Conference and spoke at this gathering.[28] The movement achieved a great triumph when Sajjad Zaheer succeeded in getting a declaration of support and a message to the conference from Rabindranath Tagore, which showed his changed outlook towards PWM. Tagore's message reads:

26. Sukrita Paul Kumar (ed.), *Ismat: Her Life, Her Times*, New Delhi, 2000, p. 131.
27. Russell, *How Not to Write . . .*, p. 78.
28. Ibid., p. 79.

To live in seclusion has become second nature to me but it is a fact that the writer who holds himself aloof from society cannot get to know mankind. Remaining aloof, the writer deprives himself of the experience which comes from mingling with a number of people. To know and understand society, and to show the path to progress, it is essential that we keep our finger on the pulse of society and listen to the beating of its heart. This is only possible when our sympathies are with humanity, and when we share its sorrow. New writers must mix with men and recognize that if they live in seclusion as I do, they will not achieve their aims. I understand now that in living apart from society so long I have committed a grave mistake. . . . This understanding burns in my heart like a lamp and no argument can extinguish it.[29]

Seeing the growing popularity of PWA, the British took serious note of its activities and tried to find out the founders of this association. J.M. Ewart, Director, Intelligence Bureau (DIB), Home Department reported that 'the membership is drawn largely from the suspecting or unsuspecting friends of a few persons such as S.S. Zaheer (the son of an ex-Chief Judge of the Oudh, Chief Court), Zainul Abedin Ahmad (the son of a DIG of police in Sind) or Pramod Ranjan Sen Gupta, son of the Public Prosecutor, Krishnanagar, Bengal'.[30] Ewart suggested that PWA was rather more than it advertised itself to be and should be approached with caution by people who did not wish to be involved in extremist left-wing politics. The association was Ewart said, 'a typical example of the methods of infiltration now being pursued by communists in all countries in accordance with the current policy of the Comintern'.[31] In order to curb the activities of PWA and to stop its expansion, the Secretary to the Government of India, Home Department, warned all local governments on 28 August 1936. The full text of the letter reads:

1. I am desired to address you in connection with an organisation known as the Indian Progressive Writers' Association. This Association held its first conference at Lucknow simultaneously with the annual session of the Indian National Congress in April 1936. Since then S.S. Zaheer, the General Secretary, and the other members of the executive committee have been active in forming local branches of the Association and such branches

29. Ibid., p. 80.
30. *Home Political*, No. 7/9/36 NAI, p. 2.
31. Ibid., p. 5.

are known to exist in Aligarh, Allahabad, Andhra, Calcutta, Hyderabad (Deccan), Poona and the Punjab. The Association also has contacts in a number of other education centres.

2. This Association owes its origin to an association of the same name formed in London about a year ago. The London Association is closely connected with and to a great extent controlled by the British section of the International Union of Revolutionary Writers. S.S. Zaheer, the secretary of the association in India, was one of the signatories to the original manifesto defining the aims of the association when it was first started in London.
3. The proclaimed aims of the association are comparatively innocuous and suggest that it concerns itself solely with the organization of journalists and writers and the promotion of interest in literature of a progressive nature. Its inspiration, however, comes from and it has close contacts with organizations and individuals who are in some cases avowed and active communists and in others are advocates of policies akin to those of the communists. There is a reason to believe that the association has already attracted interest and some support from persons of an intellectual type who are unlikely to have any sympathy with communism or other revolutionary theories. The association is, however, a typical example of the methods now being pursued by communists in all countries in accordance with the current policy of the Communist International. This method is, for a few convinced and trained communists, to establish contacts with all sorts of organizations and societies having interests in intellectual, cultural and social subjects with the object of spreading communistic ideas and gaining converts. Though it is not suggested that the Indian Progressive Writers' Association as a body is a necessarily subversive or revolutionary organization, it is desirable for the reasons given that its development should be watched with some suspicion and that it should be approached with caution by individuals who do not wish to be involved in extremist left-wing politics. I am desired to suggest, therefore, that suitable opportunities may be taken to convey about this association to journalists, educationalists and others who might be attracted by its ostensible programme.[32]

PWA continued its activities with vigour and zeal. The Calcutta conference in 1938 opened with Rabindranath Tagore's address and adopted a new constitution embodying the plans for a better and

32. Ibid., pp. 6–11.

more regular organization. It resolved to issue a quarterly journal from Lucknow, with the general secretary, Abdul Alim, as ex-officio-editor, and with an editorial board consisting of the representatives of all the important languages of India. The journal *New Indian Literature* came out in 1939 and was discontinued after two issues due to commencement of the Second World War. The other publications of PWA were: *Parichaya* (Bengali), *Naya Sahitya* (Hindi), and *Abhudaya* (Telugu).[33]

The movement was revived again in 1942 when the illegal Communist Party decided to extend its support for the war after much internal discussion, and continued until 1946–7. But the vigorous anti-communist movement launched by its one-time Congress allies in 1946–7 and the ultra left line, which the Communist Party itself adopted, radically changed the conditions in which PWA had to work.[34]

Ismat Chughtai said that her proximity to the Communist Party gave her the knowledge of class differences and sectarianism. But when her stories were branded as obscene, and when the policy of the party rigidly stipulated that progressive literature was that which was concerned with peasants and labourers, she disagreed.[35] The progressive movement started disintegrating.

PWM was the target of criticism from the very beginning. The literature created under its influence was unacceptable to conservatives and slow pacers. Critics objected to its linguistic patterns and declared it fake and fabricated. They called PWA less literary and more political, and issued an appeal asking pure and original writers to abstain from it. They charged that the progressive writers were seeking truth in the ideology of Marx and said that their thinking about Indian society was in terms of foreign societies and ideals. The ideas of PWA had their roots in alien lands.[36] But the writers of the Progressive Group continued to write. They explored a range of new themes, especially

33. *Directory of Organisations in India*, p. 243.
34. Russell, *How Not to Write*, pp. 80–1.
35. Kumar, op. cit., p. 131.
36. Raja Dhale, 'Premchand, Dalits and Dalit Literature', in *Premchand: Our Contemporary*, ed. Shiv Kumar Misra, New Delhi, 1986, p. 205.

gender issues and the destruction of social taboos, with great literary skill and keen social insight, which had a remarkable place in the world of Urdu literature as well as in the history of India.

II

BIOGRAPHICAL AND LITERARY SKETCHES OF EMINENT PROGRESSIVE WRITERS

Sajjad Zaheer

Sajjad Zaheer (1905–73). His full name was Sayyad Sajjad Zaheer, but he was popularly known as Banney Bhai. He was born on 5 November 1905 in Golaganj, in Lucknow, UP (now known as Uttar Pradesh), in a well-to-do family. He received his higher education at Oxford University. During his stay in London as a student, he was exposed to Marxism. He met several leftist writers, including Ralph Fox (1900–37), whose *The Novel and the People* became popular among those who were influenced by Marxian ideology. During his talks with Fox, the idea of a PWA was mooted. The intellectual and literary development of Sajjad Zaheer began among the elites of London. He was inspired by revolutionaries like Shyamji Krishna Verma, Vinayak Damodar Savarkar, and Madame Bhikaji Cama, who had already challenged the British Empire and had helped in founding the Ghadar Party.

Sajjad Zaheer returned to India in 1931 when communism was gaining ground in political circles.[37] These themes are described in *Angare* (1932), one of the most sensational and significant works in Indian literature. This volume was a collection of ten stories in Urdu. Sajjad Zaheer's five stories included in the book were 'Nind Nahin Aati', 'Jannat Ki Basarat', 'Garmion Ki Ek Raat', 'Dulari' and 'Phir Yeh Hangama'.[38] 'Nind Nahin Aati' and 'Jannat Ki Basarat' were extremely provocative and offensive to the sensibilities of the devout. In the first story, the protagonist meets a prostitute who makes

37. Sabir Dutt, *Fun Aur Sakhsiat* (Urdu), Bombay, 1994, p. 273.
38. Sajjad Zaheer, *Roshni Ka Safar*, ed. Naresh Nadim (Hindi), New Delhi, 1994, p. 3.

sacrilegious remarks about God. In the second story, a hypocritical priest falls asleep over a copy of Holy Book and dreams of making love to a houri in paradise.[39] His third story was about a clerk in a government office and described his needs and poverty. In 'Phir Yeh Hangama' Zaheer describe various unrelated incidents. The other stories included in the book were equally provocative and critical of the middle-class attitude towards sex and religion. Khalil-ur-Rahman, a critic, argued that youthful enthusiasm, lack of moderation, boldness, and rebelliousness pervaded these stories. Although it created an uproar and many scholars felt that it crossed the limits of moderation, the publication of *Angare* gave momentum to the formation of PWA and explored new frontiers of man–woman relations and behaviour, which were considered totally unacceptable. It opened the floodgates to Marxist and Freudian ideas in Indian literature and led to an imitation of James Joyce.[40]

Sajjad Zaheer left for London, and his co-writer, Rashid Jahan, a Muslim woman, had to face the ire of the reactionaries. A *fatwa* was issued against her in a mosque. Under pressure from religious leaders, the UP government banned the book. Before the formation of PWA in India, a meeting was held in Paris in June 1935. This was an International Congress of Writers, organized by André Gide, Henry Barbouse, Romain Rolland, and André Malraux. Most of the participants had some connection with India. Gide was the translator of Tagore's *Gitanjali*. Barbouse knew M.N. Roy, Rolland had written books on Ramakrishna and Vivekanand and was associated with Tagore and Gandhi. Sajjad Zaheer and Mulk Raj Anand were the two Indian writers present at the meeting, which was attended by a number of European writers.[41]

This conference encouraged Sajjad Zaheer to pursue his mission of forming the PWA in India. A draft manifesto was prepared by Mulk Raj Anand. Its edited version was published in the *Left Review* (London) in February 1936 and a revised version in Hindi appeared in the issue of *Hans*, edited by Munshi Premchand in October 1936.

39. Das, op. cit., p. 274.
40. Ibid.
41. Ibid., p. 87.

During this time, Sajjad Zaheer had finished his studies in London and was busy writing his novel *London Ki Ek Raat.* It was published in 1937. Zaheer had a bitter experience of British racism when he was in London. The insulting behaviour of the British towards Indian immigrants always reminded them of belonging to a slave country. In this novel, Sajjad Zaheer depicted the deplorable condition of India under imperialism and the obstacles in the way of the Indian struggle for freedom. The hero said,

> In a slave country where 80 per cent population is hungry, where the epidemics are so frequently spread that in the whole country hardly any healthy face is seen, where education is limited, where the faces of children are like dry flowers, where hunger, empty stomachs, sorrows are clearly visible on the faces of people, where sluggishness, effortlessness and hatred is evident, in these circumstances, the search for romantic gifts would be like a dream.[42]

In November 1935, a number of Indian students and intellectuals of a radical temperament gathered and drafted the original manifesto and made plans to establish PWA in India. Sajjad Zaheer returned to India. He landed in Bombay, where he spent only a few days and then went straight to Allahabad where his parents were living at the time. He remained in regular correspondence with many Indian intellectuals from 1930 onwards. The next step was to seek the support of writers and intellectuals who had already established a reputation the Indian cultural scene and if possible to get them to sign the draft manifesto of the movement.[43] Sajjad Zaheer succeeded in getting the support of great personalities like Munshi Premchand, Mohammad Iqbal, Rabindranath Tagore, and even Jawaharlal Nehru. His hopes were fulfilled when, in April 1936, the first conference of the All India PWA was held in Lucknow. Munshi Premchand delivered the presidential address. Sajjad Zaheer became the general secretary of PWA. He sent the manifesto to many young writers in other states, asking them to establish branches throughout India. His mission bore fruit and branches were opened in Aligarh, Lahore, Bombay, Hyderabad, and Punjab.

42. Zaheer , op. cit., p. 107.
43. Russell, *How Not to Write*, p. 71.

Sajjad Zaheer was a staunch communist. He was the editor of *Chingari*, published from Saharanpur; it was an Urdu monthly magazine containing socialist and Marxist ideas. (For cover page of *Chingari* see pp. 84-85). The magazine was banned by the government, which was against the development of communism in India. He jailed three times for his seditious speeches against British government. A collection of his letters written to his wife from jail, *Naqush-i-Zindan*, was published in 1942. His book *Roshnai* is a detailed account of the formation of the PWM. He wrote this book after Independence while he was in a Pakistani jail. He was entangled in the Rawalpindi Conspiracy Case as general secretary of the Communist Party in Pakistan. He was not given Pakistani citizenship even after the completion of his punishment. Hence, he returned to India and reorganized PWA. He participated in the first Afro–Asian Writers Conference in Tashkent in 1958. Since 1959 he remained the chief editor of the weekly newspaper, *Awami Daur*. He died of a heart attack in Russia in 1973. Although his writings were limited, what he wrote was of a high standard. Some of his poems were published under the title *Pighla Neelam*.[44] His writings held up mirror to contemporary society.

RASHID JAHAN

Rashid Jahan (1905–52) was the eldest of the five daughters of Sheikh Abdulla of Aligarh and Wahid Jahan Begum. She was born on 25 August 1905 in Delhi. Sheikh Abdulla was a Kashmiri convert to Islam. He attended Aligarh College and obtained a law degree. He established his practice near the college. He married the educated sister of one of his classmates from a Delhi family of Mughal descent. At that time, the plight of women, particularly Muslim women, was miserable, which deeply hurt Sheikh Abdulla. He was close to Sir Syed Ahmad, but the latter had an indifferent attitude towards women's education.[45] Due to his own efforts, Sheikh Abdulla was appointed

44. Dutt, op. cit., p. 273.
45. Shahida Banu, *Dr. Rashid Jahan: Hyat Aur Karname* (Urdu), Lucknow, 1990, p. 59.

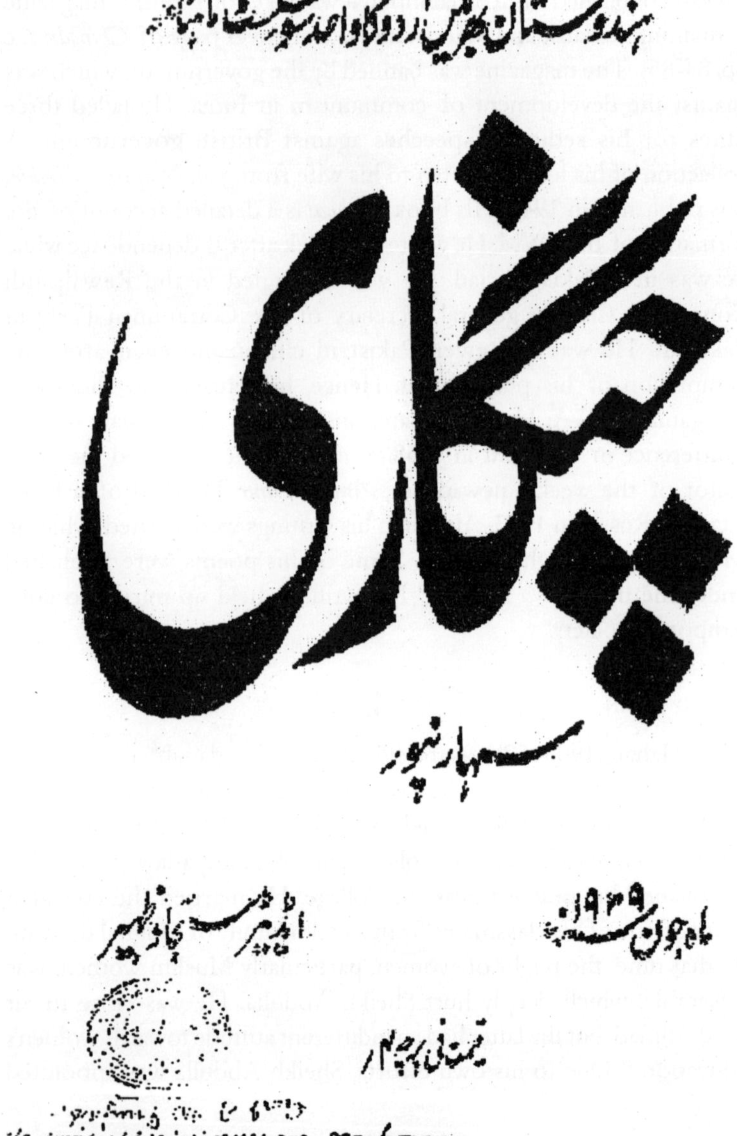
ہندوستان بھر میں اردو کا واحد سوشلسٹ ماہنامہ

چنگاری

سہارنپور

ماہ جون سنہ ۱۹۳۹ء

ایڈیٹر سجاد ظہیر

قیمت فی پرچہ ۴/

Cover page of magazine *Chingari*, Saharanpur.

عزیز دوستو!

سوشلزم کے مطالعہ کرنے اور سوشلسٹ پارٹی بنانے کے لئے یہ بات نہایت ضروری ہے کہ ایک سوشلسٹ اخبار پڑھا جائے۔

"چنگاری" اسی اہم غرض کو مدنظر رکھ کر اردو پڑھنے والوں کے لئے شروع کیا گیا تھا۔

ہندوستان میں صرف ایک ہی مارکسسٹ تھیوریٹیکل ماہنامہ اردو میں ہے۔

وہ لوگ جو سوشلزم کا مطالعہ سنجیدگی کے ساتھ کرنا چاہتے ہیں اور ایک مضبوط سوشلسٹ پارٹی ہندوستان میں قائم کرنا چاہتے ہیں اُن کے لئے نہایت ضروری ہے کہ وہ چنگاری کو اکیلے یا کسی دوسرے کے ساتھ مل کر خریدیں۔ اور کسی کا ہر پرچہ مل کر اسے پڑھیں اور اس کے ضروری مضمونوں پر بحث و مباحثہ کریں۔

جو سوالات بحث و مباحثہ کے درمیان اُٹھیں۔ اُن کو ایڈیٹر چنگاری کے پاس بھیجیں۔

آپ کے سوالوں کا جواب یا تو چنگاری میں یا خط کے ذریعہ سے دیا جائیگا۔

کوئی سوشلسٹ پارٹی یا گروہ اُس وقت تک زندہ اور منظم پارٹی یا گروہ نہیں بن سکتے۔ جب تک کہ "چنگاری" کو پڑھ کر اُس پر بحث و مباحثہ کر کے اپنی معلومات کو بڑھایا نہ جائے اور جب تک چنگاری کے دفتر سے اپنا رشتہ قائم نہ کیا جائے۔

ایڈیٹر

Secretary of the Women's Education Section of the All India Mohammedans' Education Conference in 1902. The main aim of the Women's Education Section was to start a normal school to train teachers. Some people felt that opening a primary school for the daughters of the Ashraf would be more useful and argued that this would attract more patronage. The Aligarh authorities gave the job of raising funds for the school to Shiekh Abdulla. He proved to be a born fund-raiser and organizer.[46]

In 1904, Sheikh Abdulla started the Urdu monthly, *Khatoon* (Gentle Women), as the journal of the Women's Education Section. Its purpose was to advocate women's education, with an emphasis on raising funds. The inside covers of the journal listed the aims of and the need to promote women's education. (For cover page of *Khatoon*, see p. 87.) Sheikh Abdulla encouraged women to send letters and articles written in simple and correct Urdu.[47]

The Abdullas established Aligarh Girls School in 1906. By 1914, they had raised sufficient money to build a hostel. Wahid Jahan devoted her energies to running the school and supervising the hostel. She started living in the hostel with the girls. Her efforts bore fruit and the school attracted girls from other cities. She was known as Alabi, an expression of love and respect.[48] She wrote articles, gave occasional speeches, and helped to organize women. She also raised a large family (five daughters and two sons) and superintended the girls' school and the women's college. She was a remarkable woman.

Rashid Jahan had the courage to mould public opinion. She evidently inherited this habit from her parents. She grew up in a home where all the women were involved in educational and literary pursuits. Her mother and aunts taught at the Aligarh Girls School and wrote for Urdu magazines, including their own journal *Khatoon*. The Abdullas believed so firmly in promoting women's education that they educated their own daughters generously and devotedly. According to Abdulla Begum's biography, at the time of the opening of the girls' hostel,

46. Gail Minault, *Secluded Scholars: Women's Education and Muslim Social Reform in Colonial India*, New Delhi, 1998, p. 123.
47. Ibid., p. 125.
48. Banu, op. cit., p. 65.

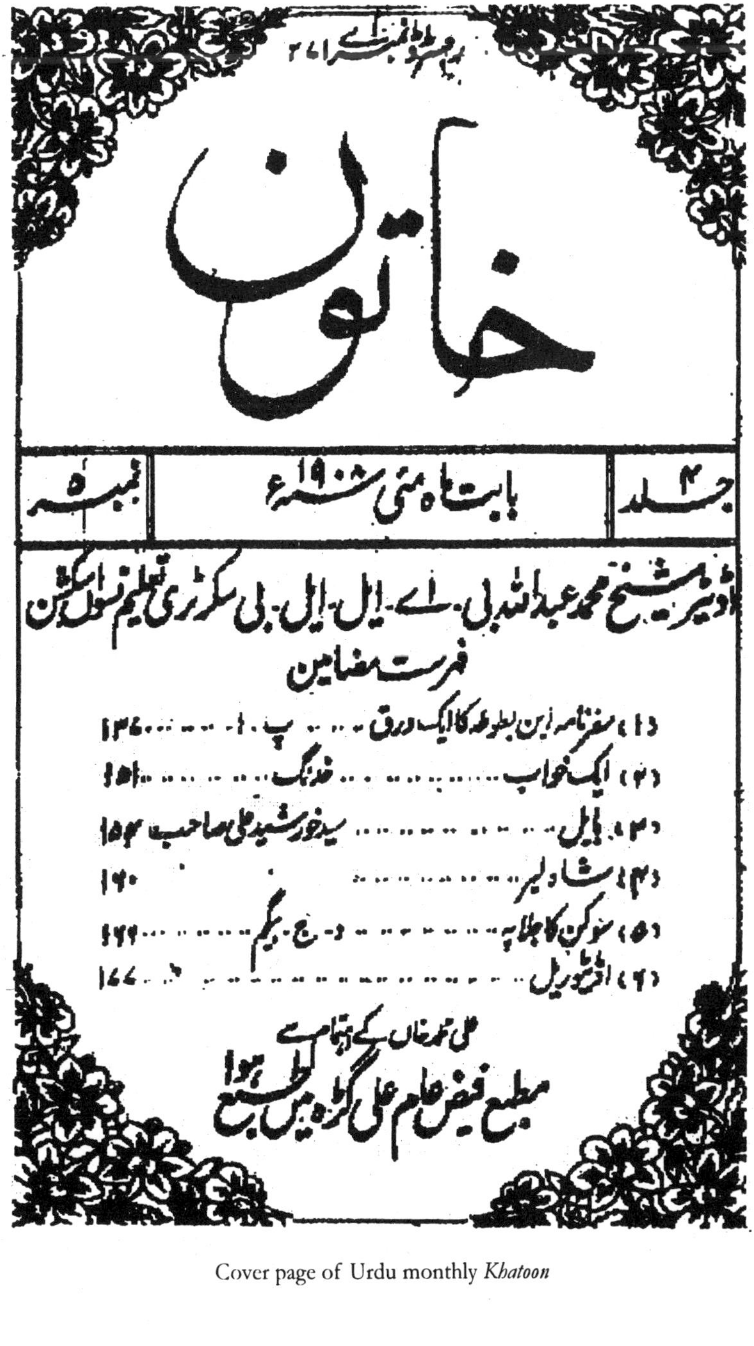

رجسٹرڈ نمبر اے ۲۷۱

خاتون

نمبر ۵	بابت ماہ مئی ۱۹۱۰ء	جلد ۴

اڈیٹر - شیخ محمد عبداللہ بی - اے - ایل - ایل - بی سکرٹری تعلیم نسواں کمیشن

فہرست مضامین

علی محمد خاں کے اہتمام سے

مطبع فیض عام علی گڑھ میں طبع ہوا

Cover page of Urdu monthly *Khatoon*

those who took admission were three daughters of Sheikh Abdulla, three were nieces of Abdulla Begum, one was her friend's daughter, and there were two others.[49] Rashid Jahan and her sisters dared to discard *purdah*, but only after leaving Aligarh to go to college. They used to wear their *burqas* to the railway station in Aligarh, but once on the train and away from home they took off their veils. Rashid Jahan and her sisters were pioneers in women's professional development. She became a doctor and an author. Two of her sisters, Khatoon Jahan and Mumtaz Jahan, served as the principals of the Aligarh Women's College. Khatoon Jahan also served as the principal of the Shekhawat Memorial Girls' College in Calcutta in the mid-1930s. Another sister, Khurshid Jahan, became an actress in films and television in Pakistan and wrote radio and television scripts.[50]

Rashid Jahan was bold and outspoken from an early age. While she was studying science at Isabella Thoburn College, in Lucknow, she distinguished herself as the author of short stories in Urdu and English. These were published in the college magazine. Her first story 'Salma' was published in the college magazine when she was seventeen years old.[51] In this story, she depicted the social condition of average Muslim families in which girls were considered an enigma. Their consent was never obtained for marriage.[52] Her radical ideas influenced her fellow students at Lady Hardinge College in Delhi, which she joined in 1924.

There she organized students to run literary classes and set up free medical clinics for the poor women of the city. But she did not give up her love of literature. She directed a play, *Lalah Rukh*, in English, which enjoyed considerable success. She completed her medical degree in 1929, with a specialization in obstetrics and gyneacology, and joined the UP Medical Services, which took her back to Lucknow.[53]

In Lucknow, the atmosphere was different; the glimpses of a pure Hindustani society could be seen here. Young people attracted by communism were trying to discover new aims and objectives. Rashid

49. Ibid., p. 67.
50. Minault, op. cit., p. 274.
51. Banu, op. cit., p. 68.
52. Ibid., p. 141.
53. Minault, op. cit., p. 274.

Jahan was also part of this generation. Responding to a call by Gandhiji, she began to wear *khadi* for some time. But attracted by revolutionary activists, she started dreaming of armed struggle.[54]

Soon she became acquainted with a politically conscious circle of young Urdu writers. These included Sajjad Zaheer, Justice Wazir Hasan's son, Ahmad Ali, and Mahmuduzzafar, the son of Dr Saiduzzafar, the principal of the Lucknow Medical College. These young progressives were devoted to both Indian nationalism and socialist revolution, and their loyalties influenced their writings. They were deeply influenced by Marxism. Rashid Jahan's writing acquired a similar influence. In addition, her medical profession brought her into close contact with women of all classes, and her writings reflected her deep social concern and compassion for oppressed women.

The four friends decided to publish a collection of short stories reflecting their social and political concerns. The result was *Angare* (Sparks or Embers, 1932), a work that became the opening salvo of the Urdu PWA. Its publication proved to be highly sensational as well as deeply significant in the history of Urdu literature. Rashid Jahan contributed two stories 'Dilli Ki Sair' (A Trip to Delhi) and 'Parde Ke Pichhe' (Behind the Veil). She portrayed the plight of *purdah* women with great economy and irony. *Angare* sparked off a bitter controversy among conventional readers, some of whom were extremely infuriated.[55] The stories were designed to challenge conservative and orthodox religious opinion. The authors sought to set a new trend in literature, moving away from sentimental language and romanticism by addressing the problems of social inequality and the life of oppressed sections such as women. *Angare* was a direct attack on social conservatism. The controversy led the UP government to ban the book. Rashid Jahan's involvement with *Angare* identified her as a rebel and made her a symbol of emancipated women among the progressives. She faced the severest blow at the hands of conservatives. A *fatwa* was issued against her in a masjid.[56]

54. Banu, op. cit., p. 70.
55. Das, op. cit., p. 274.
56. Khurshid Zehra Abidi, *Taraqui Pasand Afsane Mein Aurat Ka Tassavur* (Urdu), Delhi, 1987, p. 77.

Rashid Jahan and Mahmuduzzafar married in 1934. She continued her medical practice throughout the 1930s and 1940s. Simultaneously, she wrote stories and radio plays. Her preoccupation with medical practice and the formation and organization of the All India PWA took up much of her time. Her early death from cancer in 1952 meant that her literary output was necessarily small. As a doctor she had intimate knowledge of the lives of Indian Muslim women, which is evident in her stories and one-act plays.[57] Her many stories, which appeared posthumously, are notable for their portrayal of social themes rather than for the development of character. The pitiable position of women in the family as well as in society and the attitude of people towards disease and medical care were recurring themes. Lack of awareness made people indifferent to medical aid and led them to believe in folk medicine and superstition. In her profession she encountered many unfortunate cases either of neglect or of superstitious reliance on bogus cures.[58] She exposed these problems in the few stories she wrote. According to Hajira Begum, 'Rashid wrote twenty to twenty-five stories during 1932–52 and about twenty plays or dramas and numerous essays. *Aurat* (1937) is a collection of seven dramas and *Shola Jwala* is a collection of her short stories.'

Though Rashid Jahan did not write many stories, she will be remembered as a pioneer of a new trend in Urdu literature. Her role in *Angare* and her literary sketches jolted Indian society by boldly portraying the position of women in middle-class households.

Saadat Hasan Manto

Saadat Hasan Manto (1912–55) was born on 11 May 1912 at Samrala,[59] in Ludhiana. He received his early education at a high school in Amritsar. He had no interest in studies. He was fond of those books that teachers regarded as objectionable for students. With great difficulty he passed the matriculation at the third attempt and in the

57. Ralph Russell, *Hidden in the Lute: An Anthology of Two Centuries of Urdu Literature*, New Delhi, 1995, p. 302.
58. Minault, op. cit., p. 278.
59. Jagdish Chander Wadhawan, *Manto Nama: The Life of Saadat Hasan Manto*, New Delhi, 1998, p. 14.

third division.[60] He lost interest in studies and fell to bad company. During this period, he came in contact with Bari Alig and Ata Mohmad Chiahti, who had come to Amritsar to take up the editorship of the daily *Siv*, and joined *Masawaat,* a daily published from Ludhiana which had been founded by Ghagi Abdul Rahman.[61]

Under the guidance of Bari Alig, he translated Victor Hugo's *The Last Days of the Condemned* into Urdu and published under the title *Aseer Ki Sarguzasht* (The Life Story of a Prisoner). He also translated some stories of Gorky into Urdu. Encouraged by this success, Manto's first original story *Tamasha* appeared anonymously in *Khulk* (a magazine) in which Manto described the Martial Law of 1919 through the eyes of a child. In January 1936, he received a message from Nazir Ludhianvi, the proprietor of the weekly *Mussavar* in Bombay, to join him. To begin with, he was appointed the editor of *Mussavar* on a salary of Rs 40 per month. In 1941, Manto left Bombay for Delhi where he joined All India Radio. Among his colleagues were Upendra Nath Ashk, Krishan Chander, Devendra Satyarthi, and N.M. Rashid. His talent blossomed. He wrote more than a hundred plays that were broadcast over All India Radio in one and a half years. At the same time, he devoted his attention to story writing. He returned to Bombay in 1942 and rejoined *Mussavar.* In Bombay, he was also associated with some leading film studios, including Imperial Film Company, Bombay Talkies, and Filmistan. He wrote over a dozen films, including *Eight Days*, *Chal Chal Re Naujawan*, and *Mirza Ghalib.*[62] *Mirza Ghalib* was a great success.

Manto was a prolific writer and continued writing to the last. He wrote more than 250 short stories. His collections, *Aatish Pare* (1936), *Manto Ke Afsane* (1940), *Dhuan* (1941), *Afsane aur Drame* (1943), *Syah Hashiya* (1948), *Chughad* (1948), *Khali Dibbe, Khali Botlein* (1950), *Thanda Gosht* (1951), *Badshahat Ka Khatma* (1951), *Yazid* (1951), *Uper, Niche Aur Darmian* (1954), *Shaitan* (1954), *Sarkandon Ke Pichhe* (1954), *Namrood Ki Khudai, Sarak Ke Kinare, Phundaney, Bagair Ijazat* (1955),

60. Ibid., p. 18.
61. Ibid., p. 20.
62. Saadat Hasan Manto, *Mottled Dawn: Fifty Sketches and Stories of Partition*, tr. Khalid Hasan, New Delhi, 1997, p. 1.

Burqa (1955), *Shikari Aurtein* (1955), and *Teen Aurtein*[63] were hailed by certain people as masterpieces and ran into several editions.[64] During the period from 1934 to 1947, Manto wrote sixty-nine short stories.[65] After Partition, he left Bombay in 1947 and migrated to Lahore and remained there until his death on 18 January 1955. From 1947 to 1955, Manto wrote at great speed. Magazine editors exploited his talent to the fullest. During this period, he published twenty-two collections of short stories, one novel, five collections of radio plays, and a full-length play. Many films produced in India and Pakistan were based on his stories.[66]

Manto started his literary career by translating the stories of European and Russian masters. He was greatly influenced by Maupassant. He was also influenced by Marxian thought and Gorky's techniques. He was also associated with progressives, but his own predilections led him away. He drew his characters from the lower strata of Indian society and his stories depicted a stark reality. Though he wrote romantic and political stories, he is best known for his creations of deserted, destitute, and fallen women. He shows great sympathy for neglected and rejected women, prostitutes of filthy lanes and crowded slums. Touts and pimps rub shoulders with tarts, drawing customers into their coils. Manto unfolded their lives layer by layer, without hiding anything. He also unmasked those hypocrites who claimed to be the custodians of society and who doled out moral homilies, but who in reality were the lords of oppression and solely responsible for the degradation of women.

Manto's radically different view of literature shocked his contemporaries. No Urdu writer was so clear in his approach as Manto. Published in *Saqi*, a noted Urdu magazine, his two stories 'Kali Salwar' and 'Dhuan' came under litigation while he was working at All India Radio, Delhi. He was acquitted for the first but a case was launched

63. Dutt, *Fun Aur Shakhsiat*, op. cit., p. 303.
64. Ali Jawad Zaidi, *A History of Urdu Literature*, New Delhi, 1993, p. 401.
65. Saadat Hasan Manto, *Dastavez*, part 1, Selection and Introduction by Balraj Manra and Sharad Dutt, New Delhi, 1993, p. 475.
66. Jai Ratan (ed.), *The Best of Manto: A Collection of Short Stories*, New Delhi, 1989, p. ii.

against 'Dhuan'. Out of Manto's 250 stories, six were declared obscene, for which he was hauled up before the law time and again. Besides the above-mentioned two stories, the others that were dubbed as obscene are 'Boo' (Odour) 'Khol Do', 'Thanda Gosht' and 'Uper, Niche aur Darmian'. In his short life of forty-three years, Manto's literary life spanned over twenty-two years. Of these he spent about ten years rotting in law courts in connection with his stories. During this period, he faced great hardship and suffered physical as well as financial loss.[67]

While dragged repeatedly to the courts, Manto's patience was stretched to the utmost. On such occasions he seemed to favour the reformist role of literature. He said,

> If you cannot tolerate my stories, this means the times are intolerable. There is nothing wrong with my stories. The wrong which is ascribed to my stories is, in fact, the rot of the system, . . . if you are opposed to my literature then the best way is that you change the conditions that motivate such literature.[68]

In this statement Manto seemed to support the view that literature is a product of social conditions and that whatever the writer feels, that is created by his pen. In another defence, Manto emphasized that the *neem* leaves are pungent but they cleanse the blood. So was the case with his harsh writings.

Manto pointed out, 'A *Veshya* is a woman as well, but every woman is not a *Veshya*.' People do not go to a prostitute's quarters to offer *namaz*, they go there and buy the commodity they want to buy.[69] Manto's concern is not the commodity, but the pain, hardship, suffering, and the hollowness and loneliness of the human soul who sells the goods. Manto lamented the attitude of people who considered the very existence of women or the very nature of man–woman relations obscene. If this were so, why did God then create woman? Manto was equally critical of man-made codes of morality, which are different for both the sexes. He criticized society for not equating

67. Wadhawan, op. cit., p. 118.
68. Alok Bhalla (ed.), *Life and Works of Saadat Hasan Manto*, Shimla, 1997, p. 3.
69. Ibid., p. 16.

man and woman. 'Why should I take off the *choli* of society? It is naked as it is. Of course, I am not interested in covering it up either because that is the job of tailors, not of writers.'[70]

'Kali Salwar', 'Bapu Gopi Nath', 'Hatak', 'Boo', 'Foba Bai' and 'Burhami Ladki' are his best-known stories. Manto's fiction on India's Partition and its impact on the Indo–Pak ethos is an invaluable treasure not only of Urdu literature but also of Indian history. He moved to Pakistan in January 1948, and his greatest works were produced in the last seven years of his life. At the same time, he faced great financial and emotional hardship. Manto took stock of the tremendous and disturbing communal strife and tried to comprehend all its dimensions and put them in a proper perspective. He depicted the tragedy of Partition, particularly the effect on women who were the worst victims of gruesome communal violence.

One of Manto's greatest stories on the Partition is 'Toba Tek Singh', in which along with the transfer of population and assets, the division of lunatics also takes place between the two countries. But one Bishan Singh refused to go to India because he wanted to live in the town of Toba Tek Singh. He was left in no man's land where he died when morning broke. 'The Dog of Titwal', and 'The Last Salute' relate to the war in Kashmir after the Partition. In 'The Dutiful Daughter', 'Mozail', 'Khol Do', 'Thanda Gosht', the 'The Woman in Red Raincoat', Manto portrayed the cruel outcomes of Partition.

In addition to his finest and most powerful masterpieces on the tragic events of Partition, Manto's sketches were published under the title *Syah Hashiye* (Block Fringes). The sketches, some of them no longer than a line or two, bring out the enormity of the tragedy. These are deeply ironic and often deeply moving. In one sketch two men buy a girl because she is from a different religion, but after they have used her, they are mortified to discover that they had been cheated as 'she belongs to the same religion as they do'. 'I want my money refunded', one of them declares.[71] After the publication of the book, *Syah Hashiye* Manto was subjected to harsh personal attacks and accused of bad taste, cynicism and even cruelty.

70. Ibid., p. 6.

71. Manto, *Mottled Dawn*, pp. xxii–xxiii.

Manto argued that social oppression and economic deprivation were responsible for the plight of the various characters of his stories. He never pretended to be a philosopher and preacher. He accepted sex as one of the basic and instinctual aspects of man's existence. In 1938, he wrote to Ahmad Nadim Qasmi, 'Life should be presented as it is, not as it was or will be or ought to be.'[72] Manto left for Pakistan, but he did not find the green pastures for which he was searching. He was jailed and no one protested. He went mad and was admitted into a mental hospital. He wanted to come to Bombay, as he wrote in one of his letters to Ismat Chughtai.[73]

> You know me as a story writer and the courts know me as an obscene writer. The Government sometimes calls me a communist and sometimes a great literary figure. Sometimes the doors of livelihood are closed on me and sometimes they are opened for me. Sometimes I am declared *persona non grata* and considered an outsider. Sometimes when the powers that be are pleased, I am told that I can be an insider. I am still troubled as I have often been in the past over the question like: Who am I ? What is my status? What is my role in this country, which is regarded as the largest Islamic state?
>
> You may call my concern fictional, but for me the bitter reality is that in my country, which is called Pakistan and is very dear to me, I have yet to find a place. That is why my soul is restless. That is why I am sometimes in a lunatic asylum and sometimes in a hospital. I have still not found my rightful place in Pakistan. . . .[74]

Saadat Hasan Manto has the distinction of being the most maligned, the most controversial, and the most widely read short-story writer of Urdu. He was one of the finest writers of our age. Unfortunately he did not get the recognition he deserved during his lifetime. He was praised less and denounced more. His ruthless manner of exposing the hollowness of middle-class morality and its sordid aspects could not be digested. Manto always provoked contradictory

72. Shamim Hanfi, 'Manto: The Person and the Myth', in *Life and Works of Saadat Hasan Manto*, ed. Alok Bhalla, p. 193.
73. Ismat Chughtai, *My Friend, My Enemy: Essays, Reminiscences, Portraits*, tr. Tahira Naqvi, New Delhi, 2001, p. 210.
74. Davendra Issar, 'Manto: The Image of the Soul in Mirror of Eros', in *Life and Works of Saadat Hasan Manto*, ed. Alok Bhalla, p. 184.

responses. He was a difficult man to understand. He was touchy, introverted, and egotistical, which often left him lonely and depressed.

KRISHAN CHANDER

Krishan Chander (1913–77) was born on 26 November 1913 in Bharatpur, Rajasthan. His father, Dr Gouri Shankar, was employed in Bharatpur and after that in Poonch. Krishan Chander received his primary education in Poonch. After 1930, he went to Lahore for higher education and enrolled in the Forman Christian College. He obtained an M.A. degree in English from Punjab University in 1934.[75]

Krishan Chander's literary life started at the *Adhi Duniya*, Lahore where he was encouraged by Salah-ud-din. At this time, he was employed by All India Radio, Lahore and within one year he was transferred to Delhi and then to Lucknow. Lucknow was the centre of the PWM, so it was natural for him to associate with this movement. But dissatisfied as he was with government service, he moved to Bombay. He was deeply influenced by the PWM. He made two films. These were *Rakh* (Ashes) and *Dharti Ka Lal* (Son of the Soil)[76] in which he presented his progressive views. There was no question of success at the box office since films of this nature were not popular. These can be appreciated today not because they were hits but because of the themes with which they dealt. But it was a waste of money and energy at that time.

Krishan Chander's stature was the highest among the progressive writers who dominated the literary scene in India at that time. He used to attend the meetings of PWA regularly. He wrote novels, short stories, dramas, reports, and essays. But basically he was known as a short-story writer. He displayed a romantic flair in his short stories, which is incomparable in Urdu literature. He practised law and did freelance writing in English and Urdu for the *Ambala Tribune* and the weekly *Northern Review*. Starting with humorous stories, he switched to romantic tales. The publication of *Tilism-e-Khayal* revealed an astounding freshness, charming simplicity, and a robust frankness. He gave tongue to the lay man's aspirations, dreams, and sufferings.

75. Dutt, *Fun Aur Shakhsiat*, op. cit., p. 309.
76. Chughtai, *My Friend, My Enemy*, p. 223.

He became the most polished writer of the Progressive Group. As the leading writer of the Progressive School, he dedicated his art to revealing the capitalist and the ruling classes in all their brutality and bestiality.[77] His stories dealt with romantic, social, and psychological themes as well as political, national, and international themes. He enjoyed a larger readership in Pakistan than in India. His stories appeared in most Urdu journals. His popularity can be estimated by an excerpt from Ismat Chughtai's portrait in *Chirag Roshan Hain* (The Lamps are Lit). Chughtai pointed out that Krishan Chander's wife had a very different nature. 'Did you find her?' Krishan Chander asked. 'I found her but we did not really meet. She disappeared like the heroine from Mahal', Ismat Chughtai said, 'Is she angry with us?'

When Krishan Chander left the room for a minute, Mahendra (an Urdu writer) said furtively, 'She is angry with the whole world.'

'Why?'

'Because the world loves Krishan Ji.'[78]

His popularity had caught the attention of the masses. In Pakistan, his fame touched new heights. His works were translated into Russian and other languages. A journal in Pakistan conducted a public survey that revealed Krishan Chander was the best and most popular writer in the subcontinent.[79]

To present human suffering realistically, he occasionally disappeared for days, spending his nights on the footpaths, sharing the pain of the downtrodden by mingling with them. Ismat Chughtai says, 'When he returns with a cough and a fever, his wife thinks he has spent the night in the arms of his beloved. She doesn't know his real beloved is actually his writing whose love compels him into being oblivious to everything else.'[80]

Krishan Chander wrote more than 80 volumes of short stories, novels, travelogues, belles-lettres, and plays. His popular books are: *Tilism-e-Khayal, Anna Data, Teen Gunde, Zindagi Ke Mor Par, Tute Huye*

77. Gopi Chand Narang, *Urdu Language and Literature: Critical Perspectives*, New Delhi, 1991, p. 131.
78. Chughtai, op. cit., p. 227.
79. Ibid., p. 235.
80. Ibid., p. 230.

Tare, Shikast, Dadar Pul Ke Bachey, Ham Vahashi Hain, Hawai Qiley, Ek Gadhe Ki Sargujasht, Bawan Patte, Ek Aurat Hajar Deewane, Jab Khet Jage, Dil Ki Vadiyan, Sogain, Foot Path Ke Farishte, and *Aadhe Ghante Ka Khuda.*[81] His other notable collections are *Asman Roshan Hai, Meri Yadon Ke Chirag, Ek Violin, Samandar Ke Kinare, Chandi Ke Ghao, Kaghaz Ki Nao, Nazare, Samandar Door Hai, Ajanta Se Aage, Main Intezar Karoonga, Dil Kisi Ka Dost Nahin, Kitab Ka Kafan,* and *Ek Rupya Ek Phool.* He wrote three reportages—*Paude, Subah Hoti Hai,* and *Waraq Waraq Kho Gai Zindagi Meri.*[82] Gopi Chand Narang and Ali Jawad Zaidi estimated the number of his published books at about eighty.

Krishan Chander wrote about various problems and human relationships. He treated the art of writing as criticism of life and as a vehicle for social upliftment. Sometimes he was carried away by intense emotion and thus lacked depth. Despite his penchant for romanticism, he found the basis of storytelling in reality. His readers were pleased with his racy idealism, soft sentimentalism, and sincere exhortation. He remained tender and sympathetic towards the problems of ordinary men instead of being severe and detached. In his first collection, *Tilism-e-Khayal,* he depicted the natural scene at such length that it seems that, overlooking the harsh realities of life, he took refuge in nature. But in *Galicha, Kalu Bhangi, Mahalakshmi Ke Pul,* and *Anna Data,* he adopted a satirical tone. *Anna Data* is a story of the Bengal famine written in a very effective manner. Ismat Chughtai remarked that she had learnt to view the Bengal famine only through the lens of *Anna Data. Jab Khet Jage* deals with the problems of the Telengana peasants and their attempts to retain their land following reforms in the land tenure system. Marxian influence is also evident here.

'In a Boat over the Jhelum' and in other stories, the portrayal of the characters Angi, Buggi, Gomti, and Shama heightened the intensity of beauty and sadness mingled together. The sweetness of romance is sometimes blunted by the sharp edge of sorrow.[83] With the story

81. Dutt, *Fun Aur Shakhsiat,* op. cit., p. 305.
82. Zaidi, *A History of Urdu Literature,* pp. 399–400.
83. Krishan Chander, *Selected Short Stories,* tr. Jai Ratan, Introduction by Gopi Chand Narang, New Delhi, 1989, p. 9.

At the Hotel Firdaus, Krishan Chander's art took a new turn. Romance became idealized and worthy of being emulated.

The Partition of the country provided a new theme to writers, firing their imagination. Literature, especially Urdu literature, presented the real picture of depression, outrage, communal hatred, and other atrocities as witnessed by sensitive writers. Krishan Chander wrote stories at a breathless pace. During 1947–8 five volumes of his stories were published. They are *Ham Vahashi Hain, Ek Girja Ek Khandak, Ajanta Se Aage, Samandar Door Hai,* and *Teen Gunde*.[84]

The most notable stories are 'Ham Vahashi Hain', 'The Peshawar Express', 'Naya Madrasa', and 'Mera Bachcha'. In 'Mera Bachcha' Krishan Chander describes the Indian child as being subjected to communal prejudices from birth. In *Peshawar Express*, the train, which ran through Pakistan and India, is shown as an eyewitness to inhumane and ill deeds. Krishan Chander was more prolific among his contemporaries except Manto. It seemed that the tragic events of the Partition suited their individual styles. Manto was interested in depicting the seamy side of sex while Krishan Chander in dramatizing humanism. The literature he produced at such tremendous speed and with such missionary zeal is worthy of high acclaim. It is an invaluable treasure not only for Urdu, but also for the history of Indian literature.

There are many aspects of Krishan Chander's writing. Writing on varied subjects, he tried new experiments and techniques. He wrote a purely experimental story 'Sureeli Tasveer' and a plotless story 'The Carpet'. His language was simple and direct. Romance and stark realism mingled closely in his writings. His commitment to the ideals of human freedom and peace, and his hope for a happy future, prevailed throughout all his works.

Krishan Chander was a prolific writer. Even when he was ill, when the doctor ordered him to abstain from any kind of intellectual activity, he continued writing. He used to say, 'When I write, my mind travels to my fingers. The moment I hold the pen in my hand, my mind soars.'[85] More importantly, writing was his source of livelihood and

84. Ibid., p. 10.
85. Chughtai, op. cit., p. 237.

the cause of his popularity. Ismat Chughtai wrote about an incident that occurred while she was in Pakistan. 'It was *Id.* A boy arrived on a cycle, flustered and out of breath. "I have travelled fourteen miles and I have spent fourteen hours trying to find the house. I just wanted to find out how Krishan ji is." "He is perfectly fine," I said. He thanked me and left.'[86] At that time, Krishan Chander had suffered another heart attack and a pacemaker was installed. But he could not survive long even with the pacemaker. On 8 March 1977, he passed away. He was honoured with the Padma Bhushan by the Government of India.

Ismat Chughtai

Ismat Chughtai (1915–91) was born into a large middle-class Muslim family on 21 August 1915 at Badaun, in Uttar Pradesh. Her name was Ismat Khanam. She was the ninth of ten children. She was the daughter of Qasim Beg Chughtai, who was a civil servant in UP, and the sister of Azim Beg Chughtai who was also a noted writer, humorist, and satirist of his time. As Ismat's father had a transferable job, the family moved frequently.

Ismat and her sisters were taught Urdu and the Koran at home by an ill-tempered *ustani* (teacher) whom she hated.[87] Her older sisters went to the Karamat Husain Girls School in Lucknow, but Ismat went to Aligarh and then to the Isabella Thoburn College, Lucknow. She completed her B.A. in 1938. When she was in her teens, her father died and the family moved to Jodhpur with her uncle, who was an Inspector General of Police. During her school days, she used to go to school by train. She was rebellious from a young age and used to take off her *burqa* in the train. But when she arrived in Jodhpur, her uncle saw her unveiled, he reprimanded her for her behaviour. But she refused to listen to anyone except her father, who had died.[88] She discarded the *purdah* not only as an act of rebellion but also with the sanction of her family. Her uncle threatened to marry her off but she was keen on pursuing higher education in order to support the

86. Ibid., p. 239.
87. Minault, *Secluded Scholars*, p. 278.
88. Ibid.

children of one of her siblings who was ailing. She chose to go back to Aligarh in 1938 for her teacher training. Finding no training classes for women in Aligarh, she was prepared to attend classes with men. Several other women students were not in favour of it. They persuaded the principal of the men's training college to screen off part of the classroom so that women students could attend. Ismat obtained her B.T. in 1939.[89] She became the principal of the Raj Mahal Girls School and of the Islamia Girls School in Bareilly. Later on, she became an Inspector of the Municipal Girls Schools in Bombay.[90]

Ismat Chughtai was influenced and inspired by Rashid Jahan in her writings. She had met Rashid Jahan at school in Aligarh and was impressed by her outspoken nature and wanted to be like her, though she had been stubborn and outspoken from an early age. When she was only eight, she wept because she was not allowed to ride the white mare on which her brother rode like a prince. Her father, who was a Deputy Collector, overruled Begum Sahiba's decision and Ismat got her first ride. It was like having won a fort in a battle, she recounted later. She spent her childhood in the footsteps of her brothers, climbing trees to eat guavas, watching monkeys dance, and chasing hens.[91] Her early writing reveal the influence of her brother, Azim Beg Chughtai, an author of Urdu short stories and a humorist. He encouraged her to write and served as her first critic. Her first published work was 'Fasadi' (The Troublemaker), which appeared in the literary journal *Saqi* in 1938.[92]

Ismat had read the banned book *Lady Chatterley's Lover* by D.H. Lawrence and *Angare*, a volume of short stories by progressive writers published from Lucknow, which influenced her deeply. She discarded the *purdah*. She attended the Progressive Writers' conference in Lucknow and saw Munshi Premchand and the writers of *Angare* from a distance. She was very much a patron of PWM. She was influenced

89. Ibid.
90. Nand Kishor Vikram, *Urdu Kahanikar: Ismat Chughtai* (Hindi), Delhi, 1996, p. 13.
91. Nirupama Dutt, 'The Importance of Being Ismat Apa', *Indian Express*, 5 December 1999.
92. Minault, op. cit., p. 279.

by Marx and Freud. It was under Freud's impact that instead of moral and religious themes, the progressive writers started discussing sex with frankness and at the same time in a realistic manner.

Books had great influence on Ismat. She looked for solutions to many problems in books and found answers. 'Thousands of disappointments, countless dark moments were made bearable by these books,' she recalled. Starting from Hardy and the Bronte sisters, she arrived at George Bernard Shaw. Inspired by Shaw's dramas, she also started writing dramas. While studying at Aligarh she used to stage some of her short dramas. 'My first written work, "Fasadi" was a drama,' she said. Russian writers had the greatest influence on her in the moment of her helplessness and indecisiveness. Whenever she could not come to grips with some story and did not know where to start and where to end, she read a few stories of Chekhov for mental stimulation and her pen soon started moving. After reading she turned to talking. In a family of talkative people all sense of time was lost when two or three members got together. She enjoyed talking to everyone—shop keepers, grocers, taxi drivers, even beggars. Teasing old men and women, listening to their curses and abuses gave her a strange kind of pleasure. It helped to create a story within minutes. What she needed was to ask a few straightforward and brief questions.[93]

Ismat wrote on a wide range of subjects, including sex, social problems, politics, the fading world of the past and its loveliness, and, above all, women's issues, which she expressed in practical realism. She was a luminous star on the horizon of the new short story in Urdu. Her piercing intellect and instinct for probing beneath the surface as a fiction writer meant that she surveyed the entire social and moral scene, feudal society, and the plight of women, and tried to recreate the entirety of her complex experiences in her stories.[94]

Ismat Chughtai's best stories are drawn from the lives of women and are told largely in the specific language of women, since women

93. 'How Chekhov Kept My Pen Moving', Ismat Chughtai's delightful vignette on the art of reading, writing and listening excerpted from Sukrita Paul Kumar (eds.), *Ismat: Her Life, Her Times*, Delhi, 2000.
94. Zaidi, *A History of Urdu Literature*, p. 402.

live in a world largely separate from that of men. She had her own vocabulary and turn of phrase. Ismat wrote her early stories sitting at home. She observed the gossiping of women very closely. Its appropriateness to her themes is obvious and works powerfully in bringing readers closer to the people she portrays and makes them seem real. But some time she overdoes the use of the specific language of women, which distances the characters. So her performance is uneven.[95]

Her first short story was 'Gainda' which appeared in *Saqi* in 1939.[96] Thereafter several stories were published but the work that brought her fame or notoriety was 'Lihaf' (The Quilt), appearing just two months before her marriage to Shahid Latif, a Bombay-based film writer and director. 'Lihaf' caused a sensation and furore, for it was a frank description not only of a wife's sexual frustration but also of the woman's relationship with a female servant with whom she found emotional and sexual companionship. Consorting with a member of the lower classes was shocking enough. But the lesbian theme was too much even for progressive public opinion. Many people doubted that it was written by a woman. They were of the view that in reality it was written by a man who published under woman's name.[97] But when it was proved that 'Lihaf' was written by a woman, she was prosecuted by the Punjab government for obscenity. After trial lasting two years, the charges were ultimately dismissed.

After the trial of *Lihaf*, Shahid Latif's order to his wife to quit writing was of no avail. 'He might as well have asked me to quit breathing,' Ismat said. She continued to publish novels and short stories based on middle-class women's existence with an authenticity that no male writer could have matched and in a style that was frank, earthy, and colloquial. She depicted her characters vividly, ruthlessly, and at the same time with the deepest sympathy. Her mastery of the spoken word and her economy of form are incomparable.

Ismat wrote several novels and a number of short stories. Her first novel *Ziddi* was published in 1941. Her novel *Masooma* (1962)

95. Russell, *The Pursuit of Urdu Literature*, p. 224.
96. Vikram, op. cit., p. 13.
97. Ibid., p. 9.

examines life in an affluent Indian Muslim community and the position of the women in it.[98] Her works are as follows:

Novels: *Ziddi, Tehri Lakeer, Masooma, Saudai, Junglee Kabootar, Dil Ki Dunia, Ajeeb Adami, Bandi, Katra-i-Khoon* (novelette). She wrote *Teen Anadi* and *Nakali Raj Kumar* for Children.

Collection of short stories: *Kalian, Chotein, Ek Baat, Chhui Mui, Do Hath, Dojakh, Kanwari* (Hindi), *Badan Ki Khushboo.*

Dramas: *Dhani Banke, Shaitan.*[99] Her autobiography, *Kagazi Hai Pairahan*, describes her trial in Lahore on charges of obscenity in connection with her story *Lihaf.*

Ismat turned to writing for films and produced some screenplays. With *Arzoo,* Shahid and she became film-makers under the banner of *Filmina.* Many of their films flopped at the box office but *Ziddi* and *Sone Ki Chidiya* made a mark. In 1973 M.S. Sathyu, made *Garam Hawa*, a film based on one of Ismat's short stories. She received the president's award for the best film story. In 1976, she received the Padamshri. In 1977, she received the Ghalib Award from the Ghalib Institute for her Urdu play *Tanhai Ka Zahar.* In 1979, she was awarded the Mukhdoom Literary Award by the Andhra Pradesh Academy.[100]

Ismat Chughtai's non-fictional writings comprising essays, commentaries, and biographical sketches give readers a good idea of the artistic, political, and social milieu in which she lived and worked. She was very honest and passionate in her works. Independence and Partition are the principal backdrops against which many of her non-fictional writings unfold.[101]

Ismat Chughtai was a radical writer. She gave a new direction to the progressive movement in Urdu literature. During her entire life she fought against hypocrisy and religious fanaticism. But these were not enough for the secure existence of a radical woman in a society

98. Syed Fazle Rab, *Sociology of Literature: A Study of Urdu Novels*, New Delhi, 1992, p. 84.
99. Dutt, *Fun Aur Shakhsiat*, op. cit., p. 324.
100. Nirupama Dutt, op. cit.
101. Chughtai, *My Friend, My Enemy*, pp. iii–iv.

where religious orthodoxy was more powerful than reason. 'She will be remembered,' as Shahid Barelvi wrote in an obituary tribute, 'for her courage as a pioneer of the feminist movement in India even before it started in the West'.[102]

Rajinder Singh Bedi

Rajinder Singh Bedi (1915–84) was born on 1 September 1915 in a poor family in Disca, Sialkot in Punjab.[103] He received his primary education in Disca and then went to Lahore and passed his matriculation examination in 1931. After his matriculation, he was admitted to DAV College and passed his intermediate. But he could not complete his higher education due to the sudden death of his mother. He accepted a job as a clerk in post office in Lahore. In 1943, he resigned the job and worked in the Central Publicity Department. After that, he joined All India Radio as staff artist. After the Partition of the country, he came to Delhi. He was later appointed station director of Jammu Radio Station in 1948. But his stay in Jammu turned out to be a short one. He left for Bombay and took to writing for films. His success encouraged him to become a film director later. Among them *Dastak* became popular. The dialogues written by Bedi for films like *Mirza Ghalib*, *Devdas*, and *Anuradha* became very popular.[104]

Bedi started writing short stories during his school days. The 1930s proved a turning point in fiction writing in the country. Translations of the works of Russian writers had become common after the First World War. But Western writers, especially English and French, had impressed young writers even more. In 1932, the publication of *Angare*, an anthology of short stories, took the Urdu world by surprise. The stories, only ten in number and written by four newcomers, were characterized by a reformist politics and a spirit of rebellion against orthodoxy. With its publication the floodgates were opened to Marxian and Freudian influences. In 1935, the PWM was launched. Inspired by Marxian ideas, these writers imbibed the spirit of socialism. The manifesto of PWM was being adopted by young Urdu writers. Around

102. Das, *A History of Indian Literature*, p. 20.
103. Dutt, *Fun Aur Shakhsiat*, op. cit., p. 325.
104. Ibid.

this time, the leading trio of Urdu story writers—Saadat Hasan Manto, Rajinder Singh Bedi, and Krishan Chander—came into prominence and dominated Urdu fiction for more than two decades.

Rajinder Singh Bedi was closely associated with the progressive movement, but he was neither a diehard nor an extremist. He started writing with Chekhov as his model. He was more interested in ordinary people and presented his characters very sympathetically and tenderly. His stories are deeply rooted in the common man's real-life existence. The conflicts and problems faced by ordinary men and women in their day-to-day life are depicted with sympathy and understanding. Bedi's dexterous psychoanalysis dissects the misery and gloom in society. He did not mock it but inspired the afflicted to change their situation for the better, and to conquer the miseries of life.[105] Weaving his plots from common place themes and events, he nevertheless portrayed the characters exactly as he wanted, with ease and grace. His portrayal of the Indian wife and Indian domestic life is superb. He did not idealize woman but underlined her enduring and tolerant nature. He portrayed her hardships and sufferings with sensitivity. He presented woman in her different roles as a beloved, a wife, a daughter, a widow, a suffering soul. In his many stories, the woman, filled with a deep and abiding love, compassion and devotion, underwent various hardships and great pain to bring joy and happiness to the man, to her family and to the universe.[106]

In his stories 'Bhola', 'Chhokri Ki Loot' and 'Man Hi Man' Bedi portrayed women as widows, while in 'Terminus Se Parey' the woman appears in the role of a sister. In 'Chechak Ke Dag' the woman tolerate all hardships in all conditions. In 'Lajwanti' (Touch Me Not), Bedi portrayed a woman's suffering in different situations. She was abducted during the Partition riots and later on restored to her husband, who treated her very sympathetically and called her *devi*. He avoids talking about the past. On the other hand, Lajwanti wants him to accept her as she was before her abduction. Her husband's behaviour hurts her.

Bedi looked into woman's psyche very deeply. *Lajwanti* is perhaps his only story on the Partition. In 'Kokhjali' (Barren), 'Ek Aurat' and

105. Zaidi, *A History of Urdu Literature*, p. 402.
106. Narang, op. cit., p. 130.

'Eucalyptus' he presents woman as a complete mother. In 'Kalyani', Bedi presents sex, although with a prostitute, as the male conquering and the female surrendering as a victim.

In his novel *Ek Chadar Maili Si*, Bedi portrays a typical relationship of rural Punjab, that of a widow of elder brother entering into 'wedlock' (*chadar dalna*), that is relationship of protection with the younger brother of her deceased husband, without examining the female psyche, which may revolt against such an alliance. Bedi reveals the intricacies of the mind of the heroine who is not ready to follow such a convention. But at last she agrees for the sake of the family's prestige. In 'Grahan', Bedi employs metaphorical use of Rahu and Ketu to depict social taboos.

There are male characters also who face hardships and tolerate them with grace. The heroes of 'Garam Coat' and 'Mein Aur Mera Iman' endure many hardships. Rahman of 'Rahman Ke Jutte' is a bold male character. But some female characters like Rano, Indu, and Lajwanti have become immortal in Urdu literature as the most realistic, sincere, and sympathetic representation of Indian womanhood.

Bedi could neither write romantic and picturesque prose like Krishan Chander, nor deal with sex with the boldness of Manto. Whatever he wrote, it was with great care and after weighing each word. Once Manto said to him, 'You think too much. You think before you write, you think while you are writing and also when you have finished writing.' To this Bedi responded in a humorous tone, 'A Sikh may be lacking in many things, but he is sure of one thing: he is a good craftsman. Whatever he builds, he builds to its perfection, making sure that every part of it rings true.'[107]

Bedi wrote 66 stories. Six collections of short stories have been published. These are *Dana-o-Dam* (1936), *Grahan* (1942) *Kokhjali* (1949), *Apne Dukh Mujhe De Do* (1965), *Hath Hamare Kalam Huye* (1973), and *Mukti Bodh* (1982). Bedi wrote some dramas also. There are two collections of dramas—*Bejaan Chizein* (1943) and *Saat Khel* (1974). Bedi's novelette *Ek Chadar Maili Si* (1962)[108] became very popular. It is one of the greatest works of Urdu literature.

107. Narang, op. cit., pp. 147–8.
108. Dutt, op. cit., p. 325.

Although he did not produce many works, whatever Bedi wrote is of high quality, both linguistically and thematically. He believed that the art of writing does not emerge spontaneously from the mind like a spring from the ground. It is not that one goes to sleep at night and becomes a writer in the morning. None can claim to be a born writer. All that one can claim without any fear of contradiction is that a man may have the potential for writing, which may be an inborn gift and which can be cultivated through hard work.[109] A writer has a sensitive mind and feels more intensely than others. He can endure both praise, and pain as if he were being flayed. According to Bedi, a writer should not be satisfied with his first draft and should go in for many revisations. He believed that a good writer should have some knowledge of other arts such as music and painting.

Bedi tried his hand at poetry but without success. He said, 'I remained innocent of what poetry could teach me concerning life and its ways. On the other hand, life bestowed upon me a host of problems such as domestic bickering and the vicissitudes of daily living, which are no less arduous and intricate than the problem of falling in love.'[110] These problems create a restlessness in his mind and the result was 'Garam Coat'. An examination of Bedi's writings reveals that all his characters belonged to lower and middle-class society. He portrayed very successfully the female psyche and protected the woman's dignity. He was more interested in exploring the depths of the human mind and in making half-humorous and half-sad comments than in adapting to any predetermined line of thinking or interpretation. Most of his stories have a subtle symbolism.

R.S. Bedi has been honoured for his contribution to literature. He is the recipient of the Padamshri (1972), the Sahitya Akademi Award (1965), the Ghalib Award (1978), and several other awards.

The formation of PWA, with a view to mobilizing literature in depicting human (especially women's) sufferings, sorrows, miseries, problems and needs, was an important development in the history of India literature in the twentieth century. The writers who joined

109. Rajinder Singh Bedi, *Selected Short Stories*, tr. Jai Ratan, New Delhi, 1989, p. 253.

110. Ibid., p. 255.

this movement were many but the biographical sketches of a selected few give us an idea of their writings and attitudes. The next chapter, will examine their perceptions and attitudes towards various gender-related issues and problems.

5

Purdah and the Politics of Childbirth

Purdah remained the central theme relating to literary representations of women's life. It has been vividly described in literature, folk songs, and proverbs. *Purdah* is a Persian word, which literally means 'curtain', as in the curtain over windows and doors. The word also means veil among Muslims and Hindus. Living behind the *purdah*, or being *purdah nashin*, means the concealment of women, thus creating separation between the world of men and the world of women. At least 95 per cent of Muslim women, perhaps even more, observed *purdah* consistently and logically in the early twentieth century.[1] In the Indian subcontinent, many Hindu women also observe *purdah*, but the *purdah* of Hindus is slightly different from that of Muslims. It is estimated that 72.61 per cent of women in south-east Punjab (Haryana) observed *purdah*.[2]

Purdah among Muslim women was one way respecting them. Islam was basically a civilizing mission and it gave greater dignity to women, thus raising their status from being mere chattel and sexual objects to a life of dignity. So Islam prescribed certain norms of behaviour and styles of dressing.[3] As Arabs belonged to different tribes before Islam, it must be noted, sexual morality was quite lax. Men and women indulged in free sex. It was not considered a social evil to indulge

1. Patricia Jeffery, *Frogs in a Well: Indian Women in Purdah*, New Delhi, 1979, p. 3.
2. Prem Chowdhry, *The Veiled Women: Shifting Gender Equations in Rural Haryana 1880–1990*, New Delhi, 1994, p. 283.
3. Asghar Ali Engineer, 'Can Veil be Enforced?', *Secular Perspective*, vol. 4, no. 18, 16–30 September 2001, Mumbai, p. 1.

even in adultery. When people embraced Islam, the Prophet would take an oath from women not to indulge in adultery. To remove this laxity in sexual behaviour, the Koran prescribes punishment for adultery in verse 24.2.[4]

The Koran did only the obvious when it enjoined the faithful to keep women well covered and to give them a distinguishing mark so that they could be recognized. Thus spoke the Prophet: Tell thy wives and thy daughters and women of the believers to draw their cloaks close around them (when they go out). That will be better, so that they may be recognized (K 33: 59).[5] Thus, the avoidance of sexual feeling rather than confinement was the aim, as is borne out by the verses. The Koran also instructs believing men and women to lower their gaze and to be modest.

For Muslim women, *purdah* in the sense of complete veiling operates after the onset of puberty in relation to all men except very close kin. In northern India, for Hindus, *purdah* in this sense is largely a question of veiling only after marriage and in relation to the husband's older male kin. Hindu women do not veil themselves in the place where they are born and where their own kin live, unless their husband or one of his male relatives is present.[6] For Muslim women, a special outer covering was devised to shield or protect them from the eyes of strangers. This special garment is called *burqa*. It is almost restricted in its use to Muslim women. Hindu women can conceal themselves satisfactorily by using a shawl or by draping the end of their *sari* over their head and face.

All classes or sections, but especially lower sections, of society cannot observe or practise *purdah* for reasons of poverty and economic need. For the poorer classes, it is difficult to keep women strictly confined within the four walls of the house because they have to go out to work and earn a livelihood. Peasant women have to go out to work in the fields. In towns and cities, the poorer women have to seek domestic employment in the houses of the better off. So they

4. Ibid.
5. Jamila Brijbhushan, *Muslim Women: In Purdah and Out of It*, New Delhi, 1980, pp. 19–20.
6. Jeffery, op. cit., p. 3.

cannot live in the *zenana* or go out in *burqas*. Similarly, a poor man in a city or town cannot afford the luxury of polygamy as he has little or nothing to provide even for his only wife and family.[7] Hence, differences of wealth and status affect the nature and observation of *purdah* among different social classes.

In some homes, a curtain is indeed used to separate the *zenana* (women's area) from the *mardana* (men's area), while in others the separation is made by more solid structures. Separate apartments are constructed for men and women. This is possible for the rich people; the poor people who wish to maintain the separation can often do so by restricting entry to the home. 'If women have to leave their homes, the more wealthy may be able to transport them in curtained cars or, in shrouded sedan chairs called *palki* or *doli*. Buses and trains also provide separate areas where women may be away from the public gaze.'[8] Older Hindu women are relieved of the strictness of *purdah* but young Hindu women after attaining puberty are often given little freedom to move around outside. But they are not clad in *burqa* like their Muslim counterparts. But the general stress on bodily concealment and separation of the sexes is largely similar among Hindus and Muslims.

Concealing women behind the veil or keeping them within the walls of the *zenana* was done to maintain social distance between the sexes. For this purpose, the defenders of *purdah* like Maulana Jalal-ud-din Ansari Umri argued that men and women are like cotton and fire whose meeting is always destructive. Among the writers who presented a more reasoned defence of the *pardah* system was a well-known Egyptian scholar, Allama Farid Vajadi, and a Pakistani political and religious leader, Maulana Syed Abul Ala Maududi.[9] Vajadi and Maududi both based their defence of *purdah* mainly on scientific arguments borrowed from the biological and social sciences, especially writing on the physiology and psychology of the female sex.

> Maulana Maududi reveals that a woman by nature is a tragic being. The sex functions of her body such as menstruation, pregnancy, parturition, child

7. Mazhar-ul-Haq Khan, *Purdah and Polygamy*, New Delhi, 1982, pp. 19–20.
8. Jeffery, op. cit., p. 3.
9. Khan, op. cit., p. 20.

suckling and rearing make her physiologically unfit for any work or activity except that of bearing children and performing simple housekeeping chores. This is what he calls the biological tragedy of women.[10]

On the other hand, men have no such biological disabilities and burdens. Maududi warns those who would attempt to do otherwise. He says, 'When women are loaded equally with men with the same cultural and social responsibilities and tasks, they will inevitably cast away their natural functions. Such a state of affairs will end in the destruction of humanity itself.'[11]

The movement for the entry of women into the public sphere began in the first decades of the twentieth century. The first Muslim women who ventured out of *purdah* were all wives or relatives of those who enjoyed positions of high esteem under the British. Lady Wazir Hasan, Lady Abdul Qadir, Begum Shah Nawaz, and the Ladies of the Tyabji, Rahimtoola and Chinoy families were among those who discarded *purdah*. Suhrawardy Begum, the mother of Shahid Suhrawardy, had the distinction of being the first woman to be appointed an examiner in M.A. by Calcutta University.[12] The Nizam of Hyderabad encouraged women to discard *purdah*. In 1929, his daughter accompanied him to Calcutta and went out publicly. With the progress of the freedom movement, various Congressmen also brought their women out of *purdah*. But the discarding of *purdah* was not widespread. Many women moved about freely in cities but wore the *burqa* when they went to their villages. Others discarded their veil while on holiday in the hills and resumed it on their return.

But even this limited liberalism was not palatable to the large majority of people. Nawab Sultan Jahan Begum of Bhopal preferred to stay in *purdah*. She said,

> The problem of the seclusion of women is one of the most important and serious questions that has been engaging the thought and attention of the Islamic world for the last thirty or forty years. It has been discussed and

10. Ibid., p. 21.
11. Ibid., p. 23.
12. Ibid., p. 38.

debated much more vehemently in countries which have to a large extent come under the influence of Western civilization than anywhere else.[13]

She stated that the question of the seclusion of women has divided people into three groups: (1) those who were totally opposed to the seclusion of women; (2) those who wished to lessen the hardships of *purdah* by modifying it according to their interpretations; and (3) those who wanted to retain *purdah*.[14]

Sultan Jahan Begum wrote that in India during the 1920s,

> . . . many Muslim women have begun to regard *purdah* as an imprisonment. They have studied medicine and served their less enlightened sisters. If they had diverted their energies to some such work of public good, the evil would have possessed at least some redeeming feature, but I don't find a single instance of this among the 'progressive' section of society today. So I look upon the change with great concern and anxiety and consider it as the harbinger of our national downfall and religious degradation.[15]

In spite of the spread of education, Sultan Jahan Begum did not favour the freedom enjoyed by the women of the West. In this context, she quoted an extract from a book, *Hamari Mushkilat* (Our Problems), written by Lady Chand Rani. She says, 'Many of our brethren regard the *purdah* system as an evil and are making attempts to abolish it. But the existence of the *purdah* system shall remain necessary so long as our men do not purify their hearts.'[16] Sultan Jahan Begum stressed that it was necessary for women to observe *purdah* as it was for men to possess arms and ammunition. Just as men protect their lives and property by means of these arms, women protect their purity and chastity by means of *purdah*.[17]

Sultan Jahan Begum administered the state, travelled widely in India and abroad, and attended a party at Buckingham Palace always clad in a *burqa*. Her daughter and daughter-in-law received the finest education abroad but, according to her, the relinquishing of *purdah*

13. Nawab Sultan Jahan Begum, *Al Hijab (Why Purdah is Necessary?)*, Calcutta, 1922, p. 1.
14. Ibid., pp. 1–2.
15. Ibid., pp. 2–3.
16. Ibid., p. 12.
17. Ibid., p. 105.

was no index of a forward-looking mentality because some broad minded people did not allow their women to go out of *purdah*.

For many ladies, *purdah* was a barrier protecting them from the gaze of men. They preferred *purdah* while going out in public. As the freedom movement progressed, the strictness of observing *purdah* was relaxed. Congress leaders, intellectuals, writers, and poets began to discuss the ill consequences of keeping women confined to the four walls of the house. They called upon them to come out from the dark holes with a view to strengthening their menfolk.

The debates on *purdah*, which took place within AIWC, in which Muslim women also took part, condemned the severity of *purdah*. It was viewed as a hindrance to education and to the general development of women. The Begum of Bhopal, who had once been in favour of *purdah*, now called for a readjustment. In her presidential address to AIWC in 1928 she said: 'I have no hesitation to own that the *purdah* system as observed among the Muslims of India is not exactly Islamic and indeed very harmful to the progress of education among our girls.'[18] Begum Muzhar-ul-Haq from Bihar compared the pitiable situation of women with the Muslim women of Turkey, Persia, Afghanistan, and other Islamic countries.

Interestingly, no educated man or woman had raised a voice against *purdah* in south-eastern Punjab (now called Haryana). Neither Arya Samajists nor any social reformers or leading intellectuals paid any significant attention to the prevalence of *purdah*.[19] While in the rural areas of Punjab, *purdah* had been lifted partially or wholly, the behavioural patterns imposed by it continued to be expected or even demanded. The lifting of *purdah* in Punjab was accompanied by the withdrawal of women from agricultural labour.[20] *Purdah* was observed as a major hindrance in the uplift of both Hindu and Muslim women. Various magazines criticized the prevalent customs of *purdah*, child marriage, the inhuman treatment of widows, and other minatory

18. Karin Deutsch Karlekar, 'A Return to the Purity of Islam: Muslim Women and Social Reform in India', in *Breaking Out of Invisibility: Women in Indian History*, ed. Aparna Basu and Anup Taneja, New Delhi, 2002, pp. 91–2.
19. Chowdhry, *The Veiled Women*, pp. 284–5.
20. Ibid., p. 368.

practices. While analysing *Stree Darpan*, Kamlesh Mohan cites an extract: 'If India is to recapture its past glory and to progress, woman's potentialities ought to be given full scope for development. In order to achieve this objective, the custom of *purdah*, the inveterate enemy of woman's health, has to be discarded forever.'[21]

In the colonial period, a British settlement officer in Ambala district noted that the non-observance of *purdah* meant a presumption of immorality on the part of a woman, and according to rural male opinion, she could be turned out of the house for this act. Even now a woman who does not observe *purdah* is called *nangi* (nude) or *besharam* (shameless).[22] But only married women observe *purdah* in Punjab in the presence of their husband's kin as well as from their husband in front of others. The women extend *purdah* to most of the senior men of the village as well as to certain female affines, notably the mother-in-law or classificatory mothers-in-law. The older women can get rid of the strictness of *purdah*. Accepted as a symbol of etiquette, it imposes on women a passive and differential mode of behaviour, for example, seclusion. But *purdah* did not restrict the rural women of Punjab from working in the fields. Their participation in agricultural work refashioned the mode of observing *purdah* instead of lifting it. This mode of covering the face is known as *dhattha*, in which only eyes are left unveiled. This was acceptable for women while working in the fields.

The second aspect of *purdah* observance pertained to limiting interaction between junior women and senior males in the community. *Purdah* 'as a symbol of the sexual control of women, separates women from men among whom sexual relations are regarded with great disapproval, offers only a partial explanation of this widespread practice,' Prem Chowdhry argues.

The *Purdah* system was rather weak among the lower and upper castes. It was more commonly observed among the upper classes among both Hindus and Muslims. Differences in wealth as well as

21. Kamlesh Mohan, 'Fashioning Minds and Images: A Case Study of Stree Darpan, 1909–1928', in *Breaking Out of Invisibility: Women in Indian History*, ed. Aparna Basu and Anup Taneja, New Delhi, 2002, p. 242.
22. Chowdhry, *The Veiled Women*, pp. 287–8.

differences in context affected the very character of *purdah*. The British incursion into India brought the people into touch with a whole new set of ideas and values. The idea of upper-class women moving around freely with their faces and bosoms uncovered was totally alien to the people of the Indian subcontinent. But slowly intellectuals reevaluated their concepts and ideas with an open mind. As the freedom movement gained momentum, it became clear to intellectuals that the freedom of the country could not be possible if half the population was confined to the home.

The progressive writers highlighted gender issues. They openly depicted the dark aspects of women's lives in their fiction. *Purdah* was considered the first obstacle in the way of women's progress. Dr Rashid Jahan's two stories included in a collection of ten short stories titled *Angare* (Embers) in 1932 raised an uproar. The inclusion of these stories by a woman writer, Rashid Jahan, was something new in Urdu literature. The first of her stories was 'Dilli Ki Sair' (A Trip to Delhi) in which she portrayed a Muslim woman in *purdah*. A Muslim woman from Faridabad a town some 20 miles from Delhi, made a trip to the city with her husband. She travelled by train for the first time in her life. Hence, she was very excited. When they reached Delhi Station, her husband met a wretched station master and had to go off with him, leaving his wife sitting in her *burqa* on their luggage. She was alone, afraid, and hungry on the huge Delhi Railway Station. She witnessed through her veil the scenes at the station as if they were the wonders of the world. Two hours later, her husband returned and asked her, 'Are you hungry? Shall I bring you some *puris* or something?' She replied, 'For God's sake, take me back home. I would not go with you on a trip to paradise. A fine trip this has been!' The Faridabad train was at the platform. She asked him to sit in the train. Her husband said, 'All right, if that is what you want. If you do not want to see the sights of Delhi, don't.'[23] Rashid Jahan has portrayed in this story the helplessness of a woman in *purdah*. She is unknown to everything and everyone in this world. Invisible to the public, she is alone and helpless. The only person who can support her is the 'husband' whom she has to follow. While living in *purdah*, a woman is

23. Ralph Russell, *The Pursuit of Urdu Literature*, New Delhi, 1992, p. 208.

totally confined to herself. Rashid Jahan boldly focused on this practice.

For women to remain well-covered or to hide their breasts was considered dignified. Men dominated women, and women became treasures to be guarded above all. The *purdah* system is an extreme form of male dominance, as Rashid Jahan pointed out. It excludes women from all outdoor activities and secludes them in the female areas of the house, segregating them from all men except their closest male relatives. Women are denied freedom of action and participation in social life. *Purdah* demarcates the whole social life of men and women into two separate zones: *mardana* and *zenana*. So *purdah* did not only mean secluding women behind veils or walls but also entailed an all-encompassing ideology and code of conduct based on female modesty, which determined women's lives wherever they went.[24] In order to gain respect and status in society, women had to be as invisible as possible. Men took pride in keeping their women totally subordinated. The constitution of the family as a separate sphere facilitated the control of women through their isolation and total economic dependence on men. Within this framework of complex social restriction, *purdah* imposed an extra burden on women, because sexual control is practised in both Hindu and Muslim societies in UP and Punjab.[25] In her other stories like *Salma* and *Sauda*, Rashid Jahan attacked *purdah* and highlighted its harmful effects on women's development. She also focused on the necessity of education for girls so that they could better fulfil the demands of educated boys.

Purdah has been vividly discussed in folk culture—songs, sayings, and stories. The progressive writers emphasized on the prevalence of *purdah* in Muslim and Hindu cultures. Ismat Chughtai's story *Ghunghat* (The Veil) highlights a unique feature. In this story, a very beautiful girl, with long hair that falls below her waist, is engaged at the age of fourteen to a man of extremely dark complexion. During the engagement ceremony, he is teased by everyone. 'Dear, oh dear,

24. Dagmar Engels, *Beyond Purdah?: Women in Bengal, 1890–1939*, New Delhi, 1996, p. 2.
25. Ibid., p. 15.

the bride will be tarnished by the groom's touch. It will be like an eclipse of the moon.'

Kale Mian, terrified by such talks, runs away to his maternal grandfather's house in Jodhpur to avoid the marriage. According to him, beauty is known to beget arrogance and it is impossible for him to submit to the girl's arrogance. A concerted effort is made to make Goribi (the bride) his possession. As his wife she is supposed to do whatever he wanted.

Finally, the marriage takes place. Wedding songs on the subject of a dark groom and a fair bride are sung to tease him. When he enters the bridal chamber and sees the bride, who is enmeshed in glittering red flowers, he breaks out into a sweat. Her silken hands make his blood boil. He is overcome by an intense desire to peel off his blackness and her whiteness to remove the difference between them. The bride bends over as he extends his hands towards her veil.[26]

'All right, you lift the veil yourself,' he says. The bride drops her head lower. 'Lift your veil,' he orders her sharply. The bride is all rolled up like a ball. 'Oh! Such arrogance! Hunn'![27] The bridegroom slips his shoes under his arm and jumps out of the window and does not come back for seven years. During this span of time to prove his manhood he indulges in all sorts of vices. When his mother falls ill, Kale Mian returns home. The elders make another attempt to bring the bride and, the groom together. But again the same thing happened. Goribi, the untouched bride, waits thirty years for him.

After leading a life of debauchery Kale Mian returns home burdened with diseases. On his deathbed, he requests Goribi to come to him, so that he can die in peace. On hearing this she takes out her tattered wedding suit and puts it on, applies bridal makeup and oil to some of her grey hair and with her long veil cradled between her hands arrives at the side of the dying man.

'Lift your veil,' Kale Mian whispers. Goribi's trembling hands reach up to her veil and come down. Kale Mian has taken his last breath.

26. Ismat Chughtai, *The Quilt and Other Stories*, tr. Tahira Naqvi and Syeda S. Hameed, New Delhi, 1990, p. 2.
27. Ibid., pp. 3–4.

Goribi smashs her glass bangles. Instead of the bridal veil she pulls the white veil of widowhood over her head.

In this story Chughtai raised several social issues. First, the physical appearance of the girl is widely discussed during marriage negotiations instead of the boy's. Second, a girl is shown as having no right to exercise her individual choice and is expected to be a meek possession of the husband. She also portrayed man's false ego and stubbornness in presenting himself to his wife. Otherwise he is timid and depressed. He became a pit of all vices even then his wife is forced to live the life of a married woman loyal to the institution of marriage. She cannot divorces or remarry. When her husband returns home burdened with diseases and dies, she is pulled into widowhood. In this story Chughtai revealed how the veil became a wall in the husband–wife relationship and consumed a woman's entire life. She showed that the custom of *purdah* and loyalty to the institution of marriage both are deeply rooted in the very fibre of our culture.

Chughtai wrote,

> When the veil is abolished, a number of childish and superficial emotions, which flourish only on the basis of the imagination and which are the cause of many psychological complications, get sorted out. Reality becomes more comprehensible. Boys and girls consider each other as fellow human beings, rather than as members of the opposite sex. . . . The possibility of blind love lessens.[28]

When one talks of Manto, images from 'Toba Tek Singh', 'Kali Salwar', 'Thanda Gosht' and other well-known stories come to mind. Manto is a versatile writer. On the one hand, he talks about prostitutes and, on the other hand, he talks about *purdah*. Manto's story 'Talk about Purdah' is equally devastating. At one place he writes, 'In a tailor's shop, work is feverishly in progress, sewing *burqas*. Along with work there is chit chat. 'Why doesn't Jinnah Sahib's sister observe *purdah*?'

'Don't know?'

'The prime minister's wife also goes without a veil.'

'What is the need for the rich to observe *purdah*?'

28. Sukrita Paul Kumar (ed.), *Ismat: Her Life, Her Times*, New Delhi, 2000, p. 80.

'A maulvi should be consulted about this.'

At another place in the same piece Manto writes, 'In the coffee house, a man with long hair was saying to his friend, '*Purdah* is meaningless. A veil of ignorance, of backwardness, of anonymity, of secrecy is understandable. But a woman is none of these. Why then a veil for her?''[29]

Chughtai focused mainly on the lives of women in the specific language of women, which has its own vocabulary and phrases. In her stories 'Bahu Betian' and 'Nanhi Ki Nani' (Tiny's Granny), she presented a vivid picture of women's world and the cruel implications of various customs and traditions. The story 'Nanhi Ki Nani' is produced in detail below:

God knows what her real name was, no one called her by it. When she was a snotty-nosed girl roaming about the alleys, people used to call her 'Bufatan's kid'. Then she was Bashira's daughter-in-law and then Bismillah's mother and when Bismillah (girl) died in childbirth leaving Tiny an orphan, she became Tiny's Granny. She remained Tiny's Granny to her dying day.

There was no occupation that Tiny's Granny had not tried at some stage of her life. From the time she was old enough to hold her own cup she had started working at 'odd' jobs in people's houses in return for her two meals a day and occasional cast-off clothes. Exactly what the words 'odd job' mean only those know who have kept at them at an age when they ought to have been laughing and playing with other children. Anything from the uninteresting duty of shaking the baby's rattle to massaging the master's head comes under the category of "odd jobs".[30]

As she grew up she learnt to do a bit of cooking and she spent some years of her life as a cook. But when her sight began to fail and she began to cook lizards in the lentils and knead flies into the bread, she had to retire. All she was fit for after that was gossiping and tale-bearing. But that also was a fairly playing trade. In every *mohalla* there was always some quarrel going on, and one who has the wit to carry information to the enemy's camp can be sure of a hospitable reception. This was endless and most profitable profession. At last, she became a polished tale-bearer and accomplished beggar.[31]

29. Saadat Hasan Manto, *Selected Short Stories*, tr. Madan Gopal, New Delhi, 1997, pp. 371–2.
30. Russell, *The Pursuit of Urdu Literature*, p. 225.
31. Ismat Chughtai, 'Tiny's Granny', in *Truth Tales: Contemporary Writings by Indian Women*, ed. Susie Tharu and K. Lalita, New Delhi, 1986, pp. 167–8.

At meal times, Granny would dilate her nostrils to smell what was cooking and would reach the house.

"Lady, are you cooking *arvi* with the meat?"

"No, granny. The *arvi* you get these days does not cook soft. I am cooking potatoes with it."

"Potatoes! What a lovely smell! Bismillah's father, God rest him, used to love meat and potatoes. Every day it was the same thing. Let's have meat and potatoes and now (she would heave a sigh) I don't see meat and potatoes for months together."

Then she anxiously asked whether the lady put coriander leaves in it. Listening to 'No', she would gather her *burqa* around her and got into the garden of Hakimji on the false plea of wanting to sit in the sun, would pluck some leaves and turn back. And obviously when she had provided coriander leaves, she could hardly be refused a bite to eat.

Chughtai describes Granny a tale-bearer, liar, thief, and cheat. But she did her best to provide for her granddaughter. When Tiny grew up, Granny got a job for her at the Deputy Sahib's house. The Deputy Sahib raped her when she was only fifteen and she hardly understood what was happening. But no one dared to speak against him. Tiny went on tolerating the situation, but at last ran away after losing her Granny's most loved possession, a pillow and the scraps of stale food she stored inside it to protect it against the monkeys. The other thing she used to fuss over and worry about was her *burqa*. It was not only helpful in wrapping around one's body and keeping one's head modestly covered but it also served as one's bedclothes. Bundled up, it became a pillow. On the rare occasions when she bathed, she used it as a towel. During the five times of prayer, it was her prayer mat. When the local dogs bared their teeth at her, it became a serviceable shield for her protection.[32]

Tiny's disappearance made Granny's mind to wander. One night she passed away, sitting on her haunches on the stairs. Fixed in death, she showered continuous abuse on the world. She had never known a moment of ease.

In this story, Chughtai portrays the various aspects of a woman's

32. Ibid., p. 170.

entire life, from a child to a mother to a grandmother, in a very touching manner. She shows how *purdah* for the poor is a way of covering their weaknesses. She reveals that for a poor widow it is very difficult to protect the chastity of her granddaughter. She portrays the sorrows and pains of widowhood in a realistic way.

II

The second part of this chapter examines the politics of childbirth. I have borrowed this phrase from Dagmar Engels's book, *Beyond Purdah*. She herself has taken it from the book, *Society and Ideology: Essays in South Asian History* (1993) edited by Peter Robb. Politics is the art of fooling and oppressing others, so is the case with a woman carrying a child in her womb. She is also caught by chains of taboos and customs, and is forced to abide by them. If a mishap occurs during the period of the pregnancy, the woman is blamed for disobeying these social rules.

Hindu villages throughout the country, shared a common attitude towards women with child. Several taboos were applied to expectant women. They were forbidden to go out. They were relieved from heavy work in agriculturist families. They were not allowed to move out at particular hours of the night lest evil spirits, which are supposed to be always on the prowl, do them harm. Their domestic chores were also lightened. The pregnant woman was supposed to have noble and religious thoughts so the child she was carrying could imbibe these views. She was made to see beautiful faces so that these pleasant images could be transmitted to the child. Various rituals were performed. Eclipses during pregnancy were a matter of great concern. The parents and the in-laws of a pregnant woman worried about the effect of an eclipse and insisted that she remain in bed and not even glimpse the eclipse.[33] The sight of eclipse was believed to have an adverse effect on the child's body.

Rajinder Singh Bedi's story *Grahan* realistically portrays these social beliefs and superstitions. He took notice of all the ground realities of a society. In presenting the outer reality, Bedi also explored the

33. H.A. Rose, *A Glossary of the Tribes and Castes of the Punjab and NWF Province*, vol. I, Lahore, 1919, p. 738.

realms of suggestive symbolism, metaphor, and allusion. In *Grahan* (Eclipse) he used the power of metaphor. People believed that the moon, tortured by Rahu and Ketu, could affect a pregnant woman in the same way. Holi, a poor helpless woman, is at the mercy of her husband and mother-in-law. Her mother-in-law is the Rahu of Hindu mythology, while her husband is Ketu, both preying upon her. She is forced to give birth to children one after the other despite her poor health. During the lunar eclipse, she must follow convention. She must finish her chores before sunset and finish eating before the eclipse started. Otherwise any bowel movement could have an adverse effect on the child in her womb. Her position in the family was the worst. As she often said to herself, 'Even my younger brother-in-law thinks nothing of beating me.'[34] Her mother-in-law's jibes were more painful than her beatings. Bedi portrays here the true realities of wives in the middle-class society of Punjab and UP.

Holi's mother-in-law is least bothered about her but greatly concerned about the child in her daughter-in-laws's womb. Looking angrily into Holi's eyes she said, 'Why have you put collyrium in your eyes, you slut? Don't you know there will be an eclipse tonight? What if the child goes blind? Will a slut like you ever care to bring up a blind child?'[35] Bedi also portrays the hypocrisy of menfolk. Holi was never allowed to use her mind. Sometimes she faced a quandary. Once she asked herself, 'Should she first take the *chapattis* or wash the *dupatta*? Should she speak or keep her lips sealed? Was she a *nawabzadi* or a bitch?'[36] Because in every case she was slapped by her husband or brother-in-law or by both together.

The tyranny of society is far more cruel than the diabolical design of the eclipse. Holi's attempt to escape from her in-laws' house and seek refuge with her parents was not easy. While escaping, she fell into the clutches of Kathu Ram, whom she had known since childhood. He took her to a room in the local inn on the pretext of providing her with shelter for the night and forcibly tried to outrage

34. Rajinder Singh Bedi, *Selected Short Stories*, tr. Jai Ratan, New Delhi, 1989, p. 36.
35. Ibid., p. 37.
36. Ibid., pp. 38–9.

her modesty. In this manner a beautiful moon is ravished by Ketu, and is tarnished by one eclipse and then by another.

In *Grahan* Bedi employs myth with such telling effect as to invest the story with a down-to-earth quality. He shows various aspects of a male-dominated society and offers a realistic presentation of the *sas–bahu* and the husband–wife relationship. A pregnant woman must follow social convention blindly in order to give birth to a healthy baby rather than adhering to a proper diet. Instead of focusing on the elite or the educated, Bedi portrays a true and real picture of the masses who were far removed from any reform activities.

In this society, a son is the fulfilment of any man's existence and is an excuse for the ideological justification of male control over women. Customs and traditions governing childbirth take precedence over the woman's health. These assumptions depend on a family's caste and class background. Hindus were mostly engaged in agriculture, a poorly paid and demanding occupation. Farmers depended mostly on family labour and some hired help if the need arose or if they could afford it. The situation bred a strong desire for male progeny.[37] Second, the use of drugs like *ganja* and *charas* was mostly confined to Hindus. The desire for a son among Hindus and the difficulty in marrying of a daughter led to the neglect of girls. Although the usefulness of daughters was acknowledged, their temporary stay in the parents' home and the expense on their wedding nullified the girls' contribution. They were considered the permanent assets of their in-laws. Prem Chowdhry writes, 'The birth of a daughter in the 1920s was considered to be the equivalent decree of Rs 2,000 against her father. The heavy financial burden of marriage and in the form of dowry made sure that her death was considered fortunate.'[38]

Rashid Jahan depicts the reality of women's health in her story 'Parde Ke Pichhe' (Behind the Veil). Two married women in *purdah* are talking. Mohammadi says that she has nothing left to live for. She is in her thirties but looks seventy. Aftab consoles Mohammadi by reminding her that she has a husband, children, a home, everything.

37. Chowdhry, *The Veiled Women*, p. 48.
38. Ibid., pp. 51–2.

For a middle-class woman, these things are sufficient and she cannot expect anymore.

Mohammadi Begum is thirty-two, and is always ill. She is always under the treatment of some *hakim* or doctor. She produced a baby every year. In her words, 'I was married when I was eighteen and I have had a baby every year since then except for one year when my husband was in England for a year and another year when we had quarrelled.'[39]

Rashid Jahan portrays the helplessness of Muslim women, who have no power to make decisions of their own about having children, regard-less of their poor health. They are always ill. Consequently, their children are pale, thin, and half-starved. Mohammadi Begum knows that 'they are bound to be, when they have not had their mother's milk'. But the husband orders that the wife hire a wet nurse. 'When God has given us money, why should you be troubled.' 'It is his own pleasure he is thinking about. If the baby is with me, he would be inconvenienced. It does not matter whether it is day or night, he wants his wife. And not only his wife, he goes to other women too.'[40]

Mohammadi adds that her baby caught V.D. from a wet nurse. Pus oozed from huge blisters all over his body, but even then she was not allowed to go to him. Her anguish is evident in these words:

> I used to watch him from behind the curtain. They say, don't complain, give thanks to God. Anyway, he rotted away for two months and then died. After that I have had three more babies. I have said, again and again, I will breastfeed them, but he takes no notice of me. And he threatens that if I breastfeed the baby he will take another wife. I need a woman all the time. I am not going to stand for you spending your time fussing around children.[41]

The dialogue between Mohammadi Begum and Aftab Begum covers various gender issues and ends at the *zuhr*[42] prayer with Mohammadi's saying, 'Because of your visit I have got a lot of things

39. Ralph Russell, *Hidden in the Lute: An Anthology of Two Centuries of Urdu Literature*, New Delhi, 1995, p. 36.
40. Ibid., pp. 37–8.
41. Ibid., p. 38.
42. *Zuhr*—Midday.

off my chest. You must come a bit more often. I am ill. I can't get about anymore.'

Rashid Jahan being a doctor knew all about the health of women. In this story, she depicts the selfishness of man and his lack of affection towards his wife and children. He is portrayed worse than an animal who has no sympathy for his ill wife and sick child. The helpless mother is not allowed to go to her sick child and has to watch him longingly through the curtain. Even when she is ill, a woman is helpless and cannot deny her husband. 'The men don't care whether their wives live or die. They want their carnal satisfaction. Owing to frequent pregnancies, a woman's womb and lower limbs slip down and she is to get it put right, so that he can get the same pleasure as from a newly married wife but it slips down again. Rashid Jahan points out the harmful effect of polygamy and unequal marriage among Muslims. She draws our attention to man's hypocrisy who argues, '*Shariat* has allowed a man to have four wives. Why should not a person marry'. Girls are trained for married life. Mohammadi's daughter, Sabira, is reading Maulvi Ashraf Ali Thanavi's *Bahisthi Zevar*,[43] which her brother wants to snatch. The story revolves around women's lives and portrays their suppressed feelings and anxieties.

The proportion of females at ages 10–15 and 15–20 had a higher mortality rate because the great majority of girls got married, and during these times mortality due to early child bearing was considerable. Mortality rates among women aged 30–5 declined as older women had an easier time during child bearing.

Table 5.1[44] shows female deaths per 1,000 male deaths in 1921.

We find that comparatively fewer female children died up to age of 5, but from then onwards they died at a greater rate except in the case of those in the age group 50–60 years, when the proportion was equal. The highest mortality among females occurred in the age group 10–15 years and 15–20 years; mainly because these comprised the periods of first confinement. There was thus nothing surprising about the result. What is surprising however, was the large number of deaths among females in the age group 10–15 years. The only possible explana-

43. This book was given to daughters as part of their dowry. It describes the duties of wives towards their husbands.
44. *Census Report, Punjab, 1931*, Lahore, p. 158.

TABLE 5.1: AGE-WISE DISTRIBUTION OF FEMALE MORTALITY IN 1921

Age	No. of female deaths
0–1	968
1–5	980
5–10	1,083
10–15	1,250
15–20	1,267
20–30	1,154
30–40	1,200
40–50	1,045
50–60	1,000
60 above	771

tion is that in many cases, girls below 15 began to bear children, which led to a very high rate of mortality among them.

Let us return to the literary representation of the problems of pregnant women. Rashid Jahan's story 'Asaf Jahan Ki Bahu' examines certain aspects of traditional Muslim society. Being a doctor Rashid Jahan was greatly concerned with the health of women. In this story, Asaf Jahan, the wife of a collector, gives birth to ten children but had only one living son, Nurul Hasan. Being the only son of a wealthy father, Nurul Hasan was considered a big catch by matchmakers. But Asaf Jahan wanted to marry her son to her sister-in-law's daughter. Contrary to the prevailing social norms when female foetus are murdered, Asaf Jahan begged for a *bahu* for her son when her sister-in-law gave birth to a daughter. The entire family looked after the baby girl even to the extent of neglecting the mother.

In reality our society does not bother about the health of women who give birth to children. Rashid Jahan presents a true picture of the weak and uncared mother in our society. She also highlights the role of illiterate midwives during childbirth. A midwife who was helping Asaf Jahan's sister-in-law during a delivery remarked, 'Don't ask . . . you people act falsely. Children will be born with God's wish. What will *mams* (doctors) do? Rather than start operating. After a short while you cry for the doctor. Was there no childbirth prior to these wretched *mams* (doctors)?'[45] Rashid Jahan also focuses on the higher mortality rate among infants.

45. Rashid Jahan, 'Asaf Jahan Ki Bahu', in Shahida Banu, *Rashid Jahan: Hyat Aur Karname* (Urdu), Lucknow, 1990, pp. 206-7.

The portrayal of women and their lives within the four walls of the house and their travails during pregnancy and childbirth have been analysed by writers of progressive views. Rashid Jahan raised the issue of pregnant women's health, in stories. In 'Istkhara' she portrayed the indifferent attitude of society towards seeking medical help for women, frequent pregnancies of women and, their weakness, and maternal mortality during delivery. In 'Chhida Ki Maa' she portrayed the *sas–bahu* relationship. Chhida's mother got her son married four times, but could tolerate none of her daughters-in-law. Almost immediately after the wedding, she forced them to leave the house and later got her son to divorce them. A bahu in her eyes was not more than a toy to be used as long as a child wants it, and can be thrown out when the husband tires of it. On the one hand, she did not want her son even to talk to his wife. On the other hand, she tortured them for being unable to produce a child.

Ismat Chughtai in her story 'Sone Ka Anda' depicted a family's unhappiness at the birth of a daughter and their persistent hope for a son. In 'Chhui Mui' Chughtai portrayed the helplessness and worries of a childless woman. Even male writers could not get away from this subject. Krishan Chander's story, 'Dani' is about domestic violence. In this story, the heroine asks her husband to stop beating her because she is pregnant. Rajinder Singh Bedi's stories 'Banjh' and 'Terminus Se Parey' portray the suffering and longing of childless women. Saadat Hasan Manto in 'Khalid Mian' depicts the fear of parents about the health of their son. In 'Sarak ke Kinare' he portrays the restlessness of an unmarried pregnant girl and the indifference of the man who sowed the bitter seed in her. In 'Banjh' and 'Zubeda' Manto deals with the condition of childless women.

Female infanticide, although no longer visible as a large-scale phenomenon, was still practised by individual families or groups. Neglect of the female child was common except in areas and communities where the practice of bride price was followed. 'The birth of a girl was usually considered to be an occasion of condolence, rather than a cause of congratulation. The disappointment on the birth of a female baby to the midwife, who used to get a larger fee at the birth of a son, to the mother and to the women in attendance was equally great.'[46] Sometimes they were so disappointed that they did not touch the baby until the mother had been washed and dressed. The bathing of a girl child was also done in a slipshod manner, and the first feeding was unnecessarily delayed. As soon as the baby was able to take some kind of food, the mother stopped suckling her, partly on account of shame at having suckle to a female child and partly to have another chance to conceive in the hope of bearing a male child.

A distinction was made between boys and girls in supplying food, clothing, and medical facilities as depicted in Chughtai's novel *Terhi Lakir* (The Crooked Line). In the novel, Shaman was one of ten children. She was completely neglected by her mother, who had to stay with the father all day and night. Shaman was left to the care of a wet nurse and found solace with her. When the wet nurse left, Shaman felt orphaned. Shaman turned to her older sister Manjhu for a mother's love. When her sister got married, she suffered a serious setback and fell ill. Her eldest sister, Bari Apa, who had been widowed a few years after her marriage, had returned to her parents' house, with her two children. But Bari Apa rejected Shaman.

Chughtai portrays a realistic picture of the emotionally deprived childhood of a small girl in a house filled with siblings, nannies, servants, and parents. Her mother's aloofness, frequent changes of wet nurses, and the loneliness and neglect consequent to her sister Manjhu's marriage convinced Shaman that she was not at all loved and was fated to remain unloved.

No attention was paid to the illness of a female child unless it became serious, while the slightest indisposition in a boy upset the whole family. This neglect resulted in the death of many female infants but this was not very disturbing for the family, for they took comfort in the popular saying, 'Mothers look after the boys and God looks after the girls.'[47]

Chughtai points out that though neglected, girl infants moved about unrestricted like boys up to the age of five or seven years and that their rougher and tougher upbringing made them hardier, like the girl

46. *Census Report, Punjab*, vol. XIV, Lahore, 1911 (cited hereafter as *Census Report, Punjab*, 1911), p. 231.
47. Ibid.

Shaman. But at that age they faced restrictions and were confined more or less to the house. Shaman could not tolerate such restrictions and became rebellious. Perhaps Chughtai was portraying her own life story through this novel.

Once a young wife, whether she was twelve or sixteen years old, moved to her in-laws' house, pregnancy was eagerly awaited. Due to economic circumstances, most pregnant women were malnourished. Among some castes, they were sent back to their parents for the period of confinement. The idea was that pregnant woman needed special care and emotional support, which was considered to be available in her father's house. We have already seen the recorded figures of female deaths in Punjab. The case was no different in UP.[48]

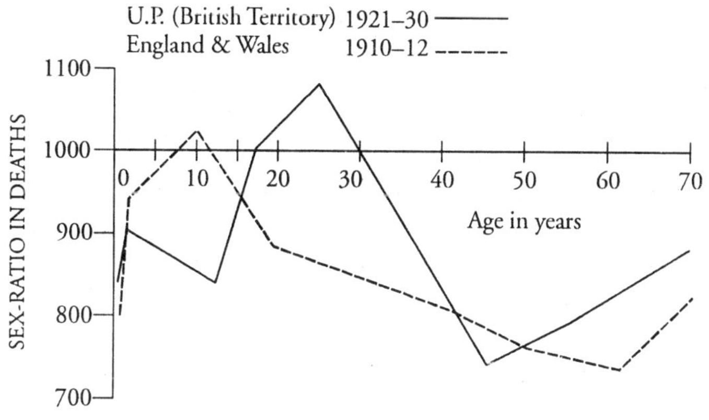

GRAPH 5.1: FEMALE DEATHS PER 1,000 MALE DEATHS AT DIFFERENT AGES.

These figures are very striking. Females outnumbered males in UP only at ages 0–5 and over 60, and the number, which averaged 902, was at a minimum between the ages of 10–15 and 15–20. Actually, more women died between the ages of 10 and 20. These figures demonstrate strikingly the dangers to which women in Punjab and UP were exposed, owing to the poor and unsanitary conditions under which they gave birth. The curve's rise between 20–30 indicates that these dangers are not limited to the birth of the first child, but continued as the result of subsequently bearing too many children

48. *Census Report, United Provinces of Agra and Oudh*, 1931, p. 267.

too frequently and as the result of disorders and diseases arising from childbirth. Girls who became mothers at 12 or 13 died of phthisis or some other diseases of the respiratory organs or from ovarian complications within ten years of the consummation of marriage. That was why the educated classes and writers started discouraging early marriage and early consummation, but their influence was restricted to the educated sections and did not reach the masses.

The great ambition of a Hindu, based on his religious teachings, was to have a son who would not only perpetuate his name but who would also after his death supply him with the ancestral obligation which he was supposed to fulfil and at the same time, relieve him of the responsibility towards his ancestors. The law of inheritance also necessitated a male issue. The Sikhs, too, prized a son, though not for the same reasons as the Hindus. Among Muslims, partly owing to their custom of succession by lineal male descent and partly because of the necessity of having a strong body of fighting men, son-preference values prevailed.[49]

After the birth of a female child, the mother's desire to conceive a male child as soon as possible by removing a traditionally accepted and natural deterrent to conception, that is, breastfeeding led her to stop suckling the female child.[50] The *garbhadan* ceremony, which was the first of the 16 *sanskars* enjoined by the *shastras*, was designed to make intercourse a sacred gift from the husband to the wife in the discharge of a sacred duty. The fulfilment of this duty lay in childbirth. So childbirth was marked by various rituals among the different communities. Charms for securing a male issue were very common among the adherents of all religions except Christians. A childless woman was cursed everywhere.

Saadat Hasan Manto in his story 'Zubeda' depicts the feelings of a childless woman with great sensitivity. This story begins: 'Zubeda was twenty-five years old when she got married. Her parents' efforts

49. *Census Report, Punjab*, 1911, p. 236.
50. Prem Chowdhry, 'Expenditure-Consumption Patterns in Rural Households', in *From Myth to Markets*, ed. Kumkum Sangari and Uma Chakravarti, New Delhi, 1999, p. 284.

to marry her earlier did not succeed as a suitable match could not be found.' Ultimately, they reconciled themselves to marrying her to a widower. He was thirty-five years old, perhaps older. He was well settled. His wholesale cloth shop brought him a good income. The marriage was a success. After Zubeda's father's death there was no one to look after her mother. Zubeda asked her husband to bring her mother to live with them. Ilmuddin readily agreed. Zubeda's mother owned some money and ornaments, which she wanted to give Ilmuddin for expanding his business and also because she was staying with her daughter.

One day, her mother said to Zubeda, 'I have been in this house for ten months but have not spent even a pie. Your father left me ten thousand rupees and jewellery worth as much. I have often thought of giving these to Ilmuddin but have saved them for a present for my grandson.'[51] Zubeda has been married for two years but there was no sign of her having a child. This situation worried her mother greatly. Zubeda was taken to a number of *hakims*. All sorts of potions were tried but nothing helped. Zubeda was fed up with this subject. She said, 'Please don't start this again. Haven't we gone through enough already?'

Her mother reprimanded, 'Don't you understand Zubeda, a child is a woman's whole existence? Though it is no one's fault. It is only a matter of God's graciousness.'

Her mother's frequent references to the need for a child made Zubeda feel like barren soil doomed forever to barrenness, where a seed will never germinate. She started dreaming of strange things. Sometimes she saw herself in a desert, with a child in her arms. Suddenly her child disappeared. Sometimes she dreamt, that she was lying on a bed made out of the flesh of children, dead or alive. Sometimes she heard the cries of a child and asked, 'Whose child is crying?'[52] Sometimes she felt there was milk in her breasts. She removed her blouse and found her breasts swollen.

Her condition was worsening, but her husband was less worried and was busy making money. One day, he found some notes lying in the milk pot. When he asked, Zubeda replied, 'These children are

51. Saadat Hasan Manto, *Selected Stories*, tr. Madan Gopal, Delhi, 1997, p. 128.
52. Ibid.

very naughty. They must have put them here.'[53] Ilmuddin understood that his wife's condition was getting worse and stopped going to the shop. He stayed home to look after her. She was worried about the business. She often said, 'If the servant embezzled our money, what would happen to our children?' Zubeda started sewing clothes for imaginary children and washing socks or knitting woollens for them.

Ilmuddin was deeply worried. One day he met a friend who faced a problem of his pregnant girl friend who needed an abortion. He asked his friend not to seek an abortion and instead to give the child to him. He told Zubeda that she was pregnant. One night, he brought the child and placed it by her side when she was asleep. Seeing the child, when she awoke, she beamed with joy, 'When did it arrive!' 'Seven in the morning,' Ilmuddin replied. She said, 'I must have become unconscious with pain.'

Next morning, Ilmuddin found Zubeda bleeding profusely. She had cut open her breasts with a razor in anger. 'All night it has been crying but there was no milk in these wretched breasts. What use are they?'[54] And lifting a finger dripping with blood, she put it into the child's mouth. Then she went to sleep forever.

In this story, Manto portrays the emotions and mental pressures of a woman without a child. Like his other masterly pieces on partition and prostitutes, he depicts with sensitivity the pain of a childless woman who can go to any extent in her desire for a child. A woman's reproductive function was highly valued and a failure to produce a child was inexcusable. Barrenness was a curse for a woman, as depicted in the story. A barren woman was considered inauspicious. Women echoed the sentiments of their men by saying, 'A barren field and a sterile woman—who will take them?' 'Without children, how can we have men?'[55] In contrast, a woman with several sons was considered *bhagyawan* (lucky).

High infant mortality rates, meant that one male (son) was considered neither safe nor sufficient for the family. Hence, no attention was given to birth control or contraceptives. In 1920s, the

53. Ibid., p. 129.
54. Ibid., p. 130.
55. Chowdhry, *The Veiled Women*, p. 130.

availability of contraceptives in India was limited. Though birth control clinics were opened in Bombay, Madras, Calcutta, Lucknow, and other cities by the Society for the Study and Promotion of Female Hygiene, uneducated rural women hardly had any access to them.[56] AIWC had discussed the issue of birth control since the 1930s, but this was limited to middle- and upper-class women. The ideals of femininity concentrated more on maternal rather than sexual role expectations. Women could be unfaithful wives but not lax mothers. A woman played a significant role by producing male progeny. For men, their maleness was derived from their mother's milk, not from their wife's sexuality. So they were committed to defending the honour of their sisters who were nurtured on the same milk. There was hardly any cultural and practical emphasis on defending the honour of the wife with whom the man enjoyed only a peripheral relationship.[57]

Childbirth took place in a special room called the *jacha ghar*. Generally, it was one of the worst rooms in the house, or a shed erected in the compound. Among the poorer classes, women's accommodation was wretched. A portion of a living room might be screened off the woman or might have to use the varandah; even the cowshed or kitchen was used occasionally. As a rule, when a separate room was assigned, it was small, dark and poorly ventilated.[58] Windows and apertures were closed with mud or stuffed with old rags.[59] This was done to prevent the entry of evil spirits into the room and to prevent mother and child from catching cold. For this purpose, a small fire was kept burning in an earthen pot at the door of the house, filling the dirty room with smoke and heat. The unhygienic condition of the *jacha ghar* increased infant and maternal mortality rates.

In middle-class families, childbirth practices were largely similar. Midwives were not trained. The condition of *jacha ghar* was poor. After

56. Mausumi Manna, 'Approach Towards Birth Control: Indian Women in the Early Twentieth Century', *Indian Economic and Social History Review*, vol. 35, no. 1, 1998, p. 40.
57. Subhadra Mitra Chanana, 'Gender and Social Space in a Haryana Village', *Indian Journal of Gender Studies*, vol. 4, no. 1, Jan–June 1997, p. 28.
58. Engels, *Beyond Purdah?: Women in Bengal, 1890–1939*, p. 175.
59. Ibid., p. 328.

delivery the umbilical cord was cut with a knife, a bamboo stick, or a shell, and disinfected with cow dung. Sometimes 'in Ludhiana it was tied with a *janeo* of an elderly man belonging to the family. If the child was a girl, the cord was tied with [the] thread of a spinning wheel.'[60] 'If a woman died within thirteen days of her delivery, she will return in the guise of a malignant spirit to torment her husband and family.' To avert this, a *shanti path* was performed at her funeral, a piece of red cloth and the grass image of her child were placed on the bier. Some people drove nails through her head and eyes while others fastened nails on either side of the door of the house to prevent her entry.[61]

The observances after birth were many, and it was difficult to distinguish between religious and social practices. The observances were less elaborate in the case of a girl child, and the idea that the birth of a girl child was a misfortune had a negative effect on the mother. Less care was bestowed upon her and observances were hurriedly conducted, if the child was not a boy.

In the first section of this chapter, the practice and forms of *purdah* in Punjab and UP have been discussed. It was observed in different forms among different classes for different purposes. Efforts to discard *purdah* had been initiated in the early twentieth century by some enlightened women. The progressive writers, especially women progressive writers, raised a strong voice against the harmful effects of *purdah* on women's health, and they themselves gave up *purdah*. This created public opinion against the practice.

The other major women's issue was childbirth. Various rituals were performed to avert harm to the child in the womb, though less care was bestowed upon the mother. The birth of a male child was a matter of pride for the mother. The progressive writers boldly depicted the problems of childbirth, women's ill health, and social taboos. These writers also portrayed the tremendous psychological strain faced by a childless woman. Hence, the progressive movement took the lead in focusing on various secret or closed aspects of a woman's world. The next chapter examines the issues and problems of brides and widows.

60. Rose, op. cit., p. 747.
61. Ibid.

6

Brides and Widows

I. BRIDES

Among the most important phases of a woman's life cycle is motherhood. Marriage was almost a universal phenomenon among all castes, especially among women in the Punjab and the UP, and their position in this respect has not changed for decades. Marriage led almost inevitably to widowhood as a result of child marriage, hypergamy, and the large age gap between husband and wife.

Child marriage was prevalent especially among the lower castes of both Hindus and Muslims. The girl, right since childhood, was invariably brought up to think to herself as *paraya dhan*. She suffered discrimination in the provision of food, clothing, and education. She was considered as belonging to another family, so she was not granted any rights in her natal family. Her *paraya* status was made clear in the marriage rituals.[1] Brahmanical theory constructs the marriage of a daughter as *kanyadan*, that is, 'the gift of the virgin', which is considered *mahadan* or great gift or charity. Child marriage was plainly intended to ensure that a girl was married before she became sexually active. The marriage of a daughter was considered a liberation for the parents from responsibility (*bandhan se mukti*); they were relieved of the burden of lifting the weight of virginity; a virgin or unmarried girl was the property of her father, the married woman was the property of her in-laws.[2] The burden of a daughter was largely the result of the financial costs of arranging her marriage and paying dowry. Large sums were

1. Prem Chowdhry, *The Veiled Women*, pp. 308–9.
2. Jonathan P. Parry, 'Ankalu's Errant Wife: Sex, Marriage and Industry in Contemporary Chhattisgarh', *Modern Asian Studies*, vol. 35, part 4, October 2001, pp. 794–5.

spent on weddings by the Jats and Rajputs, and these were a frequent causes of debt. A man would mortgage half of his landholding rather than allow his son to cross the age at which he should be married.[3] The practice of the sale and purchase of brides among the economically distressed peasantry and lower castes was also believed to be fairly common. Although the British considered the practice of selling daughters a bad custom, indeed a barbarous one, yet legally the purchase of a wife was held to be a valid necessity.[4] Sometimes parents, in order to earn the merit of *kanyadan*, married their young daughters to any man—widower, drunkard, or a man who was licentious, chronically sick, mentally unsound, or advanced in age.[5] Marriage was a universal phenomenon for women in India. Only those girls who suffered from chronic diseases were not given in marriage. It was no different among Muslims. There being no registration of marriages in India, no exact statistics are available to ascertain exactly the average age of the bride and the bridegroom at the time the marriage. The census statistics show the proportion of the population that was married, unmarried, and widowed at each age by making certain assumptions to find out the average ages at which marriages took place. In 1891, one in three Hindu women was a widow. In 1911 and 1921, the Muslim proportions were lower than those of the Hindus for both males and females. The figures for both religions showed a decline between 1911 and 1921, as shown in Table 6.1.[6]

TABLE 6.1: NUMBER OF MEN AND WOMEN MARRIED OR WIDOWED PER 1,000 IN DIFFERENT AGE GROUPS 0–5

	Brahmanic Hindus		Muslims	
	Male	Female	Male	Female
1931	24	29	25	36
1921	5	7	4	6
1911	8	11	5	9

3. *District Gazetteer, Amritsar*, vol. XX, part I, Lahore, 1914, pp. 28–9.
4. Chowdhry, *The Veiled Women*, pp. 67–8.
5. Kamlesh Mohan, 'Fashioning Minds and Images: A Case Study of Stree Darpan, 1909-28', in *Breaking Out of Invisibility*, ed. Aparna Basu and Anup Taneja, New Delhi, 2002, p. 254.
6. *Census Report, United Provinces of Agra and Oudh*, 1931, p. 303.

The figures cited in Table 6.1 indicate that there were fewer Muslim widows than Hindu widows in 1911 and 1921. This was due to the late age of marriage among Muslims. The figure was higher in 1931 because of infant marriages, which were performed to escape the consequences of the Sarda Act. In the 1930s, Muslims had a higher proportion of child marriages than Hindus. The number of persons returned as married below the age of 15 in Punjab and UP had increased at a rate more than double that of the general increase in the total population. This was in spite of the Child Marriage Restraint Act (popularly known as the Sarda Act which was passed in 1928 but did not come into force until 1 April 1930).[7] It prohibited males below 18 and females below 14 from marrying. Perhaps this Act was responsible for the increased number of child marriages in anticipation of the prohibition. It was strongly opposed. The vehement protests against the bill compelled the Government of India to suspend the Act's implementation until April 1930.

In 1929 and 1930, Punjab and UP experienced a wave of child marriages among Hindus, particularly of girls between the ages of 5 and 10. Poor parents took the last chance to arrange the marriages of their pre-pubescent daughters.[8] While conservative men of all religious persuasions were opposed to raising the legal age of marriage, women of all communities were staunchly in favour of the Act. Muslim women members of various organizations criticized child marriage, which was a hindrance to the girls receiving education. AIWC submitted a memorandum to the Viceroy supporting the Sarda Act. Early marriage of girls was in vogue in eastern Punjab, particularly in Rohtak district and in Sirmor and Bilaspur districts. The age was comparatively low in Jind, Karnal, and Hoshiarpur. It was slightly higher in Ambala, Patiala, Hisar, and Gurgaon.[9]

Blunt observed some noticeable features about marriage in 1911, namely that the marriage age was lower among the lower Hindu castes. Among Doms (plains) Luniyas, Kumhars, Pasis, Chamars, Ahirs, and

7. *Census Report, Punjab*, 1931, p. 172.
8. Karin Deutsch Karlekar, 'A Return to the Purity of Islam: Muslim Women and Social Reform in India, 1914-38', in *Breaking Out of Invisibility*, ed. Aparna Basu and Anup Taneja, New Delhi, 2002, pp. 197–201.
9. *Census Report, Punjab*, 1931, p. 174.

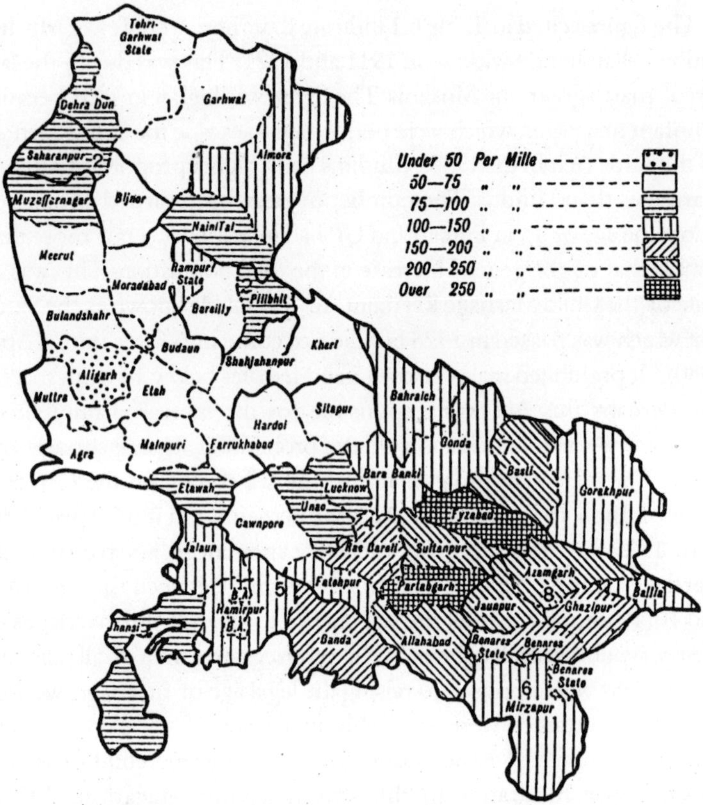

MAP 6.1: SHOWING THE PREVALENCE OF CHILD MARRIAGE BY DISTRICT AND STATE AND THE NUMBER OF GIRLS MARRIED AND WIDOWED IN THE AGE GROUP, 0–10 PER 1,000 GIRLS.[10]

Bhats, it was found to be on the higher side. Among Brahmans, Rajputs, Kayasthas, Vaishyas, Jats, and Tagas, it was at the higher end. The age groups were slightly different in the previous census compared to that of 1931. Being 0–6 and 7–13, against 0–5 and 5–12 at the time of the earlier census. But as stated earlier there was an all-round increase in infant marriages in 1931. The increase was slight in the case of the higher castes, but was very marked among the lower castes of both Hindus and Muslims.[11] The other reason for the lower age

10. *Census Report*, *United Provinces of Agra and Oudh*, 1931, p. 305.
11. Ibid., p. 307.

of marriage was the desire for raising one's social status by adopting the practice of infant marriage. In the past, the practice had been regarded as a badge of Hindu social respectability. But with the spread of education, it was realized that early marriage interfered with the education of children and youths. It became inconvenient for those who wished to pursue higher education. This factor had no effect on the lower castes and classes.

Certain religious organizations such as the Arya Samaj, Dev Dharam Samaj aimed at both religious and social regeneration of Hindus. Some reform societies were formed by important Hindu castes for the abolition of early marriage in the Punjab. These included the Rajput Sabha, the Khatri Conference, the Arorbans Sabha, the Mohyal Conference, and the Brahman Sabha. In spite of all the agitation and effort made by the reform societies, stopping early marriage did not appear to have had much practical effect.[12] It was believed that early marriage resulted in a very happy married life because of the devotion of the young wife.

Marriage has been widely discussed in literature. Though the impact of colonial values had been felt, it only scratched the surface of tradition without changing the family hierarchy among different castes and left the majority of women completely untouched. This situation provided the raw material for the writings of the progressive writers. Issues of child marriage, matchmaking, and the notion of the daughter as a burden on the father were highlighted in contemporary literature.

Krishan Chander was very sensitive to these issues. He wrote on socially reprobate and taboo subjects. His story, 'Andha Chhatarpati' portrays the imbalance in the sex ratio. Khan Sahib talks about a father who promises to marry his daughter to Chhatarpati for money. When Chhatarpati becomes bankrupt, the father refuses to marry his daughter to him. The greedy father sells his daughter to a middle-aged but rich man. 'Andha Chhatarpati' is a portrayal of the social evil of a father selling his daughter for money.[13]

Rajinder Singh Bedi's story, 'Apne Dukh Mujhe De Do' portrays the various aspects of a woman's life, that is, from her early marriage

12. *Census Report, Punjab*, 1911, pp. 266–7.
13. Shakeel Ahmad, *Urdu Afsane Mein* (Urdu), Gorakhpur, 1984, p. 224.

to her dedication to the family of her husband. It is the story of Indu, a simple village girl and her relationship with her husband, Madan, son of a post office clerk. On their wedding night, Indu wants Madan to promise to give her something. On being asked to explain, she surprises him greatly by saying, 'Give me your sorrows'. She proves to be a model wife, a model daughter-in-law, a model mother, and a model manager of the household. The larger part of the story describes incidents showing her devotion. The last section of the story focuses on the time fifteen years after the wedding. Madan loses interest in Indu and spends all his time away from home. One day when he comes home he is astonished to see his wife wearing make-up, dressing properly, and looking very attractive. They go on talking and she eventually asks him, 'Do you remember your promise?' Madan replies, 'Yes give me your sorrows.'

'You did not ask me for anything,' Indu says. 'Me?' Madan asks, surprised. 'What is there to ask you for? You give me everything.' Indu says, You should have said, 'Give me your joys.'[14] Madan understands that she does not want to be only his wife but also his beloved. He realizes that he too wants this, and the story ends.

Bedi's story 'Intermittent Fever' focused on forced marriage that was solemnized irrespective of individual choice. In north India, marriage was believed to be more or less a sacrament or a religious duty by the majority of the people. Traditionally, it is a religious rite, among the Hindus that involved two families rather than two individuals. Among Muslims, it is viewed as a contract. In both cases, the gift of a virgin girl is made by her parents to the family of a boy with whom they have agreed to contract the marriage.[15] In 'Intermittent Fever', Swati is married to Kamal. She has to forget Nabha Krishan because the selection of a spouse is not a matter of individual choice for brides or bridegrooms. Instead the decision is left to the elders of the family. When and what decision the elders take depends on various circumstances. Nabha Krishan is made to marry Madhavi. Estranged from his wife in the course of time, Nabha

14. Russell, *The Pursuit of Urdu Literature*, pp. 216–17.
15. Perveez Mody, 'Love and the Law: Love Marriage in Delhi', *Modern Asian Studies*, vol. 36, part 1, February 2002, p. 224.

seeks fame as an actor, while Madhavi is busy in taking care of their children. One day, Nabha, swathed in a blanket, goes to Swati and tells her that he has intermittent fever and says that she can throw the devil off the track.

'Nabha Babu, you must know that he is not at home. I mean Khokhi's father,' Swati replies.

'Swati,' he implores. 'Does a man in fever have any gender?'[16]

Swati prepares a concoction of tulsi leaves and makes him drink it. Nabha asks her, 'Are you happy? Did you tell him about you and me?' Swati says, 'that was a big blunder I made.' Though he loves her, when he approaches her something goes wrong, as if something had come between them. It was something that both of them unitedly feel.

Bedi has was a close observer of social issues. Individual choice has no place in marriage. Suppressed inner feelings lead to a life of compromise. In this story, Bedi portrays the woman as a truly dedicated wife who does not hide anything, including her pre-marital relations, from her husband. Though she has a soft corner for Nabha, she does not allow him to come into her home without Kamal's knowledge. Bedi portrays the complexity of husband–wife relations with great sensitivity.

It's the parents' responsibility to find a good match for their children, as the story shows. Among Hindus and Muslims alike, the parents are equally anxious to secure good matches for their sons and daughters. Direct communication between the intended partners is out of the question. Messages are usually sent through friends, priests, bhats, barbers or mirasis. Formal communication does not take place until the matter is settled. After an informal understanding has been reached, a formal ceremony called *sutr, sagai* or *kurmai* (betrothal) takes place before the wedding. Betrothal is a contract between the parents or guardians of the boy and the girl. This is almost a universal custom among both Hindus and Muslims.

The betrothal ceremony is governed by various considerations. The boy should be inherently strong and sturdy, or free from

16. Rajinder Singh Bedi, *Selected Short Stories*, tr. Jai Ratan, 1989, pp. 188–9.

hereditary disease. He should not live too far away, nor should he be a soldier or an ascetic. Countless other considerations also mattered. The girl should be a virgin, beautiful, young, and free from disease. Some girls should have a brother, otherwise according to the marriage contract her first-born son would have to be given to her father in order that the male child might become his maternal grandfather's heir.[17]

Other factors such as good reputation, a swan-like gait, fine teeth and hair, delicate limbs, a deep navel, and a soft voice also considered. The girl's legs should not be long and thin (seen as an omen of widowhood). Legs and nipples with hair were to be avoided because they would bring misfortune to her husband.

As a witness to these attitudes concerning marriage, Bedi wrote several stories. In 'Chhokri Ki Loot', he portrayed the helplessness of the girl's parents and the upper hand of the in-laws. In 'Only a Cigarette' he presented the worries of a girl's parents in searching for a suitable groom. In 'Too Tall for Marriage', he portrayed a grandmother's anxiety about her granddaughter, Munni Sohi, who was a tall girl. In this story, Bedi questioned the attitude towards a tall woman as a wife. 'Wretch, where will I find a husband for you?' Grandmother Rukmani cried and beat her head in despair over Munni Sohi who was shooting up in height.

A girl is supposed to look demure, small, and petite. Only then can she get a good match. The following comment shows the author's concern for such an unusual physical trait. 'How am I to be blamed for it?' Munni Sohi says. Like any adolescent girl who experiences puberty, Munni is ashamed of her ungainly height. There is no reason for it though. Does a tree ever feel ashamed of itself when it starts bearing fruits.'[18] Bedi shows the grandmother's worry over Munni, which compelled her to come back from the clutches of death because she has to attend to many things in this world. With tears in her eyes, she cries, 'O Munni! Will any man ever accept you?'[19]

17. Rose, op. cit., p. 783.
18. Rajinder Singh Bedi, 'Too Tall for Marriage', *Selected Short Stories*, tr. Jai Ratan, New Delhi, 1989, p. 112.
19. Ibid., p. 118.

Bedi, with feminist sensibility, wished to restore human dignity to Munni. Gautam, who is much shorter in height than Munni, approved of her as his life partner. He was so taken by Munni's height and robust body that he had fallen head over heels in love with her. The story ends with Granny's rather mischievous query when Munni comes back to her paternal house: 'How does he make up to you in bed?'[20] Bedi presents the erotic as an essential ingredient for a successful and happy married life.

After investigating all points, the betrothal is fixed for an auspicious day. Muslims avoid the month of Mohurram, while Hindus avoid Posh, Kartik and Chait. Not much money is spent on the betrothal. It is performed with only a rupee, some *gur*, often a coconut, and sometimes clothes. Taking money for a girl is strictly forbidden by the *shastras*. A proverb says *Kanjar te kasai, chut nal chut watai* (Low caste men are divided into *Kanjar* who prostitute their girls, and *kasai*, who kill or exchange their girls).[21] But the custom of accepting money for the gift of a girl prevailed in western Punjab. Among the Kirars (a term used for the Aroras), it was a general rule either to take money or to take a girl into the family in return for a girl given away.[22]

Asking for a price for the bride or the bridegroom is not authorized by the Hindu Shastras. *Kanya sulka* (bride price) was strictly prohibited, and the people who contravened the rule were condemned. But there was a noticeable increase in bride sales during the colonial period. In the official perception, bride price was compensation for the loss of the family authority, which was thereafter transferred to the husband. Recent studies regard this practice as compensatory payment to the bride's family for the economic loss they suffer on her departure.[23] The bride was supposed to be given away with befitting clothes and ornaments. The payment of bride price, and dowry made the existence of daughter a double financial burden. A good dowry, howsoever large and generous, was not considered objectionable, but when a fixed sum or a certain standard of dowry was demanded by the

20. Ibid., p. 127.
21. Rose, op. cit., p. 785.
22. *Census Report, Punjab*, 1911, p. 272.
23. Chowdhry, *The Veiled Women*, pp. 69–70.

bridegroom's family as a condition for accepting the girl's hand in marriage, the gift amounted to nothing short of *var sulka* (bridegroom's price).

The banyas as a rule paid no price for a girl up to 8 years old, but after that a 100 rupees had to be presented for every year of the girl's age, i.e. Rs. 900 if she is 9 years old, Rs. 1,000 if 10 years and so on. But girls had usually to be given away in marriage before they were 13 and so the price generally averaged between Rs. 900 and 1,500. In the eastern Punjab and in the hills, the lower classes of Brahmins also charged bride price. Poor Jats in the eastern Punjab used to accept Rs. 100–200 or sometimes as much as 400 or 500.[24]

The practice of charging bridegroom price was confined to towns and cities because high-caste families of average means often demanded a dowry of high standard to marry their sons to girls from rich families. Somehow or the other, the number of girls was higher in families that were better off, and in order to find suitable matches, combining high social status and high birth, for their girls, they had to agree to the demands of the guardians of eligible boys.

The progressive writers of the 1930s, 1940s and 1950s wrote boldly against social evils like dowry. They were very radical in their presentation of these problems. Rashid Jahan in her story 'Istkhara' described the unequal marriage of a young girl and the danger of early child bearing. 'Woh Jal Gai' depicted extravagant wedding expenditure during the marriage of Bimla and Raja Sahib. But immediately after her marriage Bimla feels estranged and commits a socially unacceptable act to satisfy her feelings, which leads to the dissolution of her marriage. Rashid Jahan described the frustration that leads Bimla to set herself ablaze in a very realistic way.

Ismat Chughtai's story 'Chauthi Ka Jorha' (The Wedding Dress) describes the worry of Kubra's mother over matchmaking for her daughter. Thousands of dowries had been adorned by her expert hands, but the wedding dress for her own daughter, Kubra, was still unfinished. It was discarded on one pretext or the other, and a new hope was kindled by starting work on a new suit. While working on a new suit, the women from the neighbourhood used to gather and sing wedding songs, sometimes about unpopular in-laws, and make

24. *Census Report, Punjab*, 1911, pp. 272–3.

dirty jokes. At that point, young unmarried girls are asked to leave the room and to cover their heads. But that only arouses their curiosity. When would they be able to laugh like this?

Kubra's father was a slight man with a bad cough. 'May this *hookkah* burn! This is the root of your coughing. Have you ever taken the trouble of looking at your grown-up daughter?'[25]

Abba glanced at Kubra's youth with a wistful look in his eyes. But a stage came when neither a doctor's prescription nor an allopath's remedy could lift him again. From that day Hameeda, the younger sister of Kubra, ceased to make demands for sweet *rotis* and proposals intended for Kubra stopped coming.

But Kubra's mother's routine continued. One day, a telegram from Kubra's uncle arrived, saying that his eldest son, Rahat, was going to be in town for police training. Amabi was beside herself with anxiety, as if a wedding party were at the door and she had not even chipped up the gold for the bride as yet. She removed her tiny clove-shaped earrings and handed over them to Bundu's mother to get one *tola* of fettered gold lace, six *masas* of gold leaf and stars, and a quarter yard of twill. The outer room was swept and dusted. Kubra whitewashed the interior room herself. The walls became white but the lime flaked the skin on her palms. Hameeda entreated after prayers, 'Please let my sister have good luck this time.' Kubra had already escaped to a mosquito-ridden chamber when Rahat arrived. A special breakfast was prepared and served. Eating simple *rotis* themselves, the women cooked sumptuous parathas, fried meatballs, and prepared biriyani for the son-in-law to be. But Rahat did not notice any of this. He ate the parathas in the early morning and returned at night to eat the meatballs. Amabi's adopted sister whispered complaints but she offered excuses, saying that the poor fellow was very shy. Hameeda was prepared to talk and please him with jokes. Rahat had no knowledge that he was being considered by the women as a prospective groom. The women believed that such bashfulness resulted in engagement of a girl whose one eye faced west and other east to a clerk in the Viceroy's office. Her father gave 15 *tolas* of gold in her dowry.

25. Ismat Chughtai, *The Quilt and Other Stories*, tr. Tahira Naqvi and Syeda S. Hameed, New Delhi, 1990, p. 96.

'Well, how can someone with fifteen *tolas* of gold and the influence to provide a job in Bare Sahib's office have any difficulty finding a boy,' said Amabi with a sigh.[26] Kubra was silent but listened to everything. The idea of a man was not born out of desire but was a question of securing food and clothing.

However, receiving no hint from Rahat or his family, Amabi arranged a *niazi* (offering of food and alms in the name of the Prophet). Girls from the neighbourhood gathered. The Moulvi Sahib had a special incantation. A special *malida* (a cake made of pounded milk, and sugar) was made to fulfil the request or desire. 'Wearing the wedding dress, laden with flowers, Kubra Apa advanced shyly. Amabi's face blossomed. Apa's eyes heavy with modesty raised, a tear of gratitude slipped. 'This was all due to your hard work, Apa's silence seemed to be saying.' Taking the *malida*, she entered Rahat's room as if she had entered a snake's hole.[27] The mountain shifted and gaped open. She moved back, but her hand was snatched and drawn into the depth of the mountain. The plate with the sacred *malida* slipped and fell over the lantern.

The next day, Rahat left for his home, after thanking Kubra's mother for her hospitality. His marriage date had been fixed. After that no eggs were fried, no parathas were warmed, no sweaters were knitted. Tuberculosis, which was pursuing Kubra, now seized her and she was quietly deposited into its lap. For her shroud, Amabi straightened the warp in the cotton folds to form a square. Though no scissors were used, innumerable scissors snipped through her heart. Her daughter's suit for *chauthi* remained incomplete, but Amabi put in the last stitch.

In this story, Chughtai raised the ever-lasting issue of dowry. A grown-up girl is viewed as a burden and as an outsider in her parents' home. It is more problematic for the poor. Hence, a daughter's mother starts collecting dowry from the time of her birth. The story also described the tradition of playing jokes by the sister-in-law on her would-be brother-in-law to prod him into proposing marriage to a woman he has never seen. She also draws attention to the practice of

26. Ibid., p. 106.
27. Ibid., p. 108.

not seeing the girl before marriage. Even today, it prevails in rural areas.

Chughtai's story 'Amarbel' (The Eternal Vine) deals with the issue of unequal marriage in Muslim society. The story is narrated by a daughter of one of the five sisters. Uncle Shujaat, a handsome man of forty, was the only brother of five sisters. He had lost interest in Bari Mumani while she was still a new bride. Unfortunately, she could not have children. To be childless is a curse for a woman even now. Hence, the sisters began searching for a new bride for their brother. 'How about our own Kaneez Fatima?' 'My dear, there is no dearth of virgins for our brother,' Asghar Khanam said, 'Why should he go running after used goods when people are ready to present their virgin daughters to him.'[28]

After a frenzied search Rukhsana's name was agreed upon. A much-heated debate took place over her physical appearance. 'If the girl is a day older than sixteen, you can hit me and give me tobacco water to drink.' 'Rukhsana is coy, like a new moon. She is slender and fragile and her complexion shimmered like crystal. Her body is like kneaded dough smeared with butter, etc.' The sisters inform Uncle Shujaat that she is twenty-five. She is a burden on the poverty-stricken home, so the uncle has to bear the expenses for both parties.

After the wedding, the uncle observes Rukhsana closely and breaks out into a cold sweat. 'She is only a child,' he exclaims to his sisters. The sisters react, 'Two or three children later, all the silver coating will wears off. When surrounded by wet diapers, little will remain of this beauty. Within ten years, she will start looking like Bari Apa. And then we'll get a twelve-and-half-year-old for our dear brother.'

In two or three years, a good diet, pretty clothes, and a doting husband produced a magical effect on Rukhsana and the new moon was transformed into a full moon. Under her magical spell, Uncle Shujaat became spell-bound. He no longer stayed out late and did not want any visitor either. Husband and wife were constantly alone with each other.

The changed attitude disturbed Shujaat's sisters and they started criticizing Rukhsana Begum. 'How long can you tie him to your *dupatta*!

28. Ibid., p. 39.

He is a man, not a baby you can keep in your lap forever.' 'It is a matter of days. She will lose all her charm as soon as she is pregnant,' they told each other.

But even after her delivery Rukhsana looked like a virgin. On the other hand, Uncle Shujaat grew older. After the birth of a daughter, the skin under his eyes hung in loose folds. His teeth became shaky, but at that same time Rukhsana's wisdom tooth appeared. The beauty and youth that had once enslaved Uncle Shujaat now began to rankle in his eyes, like a crippled child who, unable to keep up with other playmates, accuses them of cheating. When he saw Rukhsana laughing and frolicking in the company of young girls, it seemed to him that he was slowly burning to a cinder.

'You are sticking your chest out to attract young men. Why don't you find someone young for yourself ?'[29] Uncle Shujaat started spitting poison. His sisters also accused Rukhsana sometimes of wearing girl-like dresses, sometimes of not offering *namaz* five times, sometime of not being grey-haired and sometimes suspecting that she might be trying to poison their brother. But Rukhsana flourished like an amarbel, and Uncle Shujaat was like a banyan tree whose trunk is getting hollow. At last, Uncle Shujaat left the world, bequeathing the entire property to his sisters. The story ends with Rukhsana and her two children, sitting quietly, unmoved as if she were a masterpiece painted with an unparalleled brush by one of nature's most skilled artists.

In this story, Chughtai examines how an unequal marriage influences marital relations. A man wants to enjoy a young wife without caring about his own age. Other women also support him in this quest for youth and beauty in a wife. The woman is not considered a human being, an individual with her own desires, aspirations, and feelings. She is supposed to do whatever she is told. Chughtai portrays the helplessness of a young woman. She is properly cared for as long as she is prepared to fulfil her husband's wishes and demands. The longing for children remains a dominant wish. Chughtai portrays the life of a childless woman in a realistic way. This longing has important effects. First, as the traditional way of finding an heir; and second, as

29. Ibid., p. 47.

shown in the story, the erosion of beauty and youth under the burden of motherhood and domestic chores.

Chughtai's sensitive treatment of an unequal marriage is poignant. The old husband seeks to control his beautiful young wife, denying her autonomy and freedom. She is not allowed to follow her own desires. As the property of her husband, she must always obey him. The young bride seeks a formula to turn her long black hair to grey, otherwise she will be accused of enticing young men. Her youth becomes intolerable for the family, because her husband, who is more than double her age, is becoming weaker. He is unable to keep his young wife under control. The family of unequal partners is always suspicious of the young bride and forces her to get old along with her husband.

In 'Nafarat', Chughtai examines marital relations and the desire to preserve the family's reputation. In 'Ek Shohar Ki Khatir', she looks at how marriage is seen as an essential part of a girl's life. The entire life of a married woman of middle and lower classes revolves around her *maike* and *sasural*, children and husband. In 'Do Hath' Chughtai's theme is the practice of bride price. An old woman spends her entire savings on purchasing two hands, or a bride, for her son. In 'Kafir', Chughtai deals with the issue of interreligious marriage between a Hindu boy and a Muslim girl who are childhood friends and continue to like each other despite frequent quarrels. They take the extreme step of marrying in an atmosphere of communal hatred and frenzy.

Krishan Chander's story 'Aunt Isri and Her Debt' is about a deserted woman, who being a simple village girl, is not able to please her husband.

In 'Shahzada', Krishan Chander examines the social obsession with the physical appearance of a nubile girl. Sudha is plain looking. She has a swarthy complexion but a shapely figure. She is good at cooking and needlecraft, and fond of studies. Her poor father is forced to let her study further studies in the hope that this may improve her prospects of getting a good husband. The father whose marriageable daughter cannot find a suitable boy is a man frequently, irritatable and anxious. 'What kind of daughter have you borne me?' He castigates his wife. 'She does not seem to have time for anything else except her domestic chores. I have never seen her smiling. Well, just look at Kapur's daughters. They look bright and fragrant like flowers.'[30]

The girl is frustrated after being rejected by a man she likes, the prince of her dreams. She asks,

> But what was it in me that called for rejection? Did you sample the *roti* that I had made with my own hands? Did you taste my *mattar pulao*? Did you see the agony of my heart and the child that leaped out of my body? Perhaps you saw nothing but my plain face. . . . My complexion put you off but you failed to see the gorgeous colour of the sweater that I would have knitted for you. What kind of a man are you, Moti that you did not hear my laughter, that you did not see my tears and feel the caress of my fingers through your beautiful hair. Nor did you see my virgin body trembling in your arms. Tell me, what made you reject me?[31]

The plain but proud girl rejects the same prince when he eventually proposes to her after being rejected by good-looking and rich girls. She wonders, 'Why this belated offer of marriage when he was reduced to an old and ugly bald man and had become a repository of so many diseases?'[32] She had suffered a great deal. She had tolerated the evil gossip of people and the untimely death of her parents. She had killed her desires while waiting for her prince. In the end, 'She had realized that now she was nothing but a widow for the rest of her life.'[33]

Krishan Chander's Urdu novel *Ek Ladki Aur Hazar Diwane*, describes the condition of women in a gypsy community. The women had considerable freedom of movement and action but were treated like commodities owned by their husbands. They were marketable commodities, gambled away by the husbands in a game of chance. The heroine of the novel, Lachi, and her mother live with her uncle, Maman. Her father, Raggi, lost his wife and infant daughter to his brother, Maman, through gambling. Maman in turn sold Lachi to Dumaru while gambling. Owing to her physical strength Lachi protected herself from Dumaru. Krishan Chander describes an

30. Krishan Chander, *Selected Short Stories*, tr. Jai Ratan, New Delhi, 1989, pp. 95–6.
31. Ibid., p. 99.
32. Ibid., p. 107.
33. Ibid., p. 108.

interesting social custom among gypsies, in which the bridegroom lifts and carries the bride from the wedding site to his tent. If he fails he cannot claim the woman as his wife. Lachi defeated Dumaru in the performance of this test.

Krishan Chander's novel, though focused on the life of gypsies and published in 1960, remind us of the old custom of staking the wife in a game of chance, which is also described in the *Mahabharata*. A woman was free to prostitute herself to earn money for her husband and family, but in an arranged marriage her consent was not essential. Marriage was a contract and involved monetary exchange. Krishan Chander displays a romantic flair in his writings. Lachi's love for Gul, a non-gypsy boy, led her to kill Dumaru to whom she had been married through an exchange of money. She was sentenced to prison, where she lost her beauty and eyesight due to small pox. A woman's beauty is the main consideration in the marriage. After losing her looks Lachi became the victim of one and all, including Gul. After she was deserted, she led a miserable life as a blind beggar. The life of Lachi (a gypsy) was not much different from the lives of women of other communities in Punjab.

In colonial Punjab, a newly married wife was not considered a part of the husband's family. Women were always deemed outsiders. As unmarried girls, they were treated as temporary guests in their father's home. As married women, they were still seen as outsiders who were not born in their husband's village. There was little interaction between husband and wife except covert sexual intercourse to beget children. Traditionally, the position of the younger woman and the daughter-in-law in the household has been low. Until they attained the status of mother-in-law, women in Punjab were permitted little power.[34] Only women who had attained the highest status as head of the household might sit on a cot, while others sat on the ground and the young women remained standing, at least in the presence of others.[35]

34. Prem Chowdhry, 'Ideology, Culture and Hierarchy: Expenditure-Consumption Patterns in Rural Households', in *From Myth to Markets*, ed. Kumkum Sangari and Uma Chakravarti, New Delhi, 1999, p. 297.
35. Subhadra Mitra Channa, 'Gender and Social Space in a Haryana Village', *Indian Journal of Gender Studies*, vol. 4, no. 1, January–June 1997, New Delhi, p. 25.

Despite their contribution to agricultural work, women had very little money except what they had gathered by way of *shagun* in their natal village and what they had earned by stealthily disposing of the household grain when their menfolk were not at home. Otherwise, women had no control over the distribution of agricultural income, which was produced as much by them. Women had little or no say in the decision-making process, which remained primarily a male domain.[36]

The first and second decades of the twentieth century witnessed changes in the perception of womanhood. The prescribed norms for female behaviour of submissiveness, obedience, devotion and chastity had grown out of the male belief in the woman's inherent evil nature—fickleness, heartlessness, and irrepressible sexual desire. The new generation of rational and somewhat radical women from the urban middle classes regarded this cluster of womanly virtues as a unilateral construct legitimized by religious scriptures and family sanction.[37]

In the United Provinces the provision of dowry by the bride's family was widespread. Blunt pointed out that dowry was normally proportionate to the means of the bride's family and that the greatest expense was on wasteful marriage ceremonies. There was a tendency to reduce the latter but enquiries into the causes of indebtedness of agriculturists revealed that many high-caste families incurred heavy debts in connection with marriage ceremonies, whether for the dowry or for other expenditure. These expenses were beyond the means of most of the families. Little change had been observed in the attitude of Brahmans, Rajputs, and Kayasthas, towards this practice in the past many years, though among the enlightened few, the amounts were declining.

Writers, poets, and intellectuals highlighted the problems relating to women. Manto known for his bold treatment of taboo subjects also wrote on marriage. In his story 'Shadi', he highlighted the necessity

36. Chowdhry, *The Veiled Women*, pp. 268–9.
37. Kamlesh Mohan, 'Fashioning Minds and Images: A Case Study of Stree Darpan, 1909–1928', in *Breaking Out of Invisibility*, ed. Aparna Basu and Anup Taneja, p. 251.

or inescapability of marriage and the negligible scope for individual choice in traditional marriage. In 'Basit' he described the observance of early marriage. Ismat Chughtai in 'Sas' portrayed the relations between the *sas* and the *bahu* in middle- and lower-class society. Rashid Jahan's story 'Sas Aur Bahu' also focused on this issue. Growing consciousness about woman's worth led woman writers to criticize male dominance and female subjugation.

Divorce was recognized among Muslims and Christians, but among Hindus, Sikhs, and Jains, it did not enjoy religious or social sanction. According to the Hindu *shastras*, marriage was a sacred union intended not merely for procreation or mutual happiness but also for the performance of religious duties, and hence was irrevocable. By being assimilated into the husband's family (*gotra*), the wife was supposed to become incapacitated for disclaiming her connection with that *gotra* and uniting herself to another. Though there were provisions for a wife being over married (Manu IX, 80–1), if the husband kept away from the wife or she was punished and even devoured by dogs for infidelity. The wife might be abandoned if she had been married under deceit or if she was corrupt and unchaste. In eastern Punjab, among Jats, Gujjars, and Meos, if a wife ran away with another man and did not return to her former husband's house, a sum of Rs. 50–200 was paid by the man who became her second husband. This payment was called *jhagra* and severed her first husband's connection with her.[38] However, the general practice was that a husband, even if immoral, was, according to Manu, to be respected by a good wife. A wife did not merely respect her husband but also adored him as the embodiment of all that is good, indeed as God in man. The husband looked upon the wife as his predestined partner whom it was a sacred duty to please and protect.

The Jains and Sikhs followed the Hindus, but in all the other communities marriage, though a religious ceremony, was a social union capable of being terminated at the husband's will or at the instance of the wife. Among the lower castes of Hindus and Sikhs, a wife was sometimes given up on account of infidelity without any ceremony but usually on payment of a sum of money. This happened only

38. *District Gazetteer, Gurgaon*, 1910, p. 58.

when she carried on a liaison with some other man and the husband was powerless to stop it.[39]

The task of fixing the date of the marriage rested with the bride's father or guardian. When an auspicious date had been determined after consulting the *purohit*, an intimation was sent two or three months before the date, in a note usually written on a yellow paper or sprinkled with saffron or turmeric; this was called *pili chitthi* (yellow letter). If the bridegroom's family had no objection to the proposed date, preparations for the wedding began on both sides. The final invitation was, however, sent a few days before the wedding (usually between nine and 21 days). The priest, accompanied by a barber or some other attendant, conveyed this note, which contained the date, hour, and minute at which the marriage ceremony was to be performed, and asked the bridegroom's guardian to come and celebrate the wedding at the appointed time.[40] The number of *baratis* expected was also mentioned. The letter (*lagan*) was accompanied by one rupee or more in cash, along with other presents or symbols such as betelnut, coconut, and coloured threads, for the bridegroom and his family. These things were handed over in the presence of the groom and his assembled relatives. The messengers were sent back after being fed and given presents of cash, clothes, etc., according to the means of the groom's family.

Great care was taken in comparing the *gotras* before the betrothal or wedding. Among Ahirs, Brahmans, Jats (Hindu and Muslims), a man might not marry a woman belonging to his own *got*, his mother's *got*, his father's *got*. The same prohibitions applied to women.[41] These restrictions had, however, gradually broken down and there are numerous instances in the Ajnala tehsil of Jats who married within their own *got* and whose wives had been accorded full status by and in the *biradari*. The children of such marriages were treated as legitimate.[42]

In eastern and central Punjab, two types of marriages prevailed among Hindus. First, the regular marriage (*shadi byah*) with all its

39. *Census Report, Punjab*, 1911, p. 292.
40. Ibid., p. 274.
41. *District Gazetteer, Gurgaon*, 1910, p. 51.
42. *District Gazetteer, Amritsar*, 1925, p. 31.

elaborate ceremonies was performed in the case of a girl's first marriage. This evidently corresponded with the Brahma ceremony described by Manu. The second form was practised among those tribes who allowed the remarriage of widows and required none of the elaborate ceremonies of the *byah*. It seemed sufficient that the parties should consent to cohabit, and thus the *karao*, as it was called, seemed to correspond with the *Gandharva* form of marriage described by Manu.[43] Among Muslims, there was a similar distinction. The *nikah* or the Muslim form of marriage was performed in a manner that was similar to those of the Hindus. *Karao* was also similar. Side by side, four forms of customary marriages were also in vogue:

1. *Ghar byah*: performed at the house of either party.
2. *Ruti mundi*: in which the bridegroom accompanied by four or five kinsmen goes to the bride's house and brings her to his house.
3. *Madkhuia*: concubinage.
4. *Randol*: widow remarriage.[44]

The principal ceremonies of full marriage (*shadi*) were performed by all Hindu tribes with slight variations, and with the exception of the *phere* ceremony (circumambulation of the sacred fire by the couple). A proper marriage was often described as a *band baja shadi* or a wedding with a band playing or with loud celebrations. The act of drumming is ethnographically significant as it puts an emphatically public face to the event. Thus, marriage is an occasion wherein religious ritual and community celebration sanctify and acknowledge the relationship of boy and girl as husband and wife.[45] The marriage procession, which was universally in vogue, appears to be an adoption of the formalities that were probably observed originally in the case of kings or ruling chiefs only, amongst all castes, from Brahmans and Rajputs down to the lowest menials. The bridegroom, supposed to be dressed in royal robes, proceeded to the bride's house with a large retinue. The observance of the most sacred form of marriage, the one chief event in a man's or woman's life, was natural. Human

43. *District Gazetteer, Gurgaon*, 1910, p. 50.
44. Rose, op. cit., p. 795.
45. Modi, op. cit., p. 225.

vanity should be satisfied by imitating the most magnificent marriage procession that one could afford.

The custom connected with the arrival of the bridegroom to the bride's house, however, seemed to bear the traces of a curious admixture. In the case of the richer classes, the procession was not merely a prototype of a warrior chief attended by his followers, going for the performance of a peaceful religious ceremony, the groom had as his equipment arms, usually a sword or dagger (an iron stick was carried when it was not permissible by law to carry a sword, etc.), riding a horse (usually a mare) bearing a royal umbrella (*chhatar*), and having a retinue of soldiers, etc., with a band of musicians, tom-toms and processional decorations. But the decorations were a matter of course, to be plundered along the way by people while those responsible for the management of the procession were supposed to protect them. The meaning obviously was that the groom had forced his way into the bride's house against all obstructions and opposition.[46]

Among the Sikhs, marriages was solemnized according to ordinary Hindu rites, performed by a Brahman. The only difference was that the hymns of the fourth Guru known as *lawan* were sung simultaneously by women during the ceremony. Later on, a dual ceremony was adopted whereby Hindu rites were performed first and then the couple went around *Guru Granth Sahib* four times and a Sikh *granthi* read the *lawan*. The *lawan*, which are a counterpart of the four *pheras*, are known to the Sikhs as *parkarma*. This ceremony is known as the *anand* marriage. Marriages are still celebrated in the old style.

Among the Muslims, the *nikah* is performed in accordance with Muslim law by a *kazi* or his deputy. A Muslim wife can be divorced for infidelity, disobedience, blasphemy, or without assigning any cause. An annulment is effected by saying to the wife in the presence of two witnesses. 'I divorce thee' three times. Among converts from Hinduism, however, the higher castes still cherished their traditions about the indissolubility of marriage, and some Muslim tribes of foreign extraction disapproved of divorce. Among the Shias, divorce

46. *Census Report, Punjab*, 1911, p. 275.

was rare, and the long process acted as an obstacle to adopting this extreme step.[47]

Divorce was legalized under the Hindu Marriage Act of 1955. Under this Act, a husband or wife could sue for divorce if the spouse is living in adultery, has ceased to be a Hindu, or is of unsound mind. But legal divorce was considered a very serious step.[48]

II. WIDOWS

The position of women in a society is regarded as an indicator of the level of development. Socio-religious attitudes towards women are subject to change according to the male perception, the political situation, and other developments. Social reforms concerning widows were a reaction to the criticism of Hindu customs by Christian missionaries and the desire of educated Indians to alleviate the suffering of child widows kept in a state of enforced celibacy and denied the right to lead a full life.[49] With the death of her husband a woman lost her appointed place in society and became an economic and moral liability for the family, which had to provide for her and guard her chastity. But unlike the Brahmanical tradition according to which widowhood was the predestined karmic result of transgression, in rural Punjab, this was attributed loosely to *kismat* (fate), *aise karam the* (such was the fate of the woman).[50]

Widows were looked upon as victims of bad luck rather than of sin. In northern India, the widow was denied economic rights in the absence of male lineal descendants. If the widow had children, her sons succeeded to the property and she had a right only to suitable maintenance[51] and she was totally under the surveillance of the joint

47. *Census Report, Punjab*, 1911, p. 292.
48. Chowdhry, *The Veiled Women*, pp. 323–6.
49. Rajul Sogani, 'The Mirror of an Age: The Debate on Widow Remarriage in Indian Fiction, 1857-1930', in *Breaking Out of Invisibility*, ed. Aparna Basu and Anup Taneja, p. 107.
50. Chowdhry, *The Veiled Women*, p. 81.
51. Prem Chowdhry, 'Contesting Claims and Counter-Claims: Question of the Inheritance and Sexuality of Widows in a Colonial State', in *Social Reform: Sexuality and the State*, ed. Patricia Uberoi, New Delhi, 1996, p. 67.

family. The ill-treatment of a widow by her mother-in-law and other female relatives is proverbial. This harsh treatment might have been due partly to the anxiety in safeguarding the morals of young widows. In rare cases, a widowed daughter-in-law was poisoned by her mother-in-law. It was possible that a widow might be driven to desperation by ill treatment and might commit suicide by poison. But such cases were seldom heard of. If they occurred, the cause was carefully concealed and no one took notice of the event owing to the general feeling that a widow was well rid of her life of misery.[52] Among Jats and other agricultural castes, artisans, and menial classes, it was a common practice for a widow to marry the deceased husband's brother. In some cases, no distinction was made as to whether the husband's brother was older or younger than the deceased, although preferably the widow was married to a younger brother.[53]

The practice of sati (immolation of a widow on the funeral pyre of her husband) had long been outlawed. Cases of widow killing themselves immediately on hearing of or witnessing the death of the husband owing to unbearable grief, whether by poison or in some other way, though not unknown were extremely rare. Many widows were seriously shocked and tried to shorten their lifespan by deliberate exposure to privation of various kinds. Life was most burdensome for childless widows. Widows were treated harshly by their mothers-in-law and other female relatives. They were supposed to be practically dead to the world and were expected not only to eschew luxuries but to lead a life of absolute self-denial in respect of dress, ornaments, and even food. But a widow who duly observed the vows and customs of widowhood was respected even by her elders and was usually given the responsibility of managing the household and every effort was made to mitigate her unfortunate circumstances.[54]

The *Census of Punjab*, 1931 shows that there were 2,822 widows below the age of 10 years, 7,431 below 15, and 26,602 below 20. These figures are pathetic enough. But they seem insignificant when

52. *Census Report, Punjab*, 1911, p. 234.
53. Ibid., 1901, p. 282.
54. Ibid., 1911, p. 234.

we notice that in the age group above 40, every other woman was a widow.[55] There were hardly any widows under 20 in England or Wales, and their number even up to the age of 45 was almost insignificant. The small number of widows underlines the ease with which they remarried. On the other hand, the number of widows among all religious groups in Punjab presented a pathetic picture, as is evident from Diagram 6.1.[56]

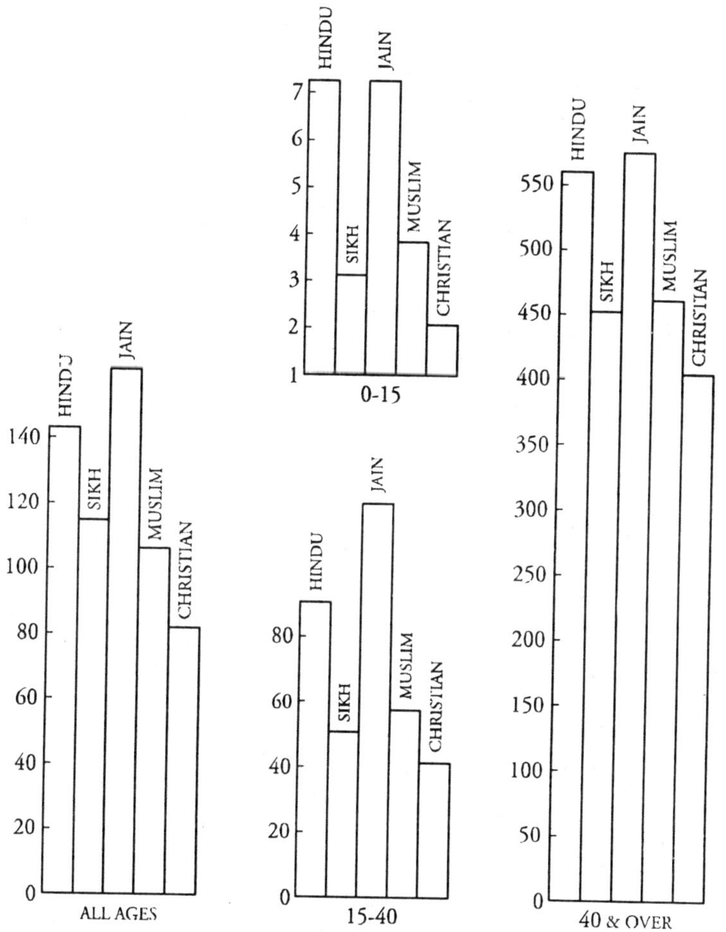

DIAGRAM 6.1: NUMBER OF WIDOWS PER 1,000 IN DIFFERENT AGE GROUPS

55. *Census Report, Punjab*, 1931, p. 186.
56. Ibid.

Diagram 6.1 shows that Jains had the highest proportion of widows at all ages, followed by Hindus. Muslims and Sikhs had almost the same number of widows. In the case of Sikhs, the proportion for all ages was slightly higher but was lower in the child-bearing period of life and in ages above that.[57]

The proportion of widows among Christians was the smallest. According to the local distribution of widows, the state of Pataudi headed the list. Hoshiarpur, Ambala, and Gurgaon also had a fairly high proportion of widows. In the caste-wise breakdown, Brahmans topped the list. Nearly one-fifth of total Brahman females were widows. The Hindu Rajputs with their feudal and military traditions came next, followed by the trading Aggarwals. Then came the Khatri, Aroras, and Jats. Among the Muslims, the high-born Syed, the martial tribes of Pathans, Awans, and Sheikhs had the highest number of widows. The Jats and the Balochs had the smallest proportion of widows. Among the Sikhs, the Jats too had the smallest number of widows. The number of widows among the Christians was very small compared to all the other castes.[58]

In the United Provinces, there were 5,912 males and 6,588 females living in British territory who had been married less than one year. Of these 89 males and 194 females were already widowed. The number increased in the age group of 0–5. At age group of 5–10, 14 per cent of males and 24 per cent of females were married. The proportion of widowers at all ages in UP was also high. This was due to higher rates of mortality among females of reproductive age. The percentage of widowers showed a marked increase in 1911–21 owing to the selective nature of the plague and influenza epidemics, which were more fatal to females, especially to those of reproductive age. The fall in that number of widowers between 1921 and 1931 was partly due to the absence of such epidemics. Since 1921, the proportion of widows in the age groups 0–10 years showed a slight increase. But there was a slight decline from 10–40 years.[59]

Widows had continued to be a popular literary subject since the passing of the Widow Remarriage Act in 1856. The Act had little effect in changing people's attitude. Among the first generation of

57. Ibid.
58. Ibid., p. 188.
59. *Census Report, United Provinces of Agra and Oudh*, 1931, pp. 295–6.

progressive writers two women, Rashid Jahan and Ismat Chughtai, wrote boldly about various issues, including widowhood among middle-class women. Rashid Jahan's story 'Garibon Ka Bhagwan' portrayed the hardships of an illiterate and poor widow with four children. She attacked various Brahmanical rituals, that a widow had to perform despite her meagre resources. At last, she realized that it was only the two hands of the poor that were her real god. In 'Faisla' Rashid Jahan described a wise widow's effort to educate her girls. But under the pressure of relatives, she had to marry her daughter at an early age. Rashid lamented the absence of women in a the decision-making process.

In his story 'License' Manto portrayed the society in a realistic manner. Abbu Kochwan, a handsome boy, used to drive the tonga. He died an untimely death. His widow, Niti, wanted to retain Abbu's tonga in his memory and asked Abbu's friends and neighbours, Dinoo and Manjle, one after the other to drive his tonga. But both were interested in Niti, not the tonga. When she refused to marry them, they refused to drive the tonga. Boldly, she drove it herself after some time, she went to the municipal committee to get a licence for driving the tonga. She was refused the licence by the city committee, instead she was given a license for selling her body. The story ends with a cry from Niti, '*Abbu, aaj teri Niti committee ke daftar mein mar gai!*'[60]

In her story, 'Kalu Ki Maan' Chughtai portrayed the other aspect of a widow's life. Here a young widow was forced to marry an old man owing to the cruel attitude of society towards widows and her penury. In other stories like 'Gainda' and 'Charpai', Chughtai focused on widows.

In her novel, *Terhi Lakir* Chughtai raised the issue of enforced widowhood. Bari Apa, who had been widowed after only three years of marriage, was sent back to her parents' house. First, consideration of family honour was bound to keep chains on the young widow's feet. Second, hope faded along with youth with the passage of time. After living for over a year with her parents, Bari Apa went to her mother-in-law. The shrewd mother-in-law, mocked by her own vanished youth, was happy that her daughter-in-law was ageing so

60. Saadat Hasan Manto, *Dastavez*, p. 31.

rapidly and was believed that she would soon be out of danger. By warning the younger woman of impending old age, she hoped to squeeze whatever life was still left in her.[61] Bari Apa was forced to maintain a silence.

In this novel, Chughtai focused on the life of married women in Indian society and the attitude of a mother-in-law towards her daughter-in-law. Bari Apa hated her mother-in-law, who had made her married life very unpleasant. She cursed her in her heart. She swore that had she any idea that her husband would die so soon, she would have covered the old crone's face with dust and made every effort to cling lovingly to those three years with her husband. Whenever he paid any attention to his wife, the old woman bristled with jealousy. Chughtai revealed the diplomatic ways by which mothers-in-law try to keep their son from their wives. If the son managed to go to his wife, the mother-in-law would immediately call the daughter-in-law to do some important chore. The daughter-in-law had to sit with a heavy heart and console herself with the thought that one day she would be rid of the old crone. But destiny was also not in her favour. She was left totally at the mercy of the old woman, along with her two children.

Chughtai described the dilemma of a young widow who had a relinquished all joys of living in keeping with demands of convention. Frustrated sexually and emotionally, lacking in proper status in her family and society, Bari Apa tolerated every injustice while bringing up her two children, her only treasures.

Among Muslims and Christians, there was no religious tenet prohibiting widow remarriage. But social customs came into play even among Muslims. Castes and tribes enjoying high social status considered it demeaning for their widows to remarry. Widows were compelled to lead a life of denial in accordance with the prevailing social norms. In many cases Muslim Jats, Rajputs, Syeds, and Pathans did not permit their widows to remarry. Evidently they had been influenced by their long association with Hindus.[62]

61. Ismat Chughtai, *Terhi Lakir*, tr. Tahira Naqvi, New Delhi, 1993, p. 146.
62. *Census Report, Punjab*, 1931, p. 188.

Widow marriage was not practised by Hindus. Restricted widow remarriage appears to have existed in Vedic times; Manu no doubt permitted the begetting of progeny by the brother-in-law or by some blood relation of the deceased husband's family under certain strict conditions. Manu permitted *niyoga* when the husband of a maiden died after their troth had been plighted. This related to an instance when the intended husband to whom a girl had been betrothed died before the marriage could take place. As betrothal was considered tantamount to marriage and one's word had been given, the relation of husband and wife was established. The girl was married without the imposition of any limitations with the brother of the deceased. But when the deceased left no brother or when owing to other circumstances it was not possible to give the girl to his brother, an option of *niyoga* was made.[63] It is possible that this provision might have been applicable to the wives of husbands who were incapable of fathering a child. But a widow with children was not supposed to remarry, but instead was condemned to leading a miserable life, as depicted by Chughtai.

Swami Dayanand was in favour of widow remarriage in the case of virgin widows and widowers. He recommended *niyoga*, which was a legally acceptable but temporary marriage. It was meant primarily for procreation. A *niyoga* marriage permitted a widow to give birth to two sons for herself, which would make them legal heirs to her husband's name and property. She could produce eight more male children for four widowers, bring them up for a few years, and then entrust them to the natural father, who would treat them as his legal heirs.[64] The custom of *niyoga*, in the case of married women did not exist as a recognized custom, even though woman of loose morals might take the law into their own hands in the event of the husband's impotence or other disability. *Niyoga* was meant for the regulation of sexuality because illicit and unbridled indulgence, in Swami Dayanand's

63. Ibid., 1911, p. 282.
64. Indu Banga, 'Social Reforms and the Gender Question in India, Late Nineteenth–Early Twentieth Century', *Proceedings of Indian History Congress*, 51st session, 1991, Calcutta, p. 545.

view, led to social degeneration, and the idea of having male children was linked with the idea that property should remain in the family. The female child had no right to inherit property.[65]

The opposition to widow remarriage evinced by Manu continued for centuries. Compulsory widowhood remained a peculiar custom among Hindus. Though the lower castes allowed widow remarriage, even among them a widow did not always remarry. Owing to the influence of Hindu association, some of the higher castes among the Muslims, whether they had converted from Hinduism or whether they claimed foreign descent, disfavoured widow remarriage. A Muslim Jat or Rajput, a Sheikh of Arab descent, or a Mughal in eastern Punjab would never think of marrying a widow. The Persian poet Sadi said, '*Rahe rast birao agarche dur ast, Jane bewah makun agarche hur ast*' (Tread the straight path safely, although it be more distant, so take not a widow as wife. Even if she be a houri).[66] But the general custom among Muslims did not enjoin enforced widowhood. Among the Sikhs too, only the higher classes followed the Hindu custom of prohibiting the widow to remarry.

In his story 'Jannat ki Basarat', Sajjad Zaheer showed that while a man was not interested in marrying a widow, a young girl was married to a widowed man in many cases. In this story, a moulvi, the father of eight children, married a young girl of twenty. The old man remained busy in the worship of God. He fasted during Ramzan, perhaps to keep himself away from his young bride. He performed *ibadat* late into night at the mosque. His wife was sleeping after extinguishing the lantern. When the moulvi returned home and searched for a match box, his young wife, in full bloom, spoke, 'Come on, sleep at once.' The moulvi thought of Adam and Hawwa, Zullekha and Yusuf, the victims of women's beauty, and set himself free from his wife's grip. Zaheer called it the age factor. But the moulvi's wife was deeply wounded and she spoke in a bitter voice, 'the rascal old man becomes a namazi. Sleep has been disturbed. Match box, match box.'[67] Zaheer's story, which was published in *Angare*, was a ferocious attack on shariat

65. Ibid.
66. Ibid., p. 233.
67. Sajjad Zaheer, *Roshni Ka Safar*, ed. Naresh Nadim, New Delhi, 1994, pp. 39–40.

law, which allows a man to enter four marriages without looking at his grey beard. Zaheer satirically portrayed the incapability of the moulvi to satisfy his young wife's desires. He also described the woman's feelings and her suppressed sexuality, which led to her anger towards the moulvi. Zaheer also focused on frequent births and the many children borne by women and their death which paved the way for the husband's next marriage.

Bedi in his stories dealt with these taboo subjects and inadmissible themes. He examined the man–woman relationship in his various stories. In *Man hi Man* he did not present a widow directly but she becomes the root cause of suspicion in the marital relations of Madho and Klarkni. Amba was a widow and Madho helped her on humanitarian grounds, which his wife did not like. Bedi showed the psychology of women and their jealous and suspicious attitude towards a widow.[68]

Bedi's *Ek Chadar Maili Si* is a realistic and moving depiction of the practice of *karewa* or *chadar dalna* in Punjab. Bedi probed the man–woman relationship with candidness. Here he portrayed with great understanding and compassion a widowed woman's life, which was bleak, an ocean of sorrows.

> O, God. May a daughter never be born even in an enemy's family. As she grows up a little, her parents wash their hands off her by driving her away to her in-laws' house. If her in-laws do not like her or are annoyed with her, they drive her back to her parents' home. She is like a ball made of clothes. When it gets drenched in its own tears, it becomes so soggy that it loses the capacity even to keep rolling.[69]

Bedi here selected a typical Punjabi social convention that of the widow marrying her deceased husband's brother for the sake of protection. He explores the heroine's (Rano's) feelings who at heart cannot adjust to the demands of a convention that takes no cognizance of her own emotional state. She cannot accept a man to whom she responds very differently than she did to her first husband. She becomes aware of her own complicated psychic state and perceive her own individual identity. But without dismissing and ignoring her

68. Shakeel Ahmad, op. cit., p. 19.
69. Rajinder Singh Bedi, *Selected Short Stories*, tr. Jai Ratan, New Delhi, 1989, p. 16.

own emotional responses in the deeper level of consciousness, she accepts marriage with her brother-in-law for the sake of protecting both herself and her family.[70]

A widow was regarded as an unproductive encumbrance, even a scourge, to the family. Her presence at certain joyful occasions and at the celebration of certain ceremonies was regarded ominous. Her lot was altogether a hard one. Hence, a widow consented to remarry owing to several reasons.

Among Muslims, widows married by the usual *nikah* ceremony. Among Hindus and Sikhs, such a practice, this practice was called *karao* or *chadarandazi* in eastern Punjab, and *karewa* or *chadarpana* in the rest of the province. Few formalities were observed in arranging widow remarriage. The widow's parents gave their consent to her remarriage to the intended husband. The widow was dressed in red and bracelets, nose ring, and earring were put on her. The man and the woman were seated together and a white sheet was thrown over the pair by a Brahman, sadhu or elder. Some gifts were presented to the woman or a rupee was placed in her hand. This occasion was celebrated with a simple meal. Bedi's novelette is a realistic depiction of this practice prevailing in Punjab.

The tradition of widow remarriage denied the widow any claim to property. By the early 1930s, reform-minded women of all religions mooted the idea of removing legal inequalities between men and women. Hindu women, whether widows or daughters, had no chance of owning property outright. Although the *shariat* gave inheritance rights to Muslim women, this was not usually practised by Indian Muslims.[71] Due to the efforts by the women reformers supported by colonial government led to the emergence of the Hindu Code Bill in the early 1940s. The Hindu Succession Act, 1956 based on the Hindu Code Bill enabled, for the first time, daughters, sisters, widows, and mother to inherit land with full property rights. The earlier limited ownership right given to women was converted into a right to full and absolute ownership. This Act was criticized by the

70. Sukrita Paul Kumar, *The New Story: A Scrutiny of Modernity in Hindi and Urdu Short Fiction*, Shimla, 1990, pp. 50–1.

71. Karlekar, op. cit., p. 190.

orthodox as *Kala Kanoon* (Black Law) and strongly disfavoured in northern India.[72]

In Punjab and UP, the custom of mock marriages, that is going through a form of marriage with an animal, a tree, or any other inanimate object, also prevailed among certain Hindu castes. This custom was based on a fear of ill luck. Mock marriages took place (1) when a widower wished to marry a third wife; and (2) when the horoscope of a girl showed that the influence of certain stars was likely to lead to early widowhood. In the mock marriage of a widow, a pitcher full of water was dressed like a boy and the girl was taken through the marriage rites with this pseudo-bridegroom. The rites were then repeated with the real bridegroom by way of an informal marriage. It was supposed that the effect of the evil star would befall the pitcher, not the bridegroom, thus averting the danger of early widowhood. This type of mock marriage was called *kumbh vivah* and was confined to the Banias of eastern Punjab. (It was reported only from Karnal.)[73]

The preceding discussion shows that the practices related to brides and widows were controlled by men and were performed to reduce men's own responsibilities and to protect and promote their own interests. On the one hand, the early marriage of a girl was a step aimed at ensuring purity of lineage, social morality, and social reputation. On the other hand, this step led to increasing numbers of widows. The condition of widows was pitiable. Having no autonomy, they were forced to marry a member of the affinal family, for example the younger brother, sometimes the older brother, of the deceased so that property could be prevented from going out of the control of the family. Thus, the sexuality of a married woman, especially a widow, was a family property or possession. This aspect of sexuality is discussed in the next chapter.

72. Chowdhry, *The Veiled Women*, pp. 301–2.
73. *Census Report, Punjab*, 1911, p. 284.

7

Sexuality

Sex in history, an American historian remarked in the early 1970s, is a 'virgin field'. Since then, the new social history has challenged our ignorance of and indifference to this subject. In ancient India, books like the *Kamasutra* presented sexuality in a frank way. The *Mahabharata* presented the love between Radha and Krishna as a form of worship. Sexuality in Indian history became a subject of historical inquiry more recently. 'Specialized studies of sex as a social experience have a long history, since at least from the time of the great pioneering sexologists and anthropologists of the late nineteenth century, and what appeared then were works which have been profoundly influential not only in describing but [also] in constructing and delineating the area to be discussed.'[1] Beginning with the progressive writers of the late 1930s, the meaning of progressivism has changed with the emergence of new problems such as the population explosion, child labour, and the sexual revolution.

The usual assumption is that sex is a definable and universal experience. Like other human propensities and desires, sexuality and sexual needs are fundamental and necessary to the human condition. Like the desire for food, the desire for sex also needs to be fulfilled, but it is the centrality given to the topic of sexuality that constitutes problems for historians for it ignores the great variety of cultural patterns that history reveals and the very different meanings given to what we label 'sexual activity'. Sexual repression is widely prevalent in India. A biology school teacher omits teaching the chapter on reproduction to save himself or herself the embarrassment of explaining sex to adolescents. 'The way in which man–woman relations

1. Jeffrey Weeks, *Sex, Politics and Society: The Regulation of Sexuality Since 1800*, London, 1981, p. 1.

were historically organized in society despite variations in arrangements and expressions reveals that there was an institutional denial of creative and free self-expression and empowerment in the public sphere.'[2]

Most historical studies on sex adopt two broad approaches, though these are not mutually exclusive. The first is the 'naturalist' approach and the second is the 'biological' approach. Both approaches have an essentialist view of sexuality. Sex is seen as an overpowering force in the life of the individual that shapes not only personal but social life as well. It is seen as a basic biological force that shapes human institutions and whose will must force its way out, in the form of direct sexual expression. If it is blocked it emerges in the form of perversion or neurosis. Kraft Ebing expressed the orthodox view in the late nineteenth century when he described sex as a 'natural instinct', which demanded fulfilment. This basic biological force must be firmly controlled by cultural and social matrices. Such an approach has the merit of appearing commonsensical in accordance with our own intimate experiences; it was largely unquestioned until recently by most theorists of sex.[3] The instinctual model was also embraced by people of, all shades of opinions, from conservative moralists to Freudians (Wilhelm Reich, Herbert Marcuse, Erich Fromm) who wanted to liberate sexuality from its capitalist and patriarchal constraints.[4]

J.H. Gagnon and William Simon have argued in their book *Sexual Conduct* that sexuality is subject to socio-cultural influences to a degree surpassed by few other forms of human behaviour. Sexuality has different approaches: the interactionist, the psychoanalytic and the discursive. But they all reject sex as an autonomous realm, a natural force with specific effects, and instead regard it as a 'rebellious energy' that has been tamed by 'social' controls.

Gagnon and Simon suggest that nothing is intrinsically sexual, or rather that anything can be sexualized.[5] In Foucault's work, sexuality

2. Pratibha Jain and Rajan Mohan (eds.), *Women Images*, Jaipur, 1996, p. 55.
3. Weeks, op. cit., p. 2.
4. Ibid., p. 3.
5. Ibid.

is seen as a historical construct. Sexuality should not be thought of as a kind of natural power, or as an obscure domain that knowledge gradually tries to uncover.[6]

Ethical and political ideas about sexuality and sexual practices are socially constructed, and are historically and contextually specific. The elements of the social construct of sexuality are not fully clear. Psychoanalysis proposes the notion of component instincts, which are unified in the complex process of acculturation. In Indian society notions about sexuality are deeply entrenched within the structures of patriarchy.[7] The state and social structures acknowledge only a limited and narrow definition and role of sexuality. Sexuality plays upon our bodies, organs, somatic localizations, sensations and pleasures, which have no intrinsic unity or 'laws' of their own. In other words, these elements are unified only through ideological constructs, and it is these elements that constitute sexuality.[8]

Sex is sex. Sex is simple. Unfortunately, when our minds and egos get involved, the issue becomes complicated. The desire to be sexual can be spiritually motivated because we love and care for a person. The desire to feel connected can also arise from feelings of hate, anger, fear, sadness, and insecurity. It can come from a desire to feel important or from a need to alleviate tension. It can come from wanting to fill a big empty space inside ourselves.[9]

The progressive writers wrote many works in various Indian languages. But the Urdu writers raised some hitherto unexamined issues related to women. As has been discussed above, the sexual urge can arise from fear and hate. In his story 'Aadha Ghante Ka Khuda' (The God of Thirty Minutes), Krishan Chander examines the love–hate relations between man and woman. He does not focus directly on sexuality, but looks at the strange love–hate relations between Kashar and Mogri. The story is about Kashar fleeing while being pursued by

6. Ibid., p. 4.
7. First National Conference of Sex Workers Organized by the Durbar Mahila Samiti, 14–16 November 1997, Calcutta.
8. Weeks, op. cit., p. 4.
9. Charlotte Davis Kasl, *Women, Sex and Addiction: A Search for Love and Power*, New York, 1989, p. 3.

Mogri's brothers. Kashar's love for Mogri was undeniable. He had never seen a girl like her. Her laughter seemed to him like apple blossoms. Mogri used to sell fruits to soldiers near Gadiali bridge. Charmed by her beauty, the soldiers used to buy all the fruits in no time. Then Kashar appeared on the scene and both disappeared in the forest. One day, her village people blew up the Gadiali bridge with dynamite. Mogri was suspected of being a spy. Kashar was shocked, and felt that something inside him has exploded.[10]

The bridge could be rebuilt but nothing could mend his shattered self. Unable to bear the gaze of his fellow soldiers, Kashar picked up his rifle and plunged into the Gadiali River. After some days he reached Mogri's house at night. He stole into her room and bolted it from inside. In the dark, he could not see her face and with great effort he smothered his desire to strike a match. He placed his burning lips on her mouth. He firmly held her mouth between his lips, making it impossible for her to raise an alarm. It was a love–hate relationship. Mogri recognized the touch of his kiss. 'A beautiful woman living dangerously had to cope with many kinds of kisses—kisses that ate into her body like termites and sucked her blood like a leech; kisses, limp insects crawling on chapped and dirty lips; kisses, diseased fumbling and lecherous, and others bold and ardent, saturated with the sap of life.'[11] Mogri recognized the kiss that knocked her heart and burst open the floodgates of love. It was a kiss for a kiss. To others she did not offer a kiss but only her cold lips.

In the semi-warmth of the midnight hour, Mogri was thrilled to the depths of her being and came into Kashar's arms with complete abandon as never before. Kashar felt as if the heavens had descended upon the earth was and the earth was taking long gasping breaths and all aquiver. Then everything went blank. The living moments had been submerged into somnolence. He awoke and picked up a dagger. Before he was carried away by emotions, he plunged the dagger up to the hilt into Mogri's heart. Mogri did not even shriek. Clasping

10. Krishan Chander, 'Those Thirty Minutes', tr. Jai Ratan, in *Breakthrough: Modern Hindi and Urdu Short Stories*, ed. Sukrita Paul Kumar, Shimla, p. 238.
11. Ibid., p. 241.

her body, he absorbed her dying spasms into his own body. And when it became still, he imprinted a kiss on her cold lips like one kissing a coffin. Unbolting the door, he crossed the courtyard and ran away.

Mogri's brothers chased him through forests and mountains. An avalanche fell upon the fleeing Kashar and his body was buried under rocks. He somehow struggled to reach his own territory. He realized that his pursuers were only half an hour behind him. He saluted the soldiers of his land and felt that this half hour was his own. He felt like a newborn for whom life had just begun. He felt like stretching out his arms and laughing aloud. Could one be so fortunate as to have half an hour, which from beginning to end one could claim as one's own? Joy surged through him. With complete abandon he relaxed his body and spread out his legs. Then he closed his eyes and waited patiently for Mogri's brothers.[12]

This story presents a complex picture of man–woman desires. On the one hand, they are in undeniable and passionate love. On the other hand, there is a deep hatred that emanates from the knowledge that they are enemies. Self-realization and self-identification take place. This story makes it clear that sex is sex. And that sex is not proof of being loved or of loving someone; sex is not proof of being attractive; sex does not make anyone important; sex does not cure problems; sex does not shore up a shaky ego and it does not save a failing marriage. Being able to seduce an attractive man or woman does not mean that a person is important, attractive, smart, virile or sexy; all it means is that the seducer is good at seduction.[13]

The story shows that a fulfilling and meaningful life does not depend on being sophisticated, handsome, rich, charming, seductive, or educated. Sex for some people is a way of filling the emptiness inside. Paradoxically, this does not satisfy their hunger. Rather it increases it and also often breeds anger and hopelessness. It does not fulfil any yearning. It affects all aspects of their lives—work, friendship, health, and peace of mind.[14]

Chughtai explored the psychology of middle-class women in a

12. Ibid., p. 3.
13. Kasl, op. cit., p. 3.
14. Ibid., p. 4.

bold way. Her story 'Lihaf' (The Quilt), which led to a court trial, portrays female homosexuality. In 'Bimar', 'Chhoti Appa' and 'Gainda', she portrays the psychology and desires of young girls and their confusing restlessness. 'Do Hath' and 'Housewife', discussed later in this chapter, present a vivid picture of female sexuality.

Chughtai's story 'Do Hath' (Two Hands) portrays, on the one hand, popular attitudes towards sexuality, and on the other hand, depicts the exploitation of women's sexuality through their sale and purchase like commodities. It focuses on a prevalent custom similar to polyandry in a realistic way. The story begins with Ram Avtar's return home after three years at the war front. He was the only surviving child out of the ten or twelve children born to his mother. She was convinced that Ram Avtar had survived because of her prayers and vows. She was happy because her son had been called to the front within a year of his wedding. Just after the wedding Gori had seemed meek and modest with her veil hanging down her face. When, her husband left, she wailed and cried for a few days. Then, little by little, her veil began lifting. This led to much gossip among the village men.

Some believed this was the result of the spring season; others said that she was a woman of loose character. Men turned to look at Gori when she walked by, with her basket perched on her waist. 'The dhobi would drop his bar of soap into the tank. The cook would turn away from his chapattis. The water carrier's pail would drop into the well and then keep on sinking. Chaprasis' monogrammed turbans would get soaked in sweat and slip down around their necks.'[15] In anger, the dhobi's wife would throw away her pot of starch, the chaprasi's wife would hit her child for clutching her breast, and the cook's third wife would have fits of hysteria.

Gori (white) was her name only. Otherwise she was as black as coal, with a broad nose, and a wide mouth. She put a lot of *kajal* in her eyes. She had a sweet voice. The old sweeperess became suspicious as soon as her son left and started keeping an eye on her daughter-in-law. But how long could she have the strength to follow her? Things took a ridiculous turn when even the *bahus* of Abbe Mian started

15. Ismat Chughtai, 'Two Hands', tr. Steven M. Poulos, in Geeta Dharamrajan (ed.), *Separate Journeys*, Bombay, 1993, p. 104.

getting jealous of Gori. If she went to sweep a room where one of their husbands was present, the daughter-in-law (*bahu*) pulled the suckling child off her breast and dashed in so that the witch could not practise magic on her husband.

When conditions become really serious, a delegation of servant women came to the old sweeperess and a 'Husband Protection Committee' was formed, to which the *bahus* of Abbe Mian extended their support enthusiastically. The old sweeperess was asked to send her daughter-in-law back to her parents. But she had no desire to send Gori away because her whole life's saving, of Rs. 200, had been spent in purchasing her chubby hand. If her father got her back, he would immediately sell her to some other sweeper for Rs. 300 or 400. The old sweeperess appealed to the other women saying that 'her daughter-in-law was not just the ornament of her son's bed, but she also had two hands and did the work of four people. Her old age was possible only because of her *bahu's* two hands.'[16] Nevertheless, the women gave the old sweeperess an ultimatum. 'If you don't make some arrangement about this trash soon, you won't be allowed inside the compound'. The old woman cursed Gori and grabbed her by the hair and beat her because she had purchased her.

A few days later, Ram Rati, the son of the younger brother-in-law of the old sweeperess, came to see his aunt and stayed on. He had been wandering about his village uselessly and his wife was still a child. As soon as Ram Rati arrived, the situation changed drastically. Gori's loud laughter became still and despite her reputation of being like an unfettered ox, she became an extremely dutiful daughter-in-law. The women around now breathed easy, but their husbands were irritated. The dhobi, the cook, and the chaprasi all started pointing out mistakes in Gori's work. But Gori took all these complaints casually. They were greatly disturbed by Ram Rati and Gori's illicit relationship. They complained to the old sweeperess, but she reacted boldly, 'No one's filth is hidden from a sweeperess. These hands have buried the troubles of many important people. These two hands, if they wished, could overturn the thrones of queens, but no. This old

16. Ibid., p. 106.

woman is no one's enemy. If someone held a knife to her throat, then perhaps she might make a mistake.'[17]

Hearing the old sweepress, the would-be assassins of her daughter-in-law got cold feet. Gori's swollen belly troubled the neighbours but brought smiles to the old woman's face. Long before Ram Avtar came back, Gori had a son. If anyone complained that this child could not possibly be Ram Avtar's, the old woman, completely ignoring the question, would start to jabber. Ram Avtar's return was a matter of great excitement among the servants owing to people's habit of interfering in the private lives of others. 'The cook put a lot of water in the pot so that he could watch the ensuing battle in peace. The dhobi took the starch off the fire and put it on a stool. And the water carrier threw the water pail down near the well.'[18]

The child was no embarrassment for Ram Avtar. Rather, he posed as if he were himself the boy's father. The *bahu* simpered like a new bride. People tried to make Ram Avtar see through these sexual games. They called him an idiot. But Ram Avtar said, 'So what? Ram Rati is my brother. He is not an outsider. It is the same blood. He'll himself use his two hands and his old age will pass easily.'[19]

This unconventional story about the evils of poverty, polyandry, sexuality, and jealousy shows that sexuality is a central issue for different sections of Indian society. Chughtai's focus on sex as means of biological reproduction points to the importance of the act as a way of earning bread for a poor family. The old sweeperess's reaction shows that there is awareness of middle-class filth that was swept under the carpet. For the poor, sexual morality is not as important as earning bread for the family.

The story points to another aspect of gender relations—*devar–bhabhi* relationship. In Punjab and UP, this relationship is portrayed in various songs, proverbs, and jokes. The Hindu joint family restricted social interaction between husband and wife.[20] A newly married wife found in her *devar* a man with whom she could talk freely; on the

17. Ibid., p. 109.
18. Ibid., p. 111.
19. Ibid., p. 113.
20. Charu Gupta, 'Impossible Love and Sexual Pleasure in Late Colonial North India', *Modern Asian Studies*, vol. 36, part 1, February 2002, p. 202.

other hand, the *devar* saw in his *bhabhi* a woman with whom he could flirt. Secondly, increasing male recruitment into the army, especially in south-east Punjab, facilitated this relationship. The *devar* was seen as a potential husband for the widowed *bhabhi* under the custom of *karewa*. Though the reason behind this custom was economic, the widespread apprehension was that the woman would turn her affections elsewhere, possibly beyond caste, that she might even refuse to obey the custom of *karewa*.

Young widows and barren women were regarded as major threats to male honour. Prem Chowdhry draws attention to a proverb that projects young widows as being responsible for sexually arousing even an old father-in-law. *Jawan rand, burhe sand* (the young widow makes old men lusty).[21] A barren woman in south-east Punjab was equated with a prostitute, where 'the sexual energy is not considered to have been exhausted by begetting several children and she [the woman] continues to remain [an] uncontrollable and dreadful force, posing a permanent menace to society'.

Chughtai, who is known for her bold and unconventional ideas regarding the man–woman relationship, portrays very effectively the hidden desires and longings of women in her fiction. The story, 'Housewife' depicts man–woman relations in the lower classes and men's control over women's sexuality. The story begins with Mirza's new maid ambling into his house. There was a commotion in the neighbourhood. The sweeper, who normally avoided work, stayed on and scrubbed the floor with great vigour. The milkman, notorious for adulterating his ware, brought milk clogged with cream.[22] These lines clearly present the male's attitude towards a poor but sexually attractive woman. Men tend to see women in purely sexual terms. Bashfulness was unknown to Lajo. From birth she had been abandoned in the streets. Begging and starving, she reached the age when she could snatch a living. Her body was the only asset that could stir young and old alike.

21. Prem Chowdhry, *The Veiled Women: Shifting Gender Equations in Rural Haryana, 1880–1990*, New Delhi, 1994, p. 119.
22. Ismat Chughtai, 'Housewife', tr. Fatima Ahmad, in *Indian Love Stories*, ed. Sudhir Kakar, New Delhi, 1999, pp. 179–91.

Mirza was a bachelor and ran a grocery shop. He had no time even to return to his home and get married. Mirza's friend Bakshi, installed Lajo in Mirza's house. He thought, 'Instead of squandering money in brothels, why not let Mirza enjoy a free dish?'[23] Though Mirza refused to have a tart at home, Lajo made herself comfortable. She swept, cooked and did all the domestic chores earnestly. Mirza was happy with his sparkling house and enjoyed spinach and potato curry and dal with onion and garlic just the way his Ammaji used to cook. However, he was afraid of incurring more expenses. He said, 'Look I'll pay your return fare. I just cannot afford a servant.' 'Who wants to be paid?' 'But'— 'Is the food hot?' Lajo asked, slipping a fresh chapatti onto his plate.

'Not the food, but I am certainly hot from head to toe!' he whispered. Lajo had fallen in love not with Mirza but with his house. She kept the house properly but Mirza's frequent visits to singing girls hurt her. Wherever she had worked, she had served well in every capacity. And here a full chaste week had passed. She had never felt so unwanted before. Several offers came her way, but she refused one and all. But Mirza could not see the volcano erupting within her. Lajo's name was on every lip. Today she slapped the milkman. Yesterday she had aimed a dung cake full on the face of the *bania.* The school-master insisted on educating her. The *mullahji* of the mosque burst into prayers in Arabic, with beseeching God to ward off impending danger.[24] Mirza was annoyed with her, or himself. One day, he saw Lajo quarrelling with a man, who slunk away the moment he saw Mirza. 'Who was that?,' he asked in the tone of a suspicious husband.

'Raghava. He was asking me how much milk he should bring from now on?'

'What did you say?'

'I said, may God hasten your funeral! Bring the usual measure.'

'Then?' Mirza was furious.

'Then I said, "Bastard, go. Feed the extra milk to your mother and sister!"

23. Ibid., p. 180.
24. Ibid., p. 182.

The scoundrel!

'Don't let him set foot here again. I shall myself fetch milk on the way home from the store.'

That night, after dinner Mirza put on a starched *kurta*, stuck a scented piece of cotton wool in his ear, and walked out. Lajo cursed the singing girls. But Mirza returned home uneasy. He was uncomfortable. He slowly lifted the hem of Lajo's skirt and pulled it down, stood indecisively for a while and then turned away. But with a quick move Lajo grabbed him. He struggled, pleaded, but she would not let him go.

Next morning, she blushed like a bride. She did her chores boldly. Mirza's looks began to improve. He felt a new lift in her gait. People knew the reason and sizzled with envy. When she fetched his lunch, the entire bazaar throbbed with her presence. So Mirza forbade her to bring lunch but his doubts assailed him. When he saw her playing with street urchins, his anger knew no bounds. Her skirt was billowing in the wind and the boy was engrossed in the skirt. It was beyond a man's tolerance. He asked her to wear tight trousers. He had grown fond of Lajo and both decided to marry. Mirza was bent upon entering a legal contract of the *nikah*. And it was solemnized.

Mirza imposed a ban on the *lahenga* and prescribed a *churidar pyjama* to avoid the display of legs, which was extremely irritating to Lajo.

> When bathing under a tap in the open, she kept wiping her tears. Mithwa, the son of the mason, climbed the terrace daily on the pretext of flying kites and watched her. She was so sad that day that she neither stuck out her thumb nor hurled a slipper at him. She wrapped the sheet around herself and went indoors[25] to wear the long trousers, which was very difficult to wear. But for Mirza this was a measure to protect her purity.

Mirza checked Lajo at every step. Her intoxicating coquetry had turned to brazenness. Mirza spent more time with his friends to avoid being labelled a henpecked husband. He installed Lajo in his house and forgot all about her. Now no one cast even a stray glance at the jute curtain except Mithwa.

One night, Mirza stayed away celebrating Dussehra. He came home the next morning and quickly went to the shop. This annoyed Lajo.

25. Ibid., p. 186.

While she was bathing, Mithwa's stare pierced her wet body like spears. When Mithwa's kite was broken and stuck to her body, she did not care, she wrapped her towel around herself and went inside. From then Mithwa was at her service at all the times. She did not waste food if Mirza did not come home to eat it. It was Mithwa who was fed. The news of Lajo and Mithwa disturbed Mirza very much and he thought of killing her to save his honour. But on Miran Mian's advice, he divorced her. When Lajo heard the news, she danced with joy but felt suffocated after some time. Thoughts of the house worried her.

One day, Mirza was on his way to the shop when Lajo waylaid him. 'Mian, shall I resume duty from tomorrow.' 'Damn', said Mirza and walked away. 'But I shall need a maidservant sooner or later, he thought. Maybe this wretch, if none other.'[26]

Lajo did not wait for his response and started cooking and sweeping. At night, she spread a jute curtain on the kitchen floor and went to sleep. Mirza felt uneasy and cursed himself. Then with a sudden, 'Damn it all,' he got up, ran across, and collected the housewife from the mat.[27]

This story portrays female sexuality and male attitude towards it. The woman is revered if she is married and remains the object of public gaze if she remains a maidservant.

While discussing men's hold over female sexuality, as depicted in this story, a question arises: Do men and women have equal claims to sexuality in their own marriage? The answer is no. Social norms about sex and sexuality do not apply equally to men and women. If at all there is any acknowledgement of sexual needs beyond procreation, it is only for men. Even if there are minor differences between one community and another, and even if in the name of modernity certain sexual mores have changed, in some places it is still men who enjoy the right to be polygamous or to seek extramarital or multiple sexual partners. A woman has always been expected to be faithful to a single man. If she dares to cross the *lakshman rekha*, she is stigmatized as *kulta* and divorced, as portrayed in this story. Her one mis-step can

26. Ibid., p. 191.
27. Ibid.

ruin the reputation of her family. A man taking sexual liberties can boast of increased strength and *purusha.* Beyond scriptual prohibition, social practices severely restrict the expression of female sexuality.

As soon as a girl reaches puberty, her behaviour is strictly controlled and monitored so as not to provoke male lust. The practice of child marriage was primarily based on this belief. There is no space for the expression of a woman's autonomous sexuality or desire. She has to cover her body to protect herself from the male gaze. In Chughtai's story, Mirza could not tolerate Lajo's billowing skirt though she was his maidservant. He had mistakenly treated her as his possession and could not digest the fact that he was attracted to her. The family, like other social institutions, is grounded within the material and ideological structure of the state and society; the basis of an ideal family is inheritance through legitimate heirs and sexual fidelity. But as the story shows, fidelity depends entirely on a woman's chastity, and she is not supposed to think beyond this sphere. A chaste wife is granted no sexuality; she is only granted de-sexed motherhood and domesticity. A woman's goodness is judged on the basis of her lack of desire and her ability to control and disguise her sexuality. It is always controlled and shaped by patriarchy in the interest of man. A woman is bound to be faithful to her husband even if married at the age of sixteen to a husband of fifty or sixty. Women's sexual needs are considered unimportant. Sexuality as mere desire is contrasted with a higher form of sexuality, that which is subordinated to conjugal duty and geared to meet the shared responsibilities of parenthood.

Chughtai criticized various aspects of sexuality. In her novel *Terhi Lakir*, she described the highly restricted relations of son and daughter-in-law. The daughter-in-law, Bari Apa, always cursed her *sas* or mother-in-law for making her married life unpleasant. Whenever she saw her *bahu* with her son, the *sas* cried, 'Arrey, I say, what is this constant fussing'. She would wrinkle her nose and taunt her daughter-in-law. Poor Bari Apa would break into a sweat with shame. Hastily she would free herself from her husband's embrace and start sorting spinach leaves.[28] It was only when the old lady realized that her son's anger had risen to a boiling point that she let Bari Apa go to him. The

28. Ismat Chughtai, *Terhi Lakir*, tr. Tahira Naqvi, New Delhi, 1995, p. 147.

conjugal duty of reproducing children had been done. Bari Apa had two children to raise. Bari Apa's daughter, Noori, has a romance despite the constant watch of her mother and grandmother. Chughtai also portrayed the psychological confusion of young Shaman towards sexuality.

Chughtai's novel *Masooma* focused on the lives of rich Muslim. Men are allowed to have many wives and maidservants to satisfy their lust. Women are restricted and are supposed to follow ethical and religious norms. Frustrated women have illicit relations inside the four walls of the house. Huzur Ali, one of the male characters in the novel, says that he had grown old and that any child born thereafter in his *haram* should not be considered his offspring.[29]

The desertion of women by their husbands is common in the Muslim community. These victims are often dragged into the whirlpool of debauchery and other sexual perversions. Masooma, the heroine of the novel, was the daughter of a deserted woman. Poverty compelled her to throw aside traditional respectable life and obliged her to sink to a vicious circle of sex and immorality. Masooma changed her name to Nilofer. She became a concubine of a rich man of repute she satisfied the lust of many people whose favour the rich man wanted to win. Chughtai's portrayal of the life of the rich exposes the lewdness of such people. Sexual exploitation led the innocent girl to alcoholism. In a state of intoxication, she could have slept with a dog.[30] Masooma was written in 1962 and portrayed the life of the rich in a metropolitan city (Bombay), but it is a unique Freudian psychoanalytical portrayal of sexuality. The novel shows how women are seen as instruments for making huge sums of money by rich people. They can degrade themselves to any extent in the pursuit of money. The situation is not much different in other parts of the country. The metropolitan cities of the provinces under study show the same sexual attitudes towards women.

'Women draw sacred attention' two feminist anthropologists have argued, primarily in connection with women's reproductive status.

29. Syed Fazle Rab, *Sociology of Literature: A Study of Urdu Novels*, New Delhi, 1992, p. 86.
30. Ibid.

Their point is that religious discourse deals with women only in relation to biological sexuality. Other constructs of sexuality are secondary. Moreover, in many religions, female sexuality is seen as contaminating and polluting, and is regarded as a potential harbinger of evil, which needs to be controlled strictly. The status of a family or *khandan* in general depends to a large extent on female chastity and purity, especially of sisters and daughters who are to be given in marriage.

The imposition of *purdah* on women has been seen as a barrier in the direct man–woman relationship. This point has been discussed in earlier chapters. Ownership of private property and maintenance of patriarchy necessitated a strict control over women's sexual labour and reproduction. Since property lines are maintained through legitimate heirs, sexual intercourse between husband and wife alone carries the potential for procreation and patriarchal sanction. Sex is seen as an instrument of reproduction, negating all other aspects of pleasure and desire intrinsic to it. Hence, sex and sexuality are given no social sanction beyond their reproductive purpose within legally sanctioned heterosexual marriage.[31]

Though Bedi does not show the boldness of Manto and Chughtai, his stories 'Bubble: The Boy Saved the Day', 'Give Me Your Sorrow', 'Maithun' and 'Bankruptcy' describe sexuality in different moulds. Bedi's story 'Kalyani' portrays the biological aspect of sexuality boldly. The birth of a male child, even by a prostitute, is seen as the victory of a woman. Sexual relations are seen as an act where the male conquers and the female surrenders as a victim. Sex becomes, then, one more area for the exercise of male power. 'Kalyani' does not present this stance only but also offers a creative exploration of the complexity of the male and female psyches.

The story describes the life of a sexually experienced prostitute, Kalyani, with Mahipat, her customer. Describing the house of a prostitute with masterly skill, Bedi recreates a vibrant and throbbing place buzzing with activity. The parrot's chanting '*Bhaj Man Ram*' is in contrast the restlessness of the loud-mouthed waiting girls. Male arrogance is seen when Mahipat reappears after having gone to a different set of girls for a change of taste. He returns to the old

31. First National Conference, op. cit.

prostitute with an incomplete image of a woman in his mind and thinks, 'After all, he himself had to complete that image as a man who is a painter of the painting which is a woman.'[32]

Mahipat restlessly observed the picture of Durga while Kalyani was away. He saw the image of Durga as Shakti, and the projection of her power in her weapon-laden arms and a bleeding head held in one of her hands. A corpse lays under her feet. His sense of guilt and fear deepened and he saw himself lying with a bleeding head. While engaged in sexual intercourse, he violently searched not for Kalyani the woman but for all womanhood.[33] He did not bother about the screaming and groaning of a woman. Rather he regarded this as a mark of masculinity. Kalyani, the symbol of womanhood, tolerated all his tortures for the sake of nurturing the bud that was born to her.

After a few moments, Mahipat regreted his behaviour. Kalyani looked at him helplessly. Helplessness and powerlessness mark a woman. She is compensated, however, with pride in being able to produce a male child. She feels victorious in annihilating the male. Despite the extreme physical torture and torment she faces, she asks for more money for the sake of her child as Mahipat has used her twice. 'Your child!'

'Yes, haven't you seen my child?'

'No. Where?' Who gave you the child?'

Kalyani giggled and then blushed, 'I wouldn't know who! . . . . May be it is yours.'[34]

Mahipat nervous, and embarrassed, barged out of the hovel, out into the open, to hide his face in the dazzling glare of the world outside.

In Bedi's portrayal, although woman emerges as an exploited sufferer (who had inward fully surrendered to the male), she is nevertheless victorious, joyful and triumphant when she produces a male child. This is perhaps the culturally determined definition of sexuality. But as Bedi portrays it, the man bows down to female power,

32. Rajinder Singh Bedi, 'Kalyani', in *Breakthrough Modern Hindi and Urdu Short Stories*, ed. Sukrita Paul Kumar, Shimla, 1993, pp. 165–74.
33. Sukrita Paul Kumar, *The New Story: A Scrutiny of Modernity in Hindi and Urdu Short Fiction*, Shimla, 1990, p. 52.
34. Bedi, 'Kalyani', p. 172.

and it is due to her great capacity for transforming a sexual act into physical form. Religious rituals and Brahmanical superiority enforced the idea of keeping women under men's control, to the extent of imposing *purdah*, thus making women socially invisible. They also propagated the notion that female sexuality should be controlled from the beginning. This idea necessitated child marriage ostensibly to protect girls from premarital or extramarital sex.[35]

Surprisingly, Indian writers have tended to shrink from writing on colonial sexualities. An analysis of sexuality in literature offers the historian an opportunity to explore relationships between the social structure and normative cultural history. For a feminist historian this is of the utmost significance. Sexuality is to feminism what work is to Marxism—that which is most one's own, yet most taken away.[36]

Before her marriage, girl's chastity is the main concern of the parents. Though expenditure on clothes is the second largest item next to food in rural households of eastern Punjab, the ideal of simplicity and austerity was especially extended to unmarried girls. According to a popular saying of eastern Punjab: *baap ke ghar beti gudar lipti achhi* (in her father's house, a daughter is best clad in simple and rough rags).

Girls were kept clad in rough clothes not only to avoid sexual provocation on the part of males but also to bury the girls' own desires under rags. A girl did not wear clothes of her own choice, because a pornographic representation of her could ostensibly engender voyeuristic pleasures among men. In contrast, male sexuality was considered self-evident, natural, aggressive, and dominating.[37]

The house plan in eastern Punjab was designed to prevent the entry of an outsider directly into the *zenana*. The most popular house plan had a *baithak* (a large outer apartment for men), a symbol of masculinity. The *baithak* was exclusively a male preserve, completely

35. Engels, op. cit., p. 75.
36. Shalini Shah, 'Gender and Sexuality in Ancient Punjab: A Case Study of the Karna Parva in the Mahabharata', in *Breaking Out of Invisibility*, ed. Aparna Basu and Anup Taneja, New Delhi, 2002, p. 24.
37. Patricia Uberoi (ed.), *Social Reform: Sexuality and the State*, New Delhi, 1996, p. xx.

out of bounds for women. The emphasis on the acquisition of a *baithak*, as distinct from the *ghar* (inner quarters for the women), was not only a symbol of the male-oriented housing scheme but also underlined the greater physical exclusion of women based on sexual segregation.[38] The *baithak* included some *charpais* (cots), potable water, *hookkah*, etc. Unmarried girls replenished the water pitcher and swept the *baithak*. Girls were treated as daughters of all villagers, as seen in the saying: *Gaon ki beti sabki beti* (The daughter of the village is the daughter of all the villagers).

The daughter-in-law was treated poorly in rural areas. A woman no better than man's shoes, inferior to him in power, wisdom, and knowledge. Men who heeded women's advice were considered to be *chutiya* (a term of abuse, literally a man with a vagina instead of a penis, therefore a weakling and coward, like a woman). This was enough to damn the household forever. No one wanted to enter into a marriage with a family where the woman dominated and the husband was henpecked.[39] A woman's advice was never taken and her appeals never heard, particularly in south-east Punjab. Beating women was an effective way of silencing their voices.

Apart from direct physical control, there were certain cultural constraints that not only controlled women ideologically but also assured their non-participation in decision-making. The custom of *purdah* was the foremost among these practices. A woman who did not observe *purdah* was called *badchalani*.

Purdah was observed as a matter of etiquette, which forced women to adopt a passive and deferential attitude and demeanour in their encounters with senior males and females. Women observed *purdah* in the presence of the senior family members even after the birth of several children. Men and women were not supposed to meet or speak during the day, but husbands went to their wives to fulfil their sexual needs at night. In most families, only a newly married couple was provided separate room. But after the birth of a child, especially a

38. Prem Chowdhry, 'Ideology, Culture and Hierarchy: Expenditure and Consumption Patterns in Rural Households', in *From Myth to Markets*, ed. Kumkum Sangari and Uma Chakravarti, New Delhi, 1999, p. 290.
39. Ibid., p. 299.

male child, they rarely got a chance to meet, having to vacate the room for a younger couple. As couples were traditionally not allowed to see and talk to each other during the day, or sometimes even for several nights, they shared few interests. Love and understanding between them developed only over a number of years. To women, marital love was beyond the sphere of individual preference and romantic love was immoral. In the early years of their marriage husband and wife were not very supportive towards each other.

> Moreover, many mothers-in-law had vested interests in their sons maintaining a conjugal distance because they were concerned with their own influence and emotional closeness with their sons. Only childbirth liberated a wife from the stigma of being the youngest and most subordinated daughter-in-law. As a mother, a woman directed her attention on the child, not on her husband.[40]

After the birth of a child, the couple rarely had the luxury of a separate retiring room.

The *Punjab Census* of 1931 shows that, as compared to the previous census, the number of occupied houses had increased by 7 per cent. As against this figure, the population had increased by 14 per cent, which indicates that the provision of new accommodation had not kept pace with the increase in population.[41] A comparison of family size in 1921 and 1931 in various districts of Punjab shows the increase of members in a family.[42]

From the 1920s, the number of literates increased slightly. In Punjab,

TABLE 7.1: SIZE OF FAMILIES IN VARIOUS DISTRICTS OF PUNJAB IN 1921 AND 1931

Districts	No. of persons per 100 houses	
	1931	1921
Amritsar	525	452
Jalandhar	511	437
Hisar	508	482
Rohtak	508	488
Ambala	434	407
Hoshiarpur	442	410

40. Engels, op. cit., p. 86.
41. *Census Report, Punjab*, 1931, p. 82.
42. Ibid.

literacy was higher among Hindus and Sikhs than among Muslims. Unlike Hindus and Sikhs, Muslims did not, to any appreciable extent, acquire literacy without going to school. The proportion of literates among the trading class of Hindus was very high. Literacy among Sikh women was higher than among Hindu women. Sikh women were literate in Gurumukhi. Literacy was low in Hisar, Gurgaon, and Karnal in comparison with Amritsar, Jalandhar, and Ambala. Although education made considerable progress during the decade (1921–31), 94 per cent of the population was illiterate.[43]

Literacy was a factor in increasing the marriage age of girls slightly. Some couples became politically involved together but there were few examples of this kind. The visibility of women in the public sphere was the main cause of sexual attraction. Women were supposed to keep themselves busy in domestic chores and, bearing and rearing children. They were not supposed to have their own desires, far less sexual desire. Their goodness lay in controlling their desire.

The progressive writers started writing on this delicate issue in the 1930s. Saadat Hasan Manto and Ismat Chughtai were prosecuted time and again in the courts for their stories. Chughtai's story 'Lihaf' (Quilt) created an uproar. This story depicts the hidden sexual desires of a woman. The heroine recalls the horrible images made by the quilt on the wall when she was sent to live with her aunt. Her delicate adolescent aunt was married to an old man, who remained busy teaching his students and raising pigeons and cocks, and forgot all about his young *begum*. Actually, he knew that he could not satisfy the young woman and was unable to give her a gift in the form of a child. The *begum* took the help of Rabbu, maidservant in massaging her body. Rabbu remained in her service the whole day. In the night, the heroine was surprised to hear the whispering of two people in her aunt's bed, but could not see and understand who could be there. She was frightened to see the elephant-like images on the wall created by the quilt. She screamed with fear and saw that the elephant had sat down. It was Rabbu, who was in a lesbian relationship with the *begum* for years to satisfy her sexual needs. 'Lihaf', considered Chughtai's most sensational story, portrayed the repressed sexual desires of a

43. Ibid., p. 59.

neglected woman and her erotic relationship with her maid. For this story, Chughtai faced an obscenity charge and underwent a trial in Lahore, which lasted two years before the case was finally dropped.

Polyandry was found in Kullu subdivision, Bushahar, and, to a smaller extent, Nahan, Mandi, and Suket. It also existed in eastern Punjab. The custom was common among Kanets, and was also found among the lower castes, the Rajputs, and other castes residing in these tracts.[44] The agrarian society of south-eastern Punjab exhibited a tolerant attitude towards certain practices involving women; here a woman was considered to have married a family rather than an individual.[45]

Polyandry was generally of the fraternal type. All brothers, and in some cases even cousins, shared a common wife. The elder brother usually had the first preference, and it was only in his absence that the younger brother could enjoy the wife's company. But when the younger brother went away for trade and other business and often visited home, the elder brother allowed him exclusive use of the wife. When all brothers stayed at home, the wife often spent her time equally, with all her husbands, but by turn, one evening being reserved for each. The house usually had two portions, one for males and other for females. When one brother wanted to enter the wife's room, he would leave his shoes or hat at the door as a sign that the wife was engaged. She was supposed to fulfil the sexual needs of her husband's brothers.

All the sons of the wife called all the husbands their fathers, and this was not a matter of shame but rather of pride. In some places, the first-born son was supposed to belong to the elder husband, the second to the second husband, and so on. In some cases, the wife was permitted to name the father of each son and if she was not particularly scrupulous, she named each time the richest of the brothers. According to M.C. Lennan, both promiscuity and polyandry were related to female infanticide, since the tribe was small.[46]

44. *Census Report, Punjab*, 1911, p. 287.
45. Chowdhry, *The Veiled Women*, op. cit., p. 111.
46. L.S. Vishwanath, 'Towards a Conceptual Understanding of Female Infanticide and Neglect in Colonial India', *Proceedings of Indian History Congress*, 55th Session, Delhi, 1995, p. 607.

The older generation remembers that the custom of sharing women among brothers was common in the 1920s. Several cases were cited from different villages where there was only one married brother and the other brothers had free access to his wife.[47] It was also at one time common for the father of the deceased husband to be a claimant of his daughter-in-law in sexual partnership and marry her.[48] The Jats in some of the eastern Punjab districts were stated to have followed the custom, though without full recognition. It has completely died out although an elder brother connived at his younger brother taking a certain amount of liberty with his wife. The popular Punjabi saying, *garib di rann jane khane di bhabi* (the poor man's wife is everyone's sister-in-law), shows that among the rural population, consisting mostly of Jats, a certain amount of liberty was allowed to the brothers of the husband. (The elder brother's wife was supposed to look after the younger brothers, while according to custom the younger brother's wife did not appear before the elder brother.)[49]

These unrecognized practices were the concomitant of female infanticide. The family was the first organization in which all things, including the wife, were owned in common. Though the elder brother headed the house, the universal custom of *karewa*, that is, widow remarriage, among the Jats shows how the younger brother (though it was not necessarily always the younger brother) or any brother used to succeed to the headship of the family on the death of the elder brother. Nothing except polyandry, which people was admitted occurred although they did not countenance it, can explain these figures. E. Joseph, Deputy Commissioner and Settlement Officer, Rohtak stated 'A most respectable Jat of my acquaintance procured his son's resignation from the army because his wife could not be trusted alone; as he explained, all his younger sons were too small to assist in dealing with the difficulty.'[50] *Karewa* was a systematic and extensive exploitation of women. However, this kind of sexual exploitation did not always go unchallenged, and at least one criminal

47. Chowdhry, *The Veiled Women*, p. 112.
48. Ibid., p. 118.
49. *Census Report*, *Punjab*, 1912, p. 289.
50. *District Gazetteer*, *Rohtak*, 1910, p. 88.

case of adultery came up in the early twentieth century in which the accused cited in his plea the existence of this social custom, which allowed him sexual access to his brother's wife.

The areas of Bushahar, Sirmor, Ambala, Kalsia, Ludhiana, Malerkotla, Ferozpur, Faridkot, and Amritsar have fewer wives than husbands. The small percentage of married females undoubtedly creates suspicion of widespread polyandry.[51] Sexuality has been acknowledged as the preserve of the powerful, not that of the dominated or the subordinate. In Haryana, however, both men and women assert that a woman, although held totally inferior and subordinate to a man (*pair ki jooti*), still exercises a kind of power over him, that is, sexual power.[52]

Our culture encourages women to attach all sorts of erroneous meanings to the sexual act. Women are taught that sex is a commodity, something that 'belongs to men and that women have to give'. Hence, many women associate shame with sexuality. Instead of being a natural act, sexuality becomes a dishonest act associated with duty and suffering. In such cases, sexual activity becomes unbalanced, and unfulfilling. But sexuality with sensuality is an elusive concept. Sex without sensuality is a mechanical experience. Sexuality is simply another part of life, sometimes in the forefront and sometimes relegated to the background.[53]

Sexuality remains an unexplored area for many women. They do not express their views about sexuality frankly. This is the story of many Indian women. On the topic of sexuality, the progressive writers openly challenged popular ignorance and wrote frankly on this aspect. Sajjad Zaheer's stories 'Jannat Ki Basarat' and 'Dulari', and Rashid Jahan's 'Parde Ke Pichhe' opened the floodgates in this direction. Saadat Hasan Manto and Ismat Chughtai carried this exploration even further. Manto's 'Thanda Gosht', 'Padhiye Kalma' and 'Sarkandon Ke Pichhe' portrayed the violent and aggressive expression of women's

51. Chowdhry, *The Veiled Women*, p. 116.
52. Prem Chowdhry, 'Lustful Woman, Elusive Lover: Identifying Males as Objects of Female Desire', *Indian Journal of Gender Studies*, vol. 8, no. 1, January–June 2001, p. 43.
53. Kasl, op. cit., p. 5.

sexuality, while 'Darpok', 'Babu Gopinath', and 'Banjh' presented men's piety and sinful behaviour. In 'Dhuan', 'Phaha' and 'Blouse', Manto presented the confused awakening of sexuality in adolescents. In 'Mustainwala', Manto portrayed male homosexuality, while in 'Khali Dibbe Khali Bottlein' and 'Bijli Pahalwan' depicted men's weakness. Manto's themes came from those hateful areas that no gentleman wants to even mention in daylight but that he may visit in the darkness of night.

In 'Thanda Gosht', Manto presents a unique combination of the victimization of women during the Partition riots and sexuality. The story for which Manto was tried in Pakistan on the charge of obscenity is about Ishar Singh, a Sikh who abducts a Muslim girl and rapes her during the riots. His jealous mistress, Kulwant Kaur, finding him unable to make love to her and becomes restive. In a fury, she screams, 'Ishar Singh, tell me the name of the bitch you have been with, who has squeezed you dry? . . . Who was that bitch?'[54]

Like a wild creature Kulwant Kaur picked up Ishar Singh's *kirpan* and plunged it into his neck. Blood came out, but, unaware of anything, she insisted on knowing the name of the woman. In a quivering voice Ishar Singh said,

> There was the house I broke into. . . . There were seven people in it, six of whom I killed with my *kirpan* one by one . . . and there was one girl, she was so beautiful. . . . I did not kill her . . . I took her away. . . . I said to myself . . . Ishar Singh, you gorge yourself on Kulwant Kaur every day. . . . How about a mouthful of this luscious fruit! I thought she had gone into a faint. . . . I decided to trump her right away . . . I threw the trump . . . but, but . . .
>
> Ishar Singh opened his dimming eyes and said, 'she was dead. . . . I had carried a dead body, a heap of cold flesh'.[55]

Describing the chilling experience, which rendered him impotent, Ishar Singh became colder than ice.

Contrary to the belief that women overcome their sexual desires, Manto portrayed a woman as a wounded lioness who became violent

54. Saadat Hasan Manto, *Mottled Dawn: Fifty Sketches and Stories of Partition*, tr. Khalid Hasan, New Delhi, 1997, p. 27.
55. Ibid., p. 29.

when she found her man unable to satisfy her passion. The portrayal of sexuality in this story reflects the boldness of a woman. She took the extreme step when she found her soul wounded. In addition to this story, Pakistani censors also considered another of Manto's stories 'Khol Do', obscene (he moved to Pakistan in January 1948). He was tried for obscenity half a dozen times, three times before and three times after Independence.[56]

Manto explored several aspects of prostitution with great intensity and insight. He wrote many stories on this issue, such as 'Hatak', 'Khushia', 'Fobabai', 'Burhami Ladki', 'Sarda', 'Das Rupaiya', and 'Kali Salwar'. His story 'Kali Salwar' discribes a prostitute who is as much religious-minded as any other woman. The prostitute, Sultana, does not get a single customer after shifting from Ambala cantonment to Delhi. In Ambala cantonment, she had no dearth of customers. Soldiers came to her, and she earned eight to ten rupees from each one of them in the space of three or four hours. But when she shifted to Delhi, her business suffered. Here not a single soldier came to her. Soldiers were good payers. During three months, only six men came to her, and from them she earned only eighteen rupees. Sultana was worried because Moharrum was quite near and she had no black *salwar* to wear on that occasion. To meet her expenses, she sold all her belongings. One day, she saw a man (Shankar) and waved out to him to come up. Shankar also had empty pockets. Sultana was obsessed with Moharrum. She said,

> For God's sake, do something! I do not care whether you steal or plunder. Get me cloth for a *salwar* at least. I have a white *boski silk* shirt, which I shall get dyed. I also have a *dupatta* of white linen—the one you gave me for Diwali. I shall get that also dyed along with the shirt. Only a *salwar* is needed. That you have to get me somehow. I will die if you don't.[57]

At last, Shankar, her poor customer, promised Sultana that on the first day of Moharrum she would get the *salwar*.[58] Shankar asked for Sultana's earrings, which she gave him happily because they were not so costly. On the morning of the first day of Moharrum, Shankar

56. Ibid., p. 1.
57. Saadat Hasan Manto, *Selected Stories*, tr. Madan Gupta, New Delhi, 1997.
58. Ibid., p. 27.

came with a packet containing a black satin *salwar*, similar to the one she had seen Mukhtar wearing. Sultana was very happy. The loss of the earrings had been compensated by the acquisition of a black *salwar*. When Sultana got ready with the dyed shirt, *dupatta*, and black *salwar*, she heard a knock at the door. She opened it. It was Mukhtar. Both women looked at each other, Mukhtar at Sultana's *salwar* and Sultana at Mukhtar's earrings. But there was silence between them. Evidently, Manto saw prostitutes as pious women burning with religious zeal.

Sexuality is a source of love, power, and spirituality as well as the source of extreme pain and self-destruction, depending on circumstances. Sexually addictive and sexually co-dependent behaviour both are directly related to childhood sexual abuse and neglect. Sexuality with sensuality and spirituality (mind, body, and spirit) brings feelings of power, joy, fullness, and contentment. Otherwise, sexuality on its own becomes a mechanical process, as in the case of prostitutes.

However, the free expression of sexuality remained a closed chapter for most Indians. The progressive writers broke this silence and eloquently described women's sexuality. This frankness earned them criticism from conservatives. But sexuality remained a central issue, particularly during the Partition riots, which will be discussed in the next chapter.

8

Women as Victims of Partition

The Partition of the Indian subcontinent and the establishment of the two independent nations of India and Pakistan was the culmination of the love–hate relationship between Hindus and Muslims. It occurred with remarkable suddenness. Only seven years from the first formal demand by the Muslim League for Pakistan to the establishment of the country. From the 1940s to today, a great deal has been written about the Partition and the violence accompanying it.[1] But an important characteristic of the Partition violence of 1947 that marks it from the earlier communal riots was the invasion of the private sphere in which women were the main sufferers. There was widespread sexual savagery; about 75,000 women are thought to have been abducted and raped by men of a religion other than their own in their own land, indeed sometimes by men of their own religion.[2]

The demand for Partition was adopted in Lahore in March 1940 for a Muslim country by an important section of Muslim leadership. The demand was articulated more widely and in a clearer way by Muslims across the subcontinent. Elections in early 1946 were largely held along communal lines, that is, on the question of Pakistan. The Muslim League performed well in the Muslim-majority constituencies all over the country and thus claimed to be the sole representative of the Muslims.[3]

In Punjab, there were two reactions to or perspectives on the

1. For a detailed bibliography on this aspect of the Partition, see Gyanendra Pandey, *Remembering Partition*, Cambridge, 2001, p. 3.
2. Urvashi Butalia, *The Other Side of Silence: Voices from the Partition of India*, New Delhi, 1998, p. 3.
3. Pandey, op. cit., p. 22.

question of Pakistan. In the countryside communal cooperation and amity prevailed, while in towns politics was structured along communal lines. The Congress was weak in Punjab, where it was identified with the interests of the Hindu urban commercial classes. So its appeal was marginal among the rural Hindu communities.[4] Hence, the Muslim League was unable to form a ministry in the Muslim-majority provinces of Punjab and the North West Frontier Province (NWFP), and managed to do so very narrowly in Sind. The Unionist Party rekindled the political approach and formed a government. Its leading members were able to maintain relative tranquillity in the countryside. The British were ready to pour considerable resources, both economic and political, to maintain peace in the countryside, which formed the major recruitment area for the Indian army. It was only when the rural Muslims deserted the Unionist Party that the conditions were created for the bloodletting of 1947.[5]

The growing belief in an independent Muslim-majority state where Islam prevailed and where equality and justice would flourish, generated great enthusiasm among the Muslim middle classes, especially the youth. The idea of Pakistan was supported by intellectuals, students, teachers, and professionals. Every word of Jinnah was digested and etched on the heart of Muslims. Pakistan was seen as the only answer to Hindu oppression. The Muslim League campaigned enthusiastically against the Congress and its leaders. The League claimed that the formation of Pakistan had two aims: freedom from Hindu oppression and freedom from foreign rule.[6] A true Muslim should be prepared to lay down his or her life for Pakistan. Those who were unable or unwilling to make sacrifice for their religion and nation were not Muslim at all, but renegades 'quislings' and *kafirs*.[7]

A momentary agreement took place in mid-1946 between the Congress and the Muslim League on the Cabinet Mission Plan to establish a loose federation, with the Muslim-majority provinces of

4. Anders Bjorn Hansen, *Partition and Genocide: Manifestation of Violence in Punjab 1937–1947*, New Delhi, 2002, p. viii.
5. Ibid., p. vii.
6. Pandey, op. cit., p. 28.
7. Ibid., p. 29.

the north-west and north-east being grouped into two federating units and the rest of India into a third, with a provision of constitutional review after ten years. But the agreement collapsed. On 16 August 1946, the Muslim League decided to organise a 'Direct Action Day'. On that day, violence broke out between Hindus and Muslims in Calcutta. Several thousand people were killed in four days. Violence spread to other areas.[8]

After Calcutta, violence was reported in its worst form in Bombay in early September and in East Bengal in early October. The communal fire spread to NWFP in January and to Punjab in March. In early March 1947, the League's agitation to bring down the Khizr Hyat Khan-led coalition government in Punjab succeeded. The fall of the Unionist government was seen as a turning point in the history of the partition of Punjab. Communal frenzy gripped the province, and the Muslim League was viewed as the creator of an independent country—Pakistan (Pure Land)—for Muslims. Demonstrations and counter-demonstrations, took place, and threats were made to fight to the finish. Violence spread to Lahore and Amritsar. In Rawalpindi and Multan, attacks were more fierce and more savage than before. In some areas, the savagery was extreme. Men, women, and children were hacked or beaten to death and their houses burned. There were cases of forcible conversion of men and abduction of women. Widespread violence and heavy casualities led to a considerable exodus of people to central and eastern Punjab by the end of April 1947. The official estimates of refugees in Punjab put the figure at 80,000.[9]

Satya M. Rai writes,

> When the Muslim League leader Mr. Jinnah suggested an exchange of population on 10 December, 1945 and again on 15 November, 1946, it was not seriously considered by the Congress leaders. Referring to the driving out of the Hindus from Noakhali, he said that the transfer of population was already in action and some machinery should be devised for effecting it peacefully.[10]

8. Pandey, op. cit., pp. 22–3.
9. Ibid., p. 24.
10. Satya M. Rai, *Partition of the Punjab: A Study of Its Effects on the Politics and Administration, 1947–56*, New Delhi, 1965, p. 72.

A Muslim student of Lucknow University in 1946–7 recalled. 'Nobody thought in terms of migration in those days. All [the Muslims] thought that everything would remain the same. Punjab would remain Punjab and Sind would remain Sind. There wouldn't be any demographic changes, no drastic changes anyway.'[11]

The announcement of the Partition plan on 3 June, with the transfer of power scheduled for as early as 15 August shocked the entire nation. According to this plan, the decision to Partition Punjab and Bengal should be taken by the legislative assemblies of the respective provinces. In Punjab, the plan received a mixed response. The Sikhs reacted strongly against it because of the fear that they would be in a minority in both Indian and Pakistani Punjab. The Shiromani Akali Dal called it 'death to the Sikhs' and declared that Sikhs wanted a free and sovereign state, with the Chenab and Jamuna rivers as its borders.[12] On 4 June, five deaths and five fires were reported in Lahore alone, and Amritsar witnessed two communal riots. The Gurgaon district was also in disorder and nearly 60 persons were burnt to death.

The decision to partition Punjab (and Bengal) was endorsed by the Congress Working Committee on 14 June. Addressing the meeting, Gandhi expressed his reluctance and sadness over the turn of events. He ended his address by saying:

> This decision puts both our religions on trial. The world is watching us. In the three quarters of the country that has fallen in our share, Hinduism is going to be tested. If you show the generosity of true Hinduism, you will rise in the eyes of the world. If not, you will have proved Mr. Jinnah's thesis that Muslims and Hindus are two separate nations. The Hindus forever will be Hindus and the Muslims forever Muslims, that the two will never unite, and [that] the Gods of the two are different.[13]

Despite Gandhi's appeal for restraint, riots in Punjab spread rapidly, between 18 November 1946 and 15 May 1947. In all 3,280 people were reportedly killed and 1,390 injured. The actual number may be higher as figures from Rawalpindi and Gurgaon were uncertain.[14]

11. Pandey, op. cit., p. 26.
12. Hansen, op. cit., p. 130.
13. Ibid., p. 132.
14. Ibid.

Fires and killings had become a daily phenomena. People were not sure whether it would be safe to stay on after Partition or not. Another uncertainty was the line of division. After a face-to-face with a Sikh leader, Giani Kartar Singh, Evan Jenkins, the Governer of Punjab reported that Sikhs would accept nothing short of the Chenab River as the western boundary. The Muslims, however, were hoping to stretch the eastern boundary of Pakistan as far as Ambala. The crucial task of drawing the boundaries was entrusted to a British official, Sir Cyril Radcliffe, who was unfamiliar with India and Indian politics.[15] However, there was little hope of a peaceful solution.

To counter the anxiety, on 24 July it was announced by the Partition Council that both India and Pakistan would guarantee protection to all citizens and that they had agreed to set up a Special Boundary Force from 1 August. Jinnah did not want the division of Punjab. When left with no choice but to accept the division, the Governor informed Giani Kartar Singh about Jinnah's assurance of religious and personal freedom for the minorities in Pakistan. Giani Kartar Singh replied that he had no confidence in Jinnah and claimed that the Sikhs were in great danger.[16] But in early 1947, Master Tara Singh and other Akali leaders came out in support of the Congress plan to divide Punjab. They called it sheer tyranny and a moral betrayal to leave the Sikhs of the western Punjab districts to fend for themselves.[17]

On 8 August, Mountbatten made it clear that Evan Jenkins would be the most competent official for handling the situation. He also agreed to wait and see the reactions to the Award Boundary Line. The daily casualities were estimated to be between 50–100. The commander of the newly established Punjab Boundary Force, Mr Auchinleck, recommended that 'the Joint Defence Council should have the authority of both the governments to declare any affected districts as a disturbed area'.[18] On 12 August, Mountbatten informed Jenkins that the award for Punjab would not be ready before the evening of the 15 August or morning of 16 August. The uncertainty

15. Ibid., p. 136.
16. Ibid., p. 140.
17. Cited in Pandey, op. cit., p. 32.
18. Rai, op. cit., p. 74.

about the boundary award led to increased violence. The people in the disturbed areas were not sure where to go. On 9 August, the first fully organized train attack took place, in which one woman and one child died and ten people were injured. The culprits disappeared into Faridkot in a jeep.[19] Law and order had broken down because in eastern Punjab there were hardly any police officers left since the Muslims constituted 90 per cent of the Punjab police force. The disarming of Muslim policemen in Amritsar made the officers and their families fearful of their safety and many had started leaving.[20]

In light of the continuing violence and breakdown of the administrative set up, the situation in the twelve districts that were to be divided, and which were home to approximately 12 million affected people, could not be controlled by the Punjab Boundary Force and its commander. The force utterly failed to protect the minorities or to organize the peaceful movement of people from one country to the other. On 11 August, Jinnah delivered his first speech to the Constituent Assembly of Pakistan, in Karachi, appealing to Hindus and Muslims to work together. But it was too late.[21] On the other hand, Congress leaders kept on appealing to the people to stay where they were.

On 15 August 1947, Jawaharlal Nehru addressed independent India: 'Before the birth of freedom we have endured all the pains of labour and our hearts are heavy with the memory of sorrows.' But the 'father of the nation' decided not to take part in the Independence day celebrations. Disillusioned by the Partition and the brutal violence, and unhappy over being sidelined by the Congress leadership, Gandhi stayed away from Delhi. He went to Calcutta to appeal to Hindus and Muslims to live in peace. However, no leader went to Punjab where thousands were being killed, abducted and raped, and where millions were on the move.[22]

Although much has been written on the Partition of India, there has been little attempt to fathom the depth of brutality with which

19. Hansen, op. cit., p. 144.
20. Ibid., p. 145.
21. Ibid., pp. 147–8.
22. Ibid., p. 155.

women were treated. As discussed earlier, women were the chief sufferers. Their relatives either killed the women or they committed suicide to save their honour by leaping from moving trains or jumping into wells.[23] The mass exodus of people had started. At the end of August, there were hardly any non-Muslims left in Lahore compared to the 300,000 who had lived there prior to the outbreak of rioting.[24]

In Sheikhupura, on 26 August, a band of Baluchi (Pakistani) soldiers organized a huge massacre of non-Muslims. Around 10,000 were killed and many girls molested. The attacks were now becoming more frequent. The abduction, molestation, and rape of women were weapons to humiliate men who were unable to protect the honour of their women.[25]

The orgy of violence and carnage, rapes and abductions, murders and killings rocked the province. M. Asaduddin notes that the human dimension of the violence—broken family, ties and sundered relations, physical disability and disease, the psychological trauma of torture, amputation, rape, abduction, and other atrocities—can never be fully quantified without taking into account the literature on Partition.[26] Though the progressive writers whose stories have been discussed in this book were not by conventional political standards, 'influential' yet they must be heard, argues Mushirul Hasan. These writers articulated the feelings and emotions of large numbers of aggrieved and tormented people who had no say whatsoever in the transfer of power to two sovereign nations. They convey to us the agony, pain, and sorrow of the people who were caught in the internecine communal conflicts.[27]

Writers writing in various languages have depicted the events of the Partition. Here, we look at selected Urdu stories of the progressive writers, particularly those that deal with gender issues. Krishan

23. Mushirul Hasan (ed.), *India Partitioned: The Other Face of Freedom*, vol. I, New Delhi, 1995, p. 9.
24. Ibid., p. 159.
25. Ibid., p. 160.
26. S. Settar and Indira Baptista Gupta (eds.), *Pangs of Partition: The Human Dimension*, vol. II, New Delhi, 2002, p. 314.
27. Hasan (ed.), *India Partitioned: The Other Face of Freedom*, vol. I, p. 9.

Chander's book of short stories called, *Hum Vahshi Hain* (We are Barbarians), was published in 1948, used a novel technique of employing unconventional narrators such as 'train' in 'Peshawar Express' or a hired killer. The story 'Peshawar Express' describes the shame and guilt of the times through an imaginative delineation of the atrocities perpetrated by each community. The story begins:

'I (a Train) heaved a sigh of relief as I pulled out of Peshawar railway station. My carriages were jam-packed with passengers, all of them Hindus. They have converged here from Peshawar, Hoti Mardan, Kohat, Charsada, Khyber, Landikotal, Bannu, Naushera, and Manshera. Overcome by grave insecurity in Pakistan, they were trying to escape to India.'[28] As the train leaves, people bid goodbye to their homeland with a heavy heart but were grateful that they were still alive and thankful that their womenfolk had escaped molestation or rape. At Taxila railway station, a ghastly sight of a procession greeted them. Each Muslim in the procession was carrying the corpse of a Hindu on his shoulders. Two hundred corpses were entrusted to the care of the Baluchi guards. They put ten to fifteen corpses in each carriage. After all this was done, the processionists ordered the station master to allow the train to move. But it was again stopped by the mob. The leader of the mob thundered, 'Line up, you infidels.'[29] They were then lifted up one by one and made to stand in line. Two hundred living corpses, their faces down, the miscreants' eyes pricking them like arrows. The Baluchi soldiers went into action. Fifteen people fell at Taxila station, which once boasted one of Asia's leading universities.

Krishan Chander describes the ghastly sight in the train in this way: 'Death had stalked through every carriage. There were corpses in the middle of each carriage, surrounded by living corpses over whom the Baluchi guard stood smiling. Somewhere a child whimpered, an old mother sobbed, a young wife moaned for her dead husband.'[30] On its way to Gujarat, the train was again made to stop. They ripped off the *burqas* of veiled women. 'We are Hindus, we are Sikhs !', the women cried. 'These people have abducted us.' But the young men only laughed and dragged the women down from the train. 'We are going to have our way with these women,' they shouted. 'Come if

28. Jai Ratan (tr.) *Krishan Chander: Selected Short Stories*, New Delhi, 1989, p. 186.
29. Ibid., p. 187.
30. Ibid., p. 188.

anyone of you has the guts to stop us.'[31] The train reached Wazirabad, a place known for its joint Hindu–Muslim celebrations of Baisakhi, but this year it was a gruesome Baisakhi. The crowd surged over the railway platform. Dancing and singing villagers formed the vanguard, and were followed by a concourse of naked women, ranging from old grannies to young virgins. The women's hair hung loose; their bodies bore marks of injuries. They walked erect as if the heavy shadow of death had completely eclipsed their naked bodies. The naked women were made to sit among the refugees. It is one of the darkest chapters in India's history. Krishan Chander describes a heart-rending event in the train. A child crawled to an old woman and said, 'Why are you sitting naked?'[32] He asked if she was returning from her bath. The woman forced back her tears. The sons of her own land had given her a sinister bath.

'And your clothes, where are they?' the child asked, 'The clothes bore the marks of marital bliss,' the old woman replied, 'They have taken them away to cleanse them of those marks.'[33]

At Lahore station, the train stopped at platform no. 1. Another train from Amritsar carrying Muslim refugees from India stopped at platform no. 2. The Muslim volunteers searched all the carriages thoroughly and took away all the gold, silver, and other valuables from the passengers. A number of Hindu refugees were butchered on the platform to complete the fatal tally. According to Krishan Chander, the situation was not very different in India. Muslims in Brahman clothes were put to the trousers test and then pierced through the chest. The mob did not spare the Deputy Commissioner of Ambala Cantonment and his family. A girl holding a book cried, 'Don't kill me. Convert me to Hinduism. I am prepared to embrace your religion. I am also willing to marry one of you.' But she was tortured to death. Her book was soiled with her blood. The title of the soaked book was *Socialism: Theory and Practice*, and the writer was John Strachey. The dead body of the girl was thrown into the jungle where it was preyed upon by jackals, crows, and vultures.

31. Ibid., p. 189.
32. Ibid., p. 190.
33. Ibid.

The story ends with a description of train's desire:

> I hate to carry a cargo of blood and flesh dripping with hatred. I will haul food grain to famine-stricken areas. I will carry coal, oil, and iron ore to the mills. The pious and simple women, secure in the love of their husbands, will cast loving glances at them and their children. . . . Then there will be no Hindu and no Muslim. They will all be workers and human beings.[34]

The crimes committed against women crossed all limits of brutality. They were openly raped and forced to walk naked in the streets. Krishan Chander has portrayed a train as a witness to the brutal violence throughout the Punjab.

In her remarkable work on the oral histories of women during Partition, *The Other Side of Silence*, Urvashi Butalia quotes a man who narrates how his father killed his sister.

> When my father swung the *kirpan* (sword) . . . perhaps some doubt or fear came to his mind or perhaps the *kirpan* got stuck in her *dupatta* (scarf), no one can say. It was such a frightening, such a fearful scene. Then my sister with her own hand removed her plait and pulled it forward . . . and my father with his own hands moved her *dupatta* aside and then he swung the *kirpan* and her body and neck rolled off and fell . . . there . . . far away.[35]

Likewise, several other non-Muslims killed their daughters to save their honour during the Sheikhupura massacre.

Mrs. Vidyawati Seth narrates her journey from Bahawalpur to India. Her daughter, who was very young and beautiful, became a problem. She had to dye her face black to save the young girl's honour.

Sudhir Kakar describes a true incident as recounted by his older brother. Sohan Lal, who had married a pretty girl five months earlier, threw himself in front of a train and killed himself. On the day of their departure, arrangements were made with a truck driver for their escape from Lyallpur. In their absence, their house was attacked. When they returned, they saw the house being looted by five husky Muslims with butcher's knives. The corpse of the younger brother was lying

34. Ibid., p. 191.
35. Butalia, op. cit., p. 171.

in the courtyard. The Muslims were bringing out packed trunks from inside the house and throwing them outside.[36]

> Then two of Muslims went inside the house and brought out Sohan Lal's wife and the leader pulled her to him. She sat on the man's lap, naked to the waist, her petticoat ripped open, and the Muslim's hairy hand, like a giant black spider, covered her thighs. After laying her on the ground next to our brother's corpse, where drops of blood still oozed from the severed neck, they raped her in turn. I was holding Sohan Lal tightly, my palm covering his mouth. If he had made the slightest sound, the Muslims would have discovered us. But I do not think Sohan Lal would have done anything. His legs were buckling under him and I had to hold him up. After they finished they ripped open her belly.[37]

Sohan Lal never said a word after it was all over. He remained mute for days as they crossed the border. Before they reached Rohtak, he killed himself.

The above-mentioned incident was not a solitary case. What the progressive writers witnessed and felt, they gave that voice. Manto was one of the most important writers on the Partition. Much has been written about the communal killings of 1947 but little of it has survived as literature. Either it was of little or no literary value or it was a weepy description of events. Manto captured and comprehended all dimensions and perspectives of human behaviour. He presented the intrinsic nobility of man as well as his barbaric and brutal acts.

Manto's stories on the Partition are unforgettable. These bring alive the most traumatic events in the history of the subcontinent. In particular, he raised issues concerning women in a very lively and open manner. He was tried for obscenity by Pakistan censors for two of his greatest stories on Partition, 'Thanda Gosht' and 'Khol Do'.

His stories like 'The Assignment', 'The Last Salute', 'Mozail', 'The Dutiful Daughter', 'The Woman in Red Raincoat', 'Toba Tek Singh', 'Open It' and 'Colder than Ice', written between 1947 and 1955, are masterpieces. 'Khol Do' (Open It) a story about a young girl who becomes a victim of atrocities during the Partition, begins:

36. Sudhir Kakar, *The Colours of Violence*, New Delhi, 1995, p. 34.
37. Ibid., p. 35.

'The special train left Amritsar at two in the afternoon, arriving at Mughalpura, Lahore eight hours later. Many had been killed on the way, a lot more injured and countless lost.'[38] After gaining consciousness, amidst screaming men, women, and children, Sirajuddin lay still and gazed at the dusty sky. He was in deep shock, which brought him back to the events of last night. Attack . . . fire . . . escape . . . railway station . . . Sakina. He rose abruptly and began searching for his daughter, Sakina, in the crowd at the refugee camp. Everyone was looking for lost sons, daughters, mothers wives, and other relatives. Sirajuddin sat away from the crowd and tried to think clearly. He was sure that Sakina's mother was dead. She had died in front of his eyes. He could hear her voice: 'Leave me where I am. Take the girl away.'[39] He could recollect that while running away Sakina's *dupatta* had slipped to the ground and that he had stopped to pick it up. Sakina had said, 'Father, leave it'. He could feel the bulge in his pocket. It was Sakina's *dupatta*, but where was she? A few days later, some young men brought back women and children left behind on the other side. Sirajuddin gave them a description of his pretty daughter. The young men assured him that if his daughter were alive, they would find her. Sirajuddin prayed for them.

On their next trip, they found a girl on the roadside. She was scared. She confessed that she was Sakina, daughter of Sirajuddin. They were very kind to her. One of them gave her his jacket so she could cover herself. But many days had passed, and Sirajuddin had no news about his daughter. One day, he saw the young men in the camp. He shouted: Had they found his daughter? They replied in the affirmative.[40]

That evening, he saw four men carrying the body of a young girl who had been found unconscious near the railway track. They were taking her to the hospital. He entered the hospital and saw the mole on her left cheek. 'Sakina,' he screamed. The doctor switched on the light and stared at Sirajuddin. 'I am her father,' he screamed. The doctor looked at the prostrate body and felt the pulse. Then he pointed to the window and said to the old man, 'open it'.

The young woman on the stretcher moved slightly with painful slowness. She unfastened the cord of her *salwar*, pulled the garment down, and opened her legs. The story ends with Sirajuddin's shouts

38. Saadat Hasan Manto, *Mottled Dawn: Fifty Sketches and Stories of Partition*, tr. Khalid Hasan, New Delhi, 1977, p. 11.
39. Ibid., p. 12.
40. Ibid., p. 13.

of joy, 'She is alive, my daughter is alive.' The doctor broke into a cold sweat.[41] In this story Manto describes a helpless girl who became a victim of Partition violence. Listening to the words 'open it' she pulled down her *salwar* and opened her legs, but her father did not notice this. He screamed with joy that his daughter was alive.

The story shows that these attacks were specifically targeted at the symbol of sexuality and reproduction. The female body presented an opportunity to conquer enemy territory. The attacks were made on two levels. First women were seen as the embodiment of community honour; and second, their bodies were seen as the site of community reproduction. The *modus operandi* included molestation, rape, stripping and parading the naked women through the streets, branding breasts and genitals with the slogan of 'Pakistan Zindabad' or 'Hindustan Zindabad', cutting off breasts, knifing open wombs, and killing foetuses. The rape and humiliation of women symbolized the sowing of seed in the enemy's womb. Women were the earth for sowing the seed as each community acknowledged the role of women as the bearer of future generations.[42] Women who were pregnant with bad seed were forced to undergo abortion to maintain the purity of the community, while others were planted with good seed of their community.

One witness said that a baby boy was snatched from his mother and then cut into two. Afterwards the mother was stabbed with a spear. Women were attacked by both communities. 'In a village in Sialkot district, the relatives of a girl were forced to stand around while she was continuously being raped.'[43]

Sudhir Kakar wrote about the cutting off the male genital and the sadistic fury directed against female breasts, which were hit repeatedly by iron rods, stabbed with knives, and lopped off with scythes and swords.[44] I remember one such event that my mother used to tell us about. In Kharkhoda (Sonepat), the infants cried with hunger and searched for their mothers' bodies, whose breasts had been stabbed

41. Ibid., p. 14.
42. Hansen, op. cit., p. 162.
43. Ibid., pp. 161–2.
44. Kakar, op. cit., pp. 3–7.

by the angry mob. The young children were thrown into a burning fire.

Sexual violence was widespread during the Partition riots in the north. One reason for this may be that undivided Punjab was comparatively a violent society. The socially approved dictum was that men used physical power to protect their *zar* (wealth), *joru* (woman or family honour), and *zamin* (land). During the Partition, people were uprooted, looted, and killed. Even children were not spared. The perpetrators showed no mercy to anyone.

In Harnoli, in Mianwali district, fierce fighting took place between Hindus and Muslims. Attacks were organized with the help of the Muslim army, which used tanks. More than half of the 6,000 inhabitants were massacred and children were snatched away from their mother's laps and thrown into boiling oil. Hundreds of women saved their honour by jumping into wells and by throwing themselves into burning houses. Girls as young as eight or ten years old were raped in the presence of their parents and killed mercilessly. Naked women with their breasts cut-off were made to walk through the bazaars of Harnoli.[45]

Another feature of the atrocities against women was abduction. About 8,000 girls and women were abducted from Harnoli alone. Both Muslim and non-Muslim leaders were apparently against mass migration, but they tacitly or openly encouraged the communal elements to undertake the cleansing of minorities. The murderers of the minority community were considered heroes and were openly defended in the law-making bodies. Justifying the massacre of Muslims in East Punjab, S. Udham Singh said in the Legislative Assembly, 'If our Hindu and Sikh brethren had not risen to defend themselves, the province of East Punjab would not have existed at all.'[46] As a result, the physical annihilation of the minority community had become a matter of determined policy on the part of the majority community in spite of declarations to the contrary. Mass exodus was the only alternative. In view of the deteriorating situation, the government thought of setting up machinery to evacuate the people. At the central

45. Ibid., p. 176.
46. Rai, op. cit., pp. 75–6.

level, the government appointed a special officer to act as a Chief Liaison Officer (CLO) on its behalf for working with the East Punjab Liaison Agency. The Joint Rehabilitation Board laid down policies with regard to the reception and rehabilitation of refugees.

The entire provincial machinery was engaged in the task of evacuation, relief, and rehabilitation. The Indian Boundary Force had failed to tackle the situation effectively. Hence, it was disbanded on the midnight of 31 August and the task of maintaining peace was taken over by India and Pakistan. At the beginning of September, casualities were very high. According to Governor Mudie, the number of refugees crossing the border daily was between 100,000 and 150,000. He blamed the Sikhs for the mass migration.[47] It was estimated that nearly 21 lakh Muslim refugees had moved to West Punjab since 1 August 1947 and during the same period 20 lakh non-Muslims had left for East Punjab.[48] About 673 refugee trains ran between 27 August and 6 November 1947 transporting 23 lakh refugees inside India and across the border. Of these 1,362,000 were non-Muslims and 939,000 were Muslim.[49] Huge foot convoys, each consisting 30,000 to 40,000 people were organized by the Military Evacuation Organization (MEO) and the Liaison Agency to move the bulk of the rural population, especially those who were still in possession of their bullock carts and cattle. East Punjab set up 21 refugee camps[50] in different districts of the province. A number of such camps were also set up in West Punjab. The refugees were to first report at the transit camps at the entry points like Fazilka, Ferozepur, Khem Karan, Atari, Amritsar, and Dera Baba Nanak from where they were to proceed to the areas allotted to them under the central plan. The number of refugees in the camps had risen to more than 7.25 lakh in November 1947. The Government of India set up

47. Hansen, op. cit., p. 167.
48. Rai, op. cit., p. 78.
49. Ritu Menon and Kamla Bhasin, 'Recovery, Rupture, Resistance: The Indian State and the Abduction of Women during Partition', in *Inventing Boundaries: Gender, Politics and the Partition of India*, ed. Mushirul Hasan, New Delhi, 2000, p. 211.
50. Rai, op. cit., p. 79.

a big refugee camp at Kurukshetra, which could accommodate more than 2 lakh refugees. A separate rescue home for women was set up in Jalandhar, with accommodation for 800–900 women.[51]

Abduction of women and children was the worst feature of the Partition violence. To counter this grim situation, both the governments realized the urgency of recovering the abducted women. After a joint tour of the affected areas by the prime ministers of India and Pakistan on 3 September 1947, it was declared that forced marriages and conversions would not be recognized. Mahatma Gandhi exhorted the government to stake their all on the rescue of abducted women. Considering the urgency of the task, a base camp was to be set up at Lahore for the recovered non-Muslim women and at Jalandhar for the recovered Muslim women.[52]

The recovery of these women was a long and difficult process. They fell into two categories. First, those who did not object to being evacuated were placed in the indisputable group. Second, some women found it difficult to leave their new surroundings where they had rooted themselves. The fear of a second dislocation and their non-acceptance by their Hindu families was a major problem. Gandhi and Nehru repeatedly appealed to Hindus to accept their sisters and daughters back. The Ministry of Relief and Rehabilitation issued a pamphlet quoting Manu to suggest that a woman who had sex with a man other than her husband became purified after three menstrual cycles and could then be taken back.[53] The other problem posed by these abducted women were the children born of their union with men of the other community. It was suggested that such children should be treated as 'war babies' and should be left behind in the country in which they were born. Older children were meant to stay with their natural father and unborn children would clearly have to be aborted. The abortion or *safaya* (cleansing) was taken up by the state, and specific hospitals were set up (Damyanti Sehgal, a social worker, names Kapur Hospital in Delhi). This hospital made vast amounts of money by conducting such cleansing operations. The

51. Ibid., p. 80.
52. Ibid., p. 81.
53. Mushirul Hasan (ed.), *Inventing Boundaries*, pp. 196–7.

project was financed out of a special budget allocated by the state at a time when abortion was not legal in India.[54] Besides, there were some cases of disputed women, which were brought before the Tribunal; in case of further differences, the matter was referred to high ranking officers in India and Pakistan for the recovery of women. The Government of Punjab appointed S.S. Madan as the Legal Adviser to the East Punjab Liaison Agency in Lahore to fight the cases of abducted women before the Tribunal set up for this purpose.[55]

The Indo–Pakistan Agreement laid down the responsibility of searching for abducted women. In order to prepare a list of abducted women and converts, the Central Recovery Office (CRO) on either side compiled the claims of relatives who had crossed the border. But no authentic list could be prepared. Around ten years after the Partition, in 1957, the search for women had almost petered out. At that time, a total of 35,863 women had been recovered from both India and Pakistan out of an estimated 45,000.[56]

Those abducted women who were childless were fearful whether they would be accepted in their old homes or not. Rajinder Singh Bedi's story 'Lajwanti' depicts the abduction and exchange of women in the Hindu community in the period immediately after Independence. The story begins: 'After the bloodbath of the Partition, the wounded, whose number was legion, wiped the blood from their bodies and, rising to their feet, turned their attention to those who though looking unharmed had their hearts full of anguish.'[57] Refugees were being settled. A movement to recover abducted women and to restore them to their homes now began. The orthodox were strongly opposed to reinstating these abducted women, and many of the less orthodox too could not bring themselves to take back wives and daughters who had been defiled by men of the other community. A committee was set up to campaign against such ideas and to create an atmosphere in which such abducted women would be received with

54. Ibid.
55. Rai, op. cit., p. 82.
56. Hansen, op. cit., p. 179.
57. Rajinder Singh Bedi, *Selected Short Stories*, tr. Jai Ratan, New Delhi, 1989, p. 51.

love and dignity by their families. Babu Sunder Lal was the secretary of this committee. His own wife had been abducted. He led the procession to mobilize support and worked day and night for its success.

Sunder Lal had never been a model husband. He had treated his own wife Lajwanti very harshly and had always kept strict eye on her. Lajwanti was a country girl. She was delicate and slender like a branch of the mulberry tree. But her slimness was not because of ill health but because of her inherent strength. She could easily carry heavy loads without a scowl on her face. But Sunder Lal was a quick-tempered man, who often lost his temper and quite often beat her. She on her part did not regard such ill treatment by her husband as anything very unusual. Like other village girls, she knew that all husbands beat their wives and if any woman rebelled against it, the girls themselves would say, 'What sort of man is it who can't keep his women under control?'[58]

The beating of women was mentioned in the folk songs of rural areas. Sometimes Lajwanti herself sang:

No city boy for me,
He wears heavy boots
And I have such a slender waist![59]

But she caught sight of a city boy and ended up marrying him. The city boy was Sunder Lal. Lajwanti had become used to his beatings. Even after the most violent quarrel, Sunder Lal had only to smile once and she would be unable to restrain her laughter, would run to him, and fling her arms around his neck and say, 'If you hit me again I won't speak to you.'[60] It was obvious that she no longer gave a thought to a beating by Sunder Lal.

One day, Lal Chand told Sunder Lal that he had seen Lajo Bhabi at the Wagah border. He had identified her because of a tattoo mark on her chin and another on her cheek. He said, 'She came in exchange of abducted women between India and Pakistan.'

58. Russell, *The Pursuit of Urdu Literature*, p. 218.
59. Bedi, op. cit., p. 52.
60. Russell, op. cit., p. 218.

It was a fair exchange, right on the Wagah border. Pakistan and India counted out sixteen abducted women each. But there was a rumpus. The Indian volunteer complained that the women being handed over to India were middle aged and old. Then one of the Pakistani volunteers pushed Lajo forward. 'Call her old, do you?' he asked. 'Have a look at her. Are any of the women you have passed on to us comparable to her?

After a day, Lajo was brought back, dressed in Muslim clothes, afraid and trembling in case Sunder Lal refused to take her back. But the slogan of his movement was 'Dil Mein Basao', give them a place in your hearts. Sunder Lal had said to himself, 'Only let Lajo come back. I will really and truly make a home for her in my heart.'[61]

Now he no longer called her Lajo but addressed her as *devi*, a standard Hindu form of respectful address. He resolved never to ask her about her experiences when she had been abducted. All he ever asked her was: 'Who was it?' Lajwanti lowered her eyes and replied, 'Jumman', 'Did he treat you well?'

'Yes.'

'He did not beat you?'

Lajwanti laid her head on Sunder Lal's chest and said, 'No.' Then she said, 'He didn't beat me, but I was more afraid of him than I was of you. Even when you beat me I was never afraid of you. . . . You won't beat me anymore?'

'No, *devi*, I won't beat you anymore.'

But Lajwanti didn't want to be his *devi*. She wanted to be his wife, just as she had been before.

The story ends: 'Sunder Lal has given her shelter under his roof but had he accepted her? She was living and yet rootless. Sunder Lal had neither eyes to see her tears nor ears to hear her sighs.'[62]

Bedi's primary intention in the story is to highlight the plight of women in a society in which men are obsessed by preserving or saving their own honour and where women's deepest feelings and needs are considered irrelevant. He also shows the complexity of people's emotions. On one side, Sunder Lal opposes traditional attitudes and,

61. Ibid.

62. Bedi, op. cit., p. 6.

on the other, he does not understand Lajwanti's pain. Bedi presents heart-rendering events during the Partition, especially the hair-raising episode of abduction and exchange of women like commodities.

The recovery of abducted women presented many difficulties:

1. They frequently changed hands from one man to another. So no up to date information about their whereabouts could be recorded.
2. Many abducted women were sent to Pakistan-occupied Kashmir or to some other tribal areas or to closed districts, which did not allow the entry of Indian officers.
3. Some were abducted by influential Pathans, for example, a *pir* was stated to have 30 girls in his possession, an MLA was said to have 115 with him, a former Registrar controlled 70, and another MLA had in his possession nearly 800 non-Muslim abducted girls.
4. Many girls were reported as having being killed in riots. Sometimes Pakistan police officers were the culprits. While Pathans sold the abducted non-Muslim girls for Rs. 10 or Rs. 20, they kept quiet. Some girls fell victim to their lust in the camps.
5. The foremost problem was psychological, which is shown by Bedi in his story 'Lajwanti'. Many of these women married to abductors and adjusted to their new life. Many became pregnant during the evacuation. They were apprehensive about being accepted back by their families and communities. So when they were forced to evacuate, a number of them escaped from the transit camps and plunged into the darkness.[63]

The Partition atrocities were not limited to women alone but also affected men. Men were castrated and their genitals were cut-off, just as women's breasts were removed. This act revealed the conscious desire to destroy the hated enemy by eliminating the means of its reproduction and the nurturing of its infants.[64]

Many children were killed or were left behind by fleeing relatives or were orphaned. Others were abducted along with their mothers. Such children were handed over to the claimants. But some children were born during the period of the abduction of their mothers. In

63. Rai, op. cit., pp. 82-5.
64. Kakar, op. cit., p. 37.

such cases, the first preference for the future custody of the child was given to the father and if he were unwilling to care for the child, then the child was given to abductor.[65]

The Partition left a deep wound on people's minds, bodies and souls. Incidents of retaliation were common particularly in the case of train attacks. Whenever a 'ghost train' laden with corpses arrived on one side, the other side would immediately send a train with dead bodies back. According to a British officer, the murder, brutality, looting, ill treatment of women and small children in evacuee trains exceeded even the atrocities committed in Belsen and other cruelties created by the warped Nazi mind.[66]

The uprooting of people from their motherland could never be easy. The idea of Pakistan was a thrilling one, but the implementation of the Partition plan was destructive and genocidal. Governor Jenkins said, 'it would be difficult enough to Partition within six weeks a country of 30 million which has been governed as a unit for 98 years even if all concerned were friendly and anxious to make progress'.[67]

In Mewat, riots occurred between the dominant landholding community of Hindu Jats and the cultivating community of Muslim Meos, which raged from May 1947 and reached a climax in October–November 1947. Some of the worst outrages against the Meos occurred in the states of Alwar and Bharatpur. On 17 November, a column of 80,000 Meos was said to be on its way to Pakistan, but two days later they returned, having decided that the risks in Indian Mewat were smaller than those involved in trying to reach and settle down in Pakistan.[68]

Such cruel and wicked happenings moved the writers. The progressive writers described these black deeds vividly and movingly. The departure of people from their motherland was very painful. Chughtai's story, 'Roots' depicted the pains and sorrows faced by people who were uprooted from their land. The story begins:

65. Rai, op. cit., p. 86.
66. Hansen, op. cit., p. 168.
67. Ibid., p. 139.
68. Pandey, op. cit., p. 39.

Everyone's face was ashen. No food was cooked. It was the sixth day the children had been out of school and at home. . . . The same old scuffles, wallops, wrestling, and somersaults, as if 15 August had never come. The fools did not realize that the British were gone, leaving behind as they departed a deep wound that would not be healed for years to come. The surgery on Hindustan has been performed with crippled hands and blunt scalpels so that thousands of arteries have been slit, a river of blood is flowing, and no one has any stamina left to stitch the wounds up.[69]

Everywhere the atmosphere was gloomy and tense. Muslims felt that they were under house arrest. After having lived together for centuries, no one could identify them as Hindus or Muslims. Chughtai portrayed the relationship of the family of Roop Chand and her own, which had lasted for three generations. Though they supported different political parties, their friendship and love remained unchanged.

Abba and Roop Chandji, who had retired from the hospital, were good friends. Now his practice was limited to treating Chughtai's family. When anyone sneezed, he or she was dispatched to Doctor Sahib or Doctor Sahib himself reached their house without delay. The fun would start when Amma did not feel well. She would tremble fearfully.

'No, no, I am not going to be treated by that joker,' she would say. But who would ignore the doctor at home? So the moment the doctor heard Amma was ill, he came running. 'Well, if you are going to eat all the *pulao* and *zarda* by yourself you will get sick,' he teased her.

'You think everyone is as greedy as you are!' she grumbled. 'I say the illness is just an excuse. Bhabi, why don't you just send for me! I shall come. Why do you carry on this charade?'[70] His eyes twinkled mischievously. Cursing him, Amma would pull her hand away and Abba would smile.

Beyond this medical transactions Abba and Roop Chand Chacha helped each other in dealing with family problems. But ever since 15 August, when the tricolour had been hung at Doctor Sahib's house

69. Ismat Chughtai, 'Roots', tr. and ed. Muhmmad Umar Menon, in *An Epic Unwritten*, New Delhi, 1998, p. 189.

70. Ibid., p. 193.

and the Muslim League flag had gone up at the Chughtai's house, a chasm had appeared. From that day Ammaji lost her voice. She gazed with sorrow at the frightful depth of this chasm and trembled. When after having lost everything to looters, Bari Bahu's parents arrived with much difficulty from Bahawalpur and when Nirmala's in-laws came from Lyallpur nearly half dead, the chasm widened. Without discussing the matter, Bari Bhabi began packing her luggage.

'Don't touch my trunk,' Amma finally spoke. Everyone was dumbstruck.

'You won't go,' Bare Bhai asked tartly.

'My goodness, may I be cursed! Why should I go to die among the Sindhi women? Those wretches flapping their wide pyjamas as they run about!'

'So go to Sanjhle in Dhaka.'

'Then go to Rawalpindi, to Farida's,' Khala said. 'May God forgive me! May God save everyone from the Punjabis. It is the language of hell they speak.' Her tongue loosened.

'What is this childish talk?' The leader of the National Guard spoke irately. 'No one is making any sense. Do you want us to stay here and be killed?'[71]

'You people go. There is no reason for me to go. These are my last days,' Amma said.

'Amma is senile. Her wits aren't about her at this age,' Manjhle Bhai whispered into his brother's ear.

'What does she know about the cruelty that is being inflicted on innocent people?'

If Amma had a sharp tongue she would have said, 'Where is that country that was ours, whose soil gave us birth, the soil in which we rolled about and grew up? If it is not our country, then how can a place where you live for four days become our country? . . . Is it a country or a pair of shoes which if they are a little tight are discarded in favour of another pair?'[72]

But when her sons, daughters, son-in-law, daughter-in-law, and grandchildren began boarding the lorries, Amma's heart broke into a

71. Ibid., pp. 196–7.

72. Ibid., p. 198.

million pieces. Her tearful eyes gazed at the lorries and her house. After the departure of her family, she looked into each room, remembering all the signs of life. The corner where tens of umbilical cords were buried. Ten souls had taken the first breath of life here. At night there was silence all over. Roop Chand's wife brought a food tray but it remained untouched. Who knows how many distressing thoughts, finding her alone, fell upon her all night long? Trains were being attacked, and passengers cut down. The crop that she had irrigated with her blood for fifty years had gone into exile in search of new fields. All night she confronted images of the lacerated, wounded bodies of her grown-up daughters and other family members until sleep overtook her.

When she opened her eyes, she realized there was a familiar touch upon her pulse.

'Arey, Bhabi, I will come if you send for me. Why do you have to undertake the charade?, Roop Chandji was speaking behind the curtain.'

'And Bhabi today I must have my fee. Look, I have brought your good-for-nothing sons all the way from the colony junction. They were running away, the scoundrels.'[73]

The aged lips fluttered with renewed life. She sat up. For a moment, there was silence. Then two red hot gems rolled down and fell on Roop Chandji's wrinkled hands.

In her story 'Roots' Chughtai portrayed the pains and sorrows of people's departure from their roots in a very realistic manner. She also described the bond between Muslim and Hindu families, which remained unbroken after a temporary rupture. Chughtai was an optimist seeking to unite Hindus and Muslims as they had lived for centuries.

There is a dearth of material on the victimization of women during the Partition, but literature fulfils this gap to some extent. Hindi writers have contributed little on this issue, but Urdu, Punjabi, and Bengali literature have enriched the history of the events of 1947 and after. A wide range of topics and problems pertaining to the Partition and its aftermath that were uncovered so far have been covered in and through literature.

73. Ibid., p. 202.

Progressive writers revealed the pains and sorrows of dejected and rejected women. They wrote with great sensitivity. Mushirul Hasan argues that the official records do not reflect the pain and agony, fear and anxiety, dismay and disillusionment of the people, but this is something that literary writings do most eloquently.[74]

It is impossible to make an accurate estimate of the total loss of life or the extent of damage to property and the number of women who suffered. The fact-finding organization examined nearly 15,000 witnesses, who bore testimony to the murder of 50,000 non-Muslims. This is only a small part of the total devastation caused. Thousands of villages were not included in the collected data. Out of a total 19,914 villages in West Punjab, only 2,094 were covered by the evidence collected by the fact-finding organization.[75] The people of many villages were converted to Islam, so they were also not included in the official figures. Communal riots, refugees, and their miseries, their rehabilitation, conversion, rape and abduction, the recovering of Hindu women and the rehabilitation, the psychological suffering of individuals and families cannot be fully understood without the help of literature. The portrayal of Partition in literature reveals the physical suffering and the psychological pain experienced by the people.

74. Mushirul Hasan and M. Asaduddin (eds.), *India Partitioned: The Other Face of Freedom*, vol. II, New Delhi, 1995, p. 9.
75. Gopal Das Khosla, *Stern Reckoning: A Survey of the Events Leading up to and Following the Partition*, New Delhi, 1999, p. 298.

9

Evaluation

History and literature both endeavour to reflect the truth. In history, however, conclusions drawn from facts are not accorded any finality. In the light of new facts, the truth of history may be modified or changed altogether. Thus, the question of truth is more open in the case of history. Any new piece of information—be it in literature or in any other source—can reorient our understanding of the past. Contrary to the widely held assumption of its innocence, literature is a vital instrument for the insertion of individuals into the perpetual and symbolic forms of dominant ideology formation, although this function is accomplished with a seeming naturalness, spontaneity, and immediacy, which is not possible in any other ideological practice.[1] Literature created under the PWM provided new vistas to our social history. Progressive ideas were spreading throughout the world. These were influenced by a varied ideologies. The period between the First World War and the beginning of the Second World War offered the safest possible contrast to the serenity and complacency of the Victorian era. The end of the First World War witnessed the preliminary tremors of the economic depression. Hitler's attempt to create a new European order in which Germany, not England, would dominate, brought about a resurgence of English patriotism.

The impact of Marxian ideas on young minds was also an important stimulus. It gave young people a clearer perception of the potential for change in the present situation and enabled them to envisage a definite programme for building a new society. The continuous exploitation of workers by capitalists aroused dissatisfaction among

1. Mushirul Hasan and M. Asaduddin (eds.), *Image and Representation: Stories of Muslim Lives in India*, New Delhi, 2000, p. 1.

them, providing them with a strong basis for organizing trade unions. In India, the emergence of progressive ideas may be dated from the beginning of the twentieth century. Contrary to the worldwide phenomenon of progress in the political arena, in India the movement associated itself with gender issues and social justice. The progressive writers were influenced by Marx, even if Marx had not explicitly discussed gender issues. The PWM, in contrast to the world outside, concentrated on these social and allied issues. From the beginning of the twentieth century, several women activists like Rameshwari Nehru, editor of *Stree Darpan* (1909), focused on gender problems. Munshi Premchand highlighted many grass-roots realities faced by women in their day-to-day life. This group of socially conscious writers did not borrow this ideology of progressivism in literature from any outside source; their progressivism grew out of their own experiences as participants in Indian social life. Socialist ideas spread very rapidly; the British realized the gravity of the situation and arrested the people whom they considered suspect under the Kanpur Conspiracy Case and again under the Meerut Conspiracy Case. The literature produced to propagate these ideas was closely related to the common man and his problems.

The PWM adopted pronounced political stance from the very beginning and maintained a deeply humanistic outlook through-out its heyday. In 1932, four young progressive writers, namely Sajjad Zaheer, Rashid Jahan, Ahmad Ali, and Mahmuduzzafar, who were dissatisfied with the mildly reformist approach of the existing trend in literature, brought out an electrifying anthology of ten short stories in Urdu titled *Angare*. These stories were consciously revolutionary, openly ridiculing outmoded religious practices and highlighting the oppressiveness of traditional social institutions and attitudes, especially those relating to women. The establishment of AIPWA in 1936 in Lucknow thanks to the efforts of the radical intellectuals Sajjad Zaheer, Ahmad Ali, Rashid Jahan, and others provided a platform for these writers. The Lucknow manifesto stated, 'We want the new literature of India to make its subject the fundamental problems of our lives.'[2]

2. Keki N. Daruwala, 'The Craft of Manto: Warts and All', *Life and Works of Saadat Hasan Manto*, ed. Alok Bhalla, Shimla, 1997, p. 57.

The PWA influenced poets and writers of most Indian languages, but its impact on Urdu was tremendous. The poets associated with this movement included Faiz Ahmad Faiz, Asrar-ul-Haq Majaz, Ali Sardar Jafri, Jan Nisar Akhtar, Makhdum Mohiuddin, Ahmad Nadim Qasmi, Sahir Ludhianvi, and Kaifi Azmi. Among fiction writers the chief supporters were K.A. Ashraf, Krishan Chander, Saadat Hasan Manto, Rajinder Singh Bedi, Ismat Chughtai, K.A. Abbas, Akhtar Hussain Raipuri, Upendra Nath Ashq, and Aziz Ahmad. Munshi Premchand was among the founding members of PWA. It also enjoyed the patronage and blessings of Hasrat Mohani, Josh Malihabadi, and Raghupati Sahai Firaq. To produce a complete list of the poets and writers who contributed to the growth of the unique literary movement after the Aligarh movement is like trying to count stars. Jawaharlal Nehru, Acharya Narendra Dev, and Maulvi Abdul Haq signed the PWA manifesto.[3] Iqbal expressed his sympathy with the aims of PWA, but he soon passed away, on 20 April 1938. Rabindranath Tagore sent a written message supporting the aims of PWM and expressed his sympathy with the movement. It was a shared belief among all writers that by 'remaining aloof, a writer deprives himself of the experience which comes to him by mingling with a number of people. To know and understand society and to show the path to progress, it is essential that we keep our finger on the pulse of society and listen to the beating of its heart. . . .'[4]

The main aim of the founding members was to win the support of the most prominent writers of the day, including those with the greatest reputation and those whose association with the PWA could be helpful in attracting the support of many others. And they were remarkably successful in this endeavour.

The emergence of PWA was not without controversy. The progressives were called anti-god, anti-religion, anti-morality, and, of course, anti-government. They were also charged with reducing art to mere propaganda and disregarding the accepted norms and traditions of Urdu literature and poetry. The literature created under

3. Ali Jawad Zaidi, *A History of Urdu Literature*, New Delhi, 1993, p. 350.
4. Ralph Russell, *How Not to Write the History of Urdu Literature and Other Essays on Urdu and Islam*, New Delhi, 1999, p. 80.

the impact of PWA was called fabricated and false. Akhtar Ali Tihari, Jafar Ali Khan Asar, Krishan Prashad Kaul, and Rashid Ahmad Siddiqi all formed a joint front against progressivism. But Majnoon Gorakhpuri and Ehtesham Hussain stood in its defence. A.A. Saroor, Mumtaz Hussain, Ibadat Barelvi, Mohammad Ali Siddiqi, Syed Mohamad Aqil, and Sibte Hasan widened the base of literary appreciation through their criticism.[5] The PWA continued to overcome all hurdles until 1947, when it was wound up by the progressives at the Hyderabad session. This was done for three main reasons. First, it was felt that it was not possible to go beyond what they had already gained.[6] Second, the PWA had become a mere platform for propagating communism. Third, the progressive writers had dispersed, some of them turning to the classics and others adopting a romanticist and escapist attitude instead of focusing on the fundamental realities. After having shifted to Bombay in the 1950s and 1960s, the writings of PWA members started showing the strong impact of urban life of metropolitan cities. The PWA was revived, with new writers joining it because its spirit was still alive in spite of the setback it had received.

The major aim of this study is to identify social radicalism in the Urdu progressive literature, of the period from 1930s to the 1950s in three areas: themes, characterization, and craft of writing. Turning to themes, it may be said that progressive literature reflects an unprecedented awareness of concern with, and sensitivity to gender issues and problems. For example, the practice of *purdah* in the Indian subcontinent among both Hindus and Muslims, was one of the themes of PWA writings. Although some high-ranking Muslim women such as Lady Wazir Hasan, Lady Abdul Qadir and Begum Shahnawaz ventured out without *purdah*, the number of such women was limited. The progressive writers considered *purdah* the first obstacle in the progress of women. Dr Rashid Jahan portrayed the helplessness and sorrows of Muslim women in *purdah* in bold and

5. Zaidi, op. cit., pp. 352–3.
6. Sadiq-ur-Rehman Kidwai, 'Taraqui Pasand Tehreek, Manifesto Ki Roshni Mein' (Urdu), in *Taraqui Pasand Adab: Pachas Sala Safar*, ed. Qamar Rais and Ashoor Kazmi, New Delhi, 1987, pp. 110–11.

frank words. She created a sensation in Muslim society. Recalling an incident from her college days, Ismat Chughtai observed, 'A *mullah* whose name was Shahid Ahrarvi launched an attack on the girls' college. He brought out a paper to launch a tirade against the Abdulla family, calling the girls' college a whore-house and demanded that it should be closed down immediately. He also published an obscene caricature of Rashid Apa and other writers.'[7] A *fatwa* was issued against her by the mosque. This shows that a literary appeal by progressive writers to discard *purdah* seemed very radical to the orthodox and conservatives. Although I could not locate any novels dealing with the *purdah* issue directly, the theme was present implicitly in most of the short stories, especially those by progressive women writers such as Rashid Jahan and Ismat Chughtai, who used their pen forcefully while writing on this issue. Both these women writers had themselves discarded *purdah* and wrote many stories dealing with the issue.

The theme of portraying women within the domestic space covers the two phases of their experiences: pre-marital and post-marital. Marriage plays the most crucial role in a woman's domestic life. In her married life, childbirth is an important aspect. The unhygienic conditions in which a woman has to give birth, the taboos and prejudices faced by the expectant woman and the girl child, and the discriminatory behaviour of the family towards a woman who gives birth to a female child as also towards a barren woman were popular themes in literature. These were widely and boldly discussed by progressive writers, who gave voice to these feelings. Dr Rashid Jahan, a doctor by profession, was familiar with the poor health and mental instability of women during their pregnancy. Her stories 'Parde Ke Pichhe', and 'Asaf Jahan ki Bahu', and Rajinder Singh Bedi's 'Grahan', 'Barren' and many other stories, which have been analysed in this study, show the attitude of writers towards gender issues. Saadat Hasan Manto's 'Zubeda' is a powerful depiction of the plight of a childless woman.

The other important theme chosen by the progressive writers relating to women's position in society was the marital code and the oppressive authority of the husband and the in-laws. The suffering of a woman,

7. Sukrita Paul Kumar (ed.), *Ismat: Her Life, Her Times*, New Delhi, 2000, p. 77.

particularly a newly wedded girl, is an old theme in folk literature. The nature and intensity of the suffering and ill-treatment of married women at the hands of the in-laws, the *sas–bahu* relationship, the birth of a girl child, the social norm of a girl's expertise in domestic chores are widely portrayed and critically examined in their works.

Another important aspect of gender injustice suffered by women relates to the state of widowhood. As marriage was a universal phenomenon among all castes of Hindus and Muslims, this situation arose inevitably in many cases because of the incidence of child marriage, hypergamy, and the large age gap between husband and wife. In Punjab and UP, widow remarriage was prevalent among Muslims, Sikhs, and among some castes of Hindus.

While the treatment of the problems relating to premarital and extramarital love shows considerable variation in the attitudes of the progressive writers dealing with these issues, their attitude towards the position and problems of widows was more or less similar. The suffering widow became a victim of poverty and lust, hence many widows preferred remarriage, and the authors dealing with this issue advocated the right of a widow to remarry. In his story 'Man Hi Man', Rajinder Singh Bedi portrayed the situation of a widow who becomes the root cause of suspicion in the marital relationship of Madho and Klarkni. In *Ek Chadar Maili Si*, he portrayed with approval the practice of widow remarriage by having the male protagonist put a chadar on his brother's widow. Saadat Hasan Manto portrayed the cruel attitude of society towards a widow in 'License'. Although it had originated in the patriarchal concern for protecting family honour and property, there was some space for the recognition of the validity of a widow's desire for remarriage.

A woman's sexuality had not received proper attention from social thinkers and creative writers, and it had remained a neglected matter. It was the progressive writers who raised their voices on this issue in a bold way. None of the writers whose works are discovered in this study minced their words when dealing with this theme. The classical and pre-colonial literature in various languages had a strong erotic component, but women's sexuality was seen from a patriarchal viewpoint and was not treated as a normal and legitimate aspect of human desire. In the nineteenth century, the subject was almost totally ignored and had become a taboo. Any representation of sex was considered reprehensible on the ground that it was the symptom of the wicked influence of Western literature. However, sex began to appear in Urdu literature in the beginning of the 1930s.

The confusion of adolescents about sex, the anxiety of a girl of marriageable age and her parents, woman's attitude towards sexuality, emotionally and sexually frustrated women, men's hold over women's sexual desires, prostitutes and widows these were the topics that had never been discussed in literature before. These themes were considered entirely private matters and no one prior to the progressive writers had peeped into this private sphere.

Dozens of stories depicted this theme. No writer discussed this aspect of human life with the courage and sensitivity displayed by the progressive writers. Manto and Ismat Chughtai will remain incomparable for their bold representation of the problems arising as the result of the assertion of human dignity by women who were victims of patriarchy.

The traumatic experiences of women who had suffered bloodshed at the advent of the long-awaited 'freedom', was another important theme. The gruesome reality of Partition, which brought in its trail large-scale massacres and the mass exodus of panic-stricken people, has been vividly portrayed in the writings of the progressive writers. Rapes, abductions, and brutal killings of women were committed all over. Women were killed either by murderers or by their own relatives or sometimes they committed suicide to save their honour. The progressive writers gave a realistic presentation of this traumatic experience of women during the Partition.

Under the impact of this literary movement, literature covered all important aspects of social life. Munshi Premchand was the first story writer to give a new direction to Urdu fiction. With the emergence of the PWA, a wide range of themes appeared in the writings of the progressive writers. They wrote frankly on topics related to women in a patriarchal society.

The progressive writers of the period 1930s–1950s laid the foundation for studies on sex, sexuality, and other crucial issues. The women progressive writers took the lead in portraying gender issues and held up a mirror to society to see its ugly face. They criticized the existing social structure of Indian society. Until now none had dared to highlight social issues with the boldness of the progressive writers. That is why they were sometimes called radicals. Owing to the treatment of social themes from a radical and ostensibly leftist point of view, the literature produced by the progressive writers is often described as 'socialist'. The PWM faced severe criticism at the hands of the orthodox and conservatives because of this perception, but its treatment of some crucially important social themes, particularly those involving discrimination and gender injustice, will always be viewed as valuable.

The progressive writers drew their characters from the lower strata of society, people such as sweepers, the poor, prostitutes, neglected and de-jected women, and widows. These characters were portrayed realistically, without beautification. The progressive writers did not idealize or embellish their characters. Because of its focus on the common man, this movement gained momentum. Simultaneously, it was criticized by conservatives for attacking old established social customs and norms.

The treatment of issues taken up in literature may be palatable or repulsive, it may be suggestive or direct. Most of the progressive writers were not suggestive in their approach, but they presented the issues with bold emphasis. Among these writers Dr Rashid Jahan was suggestive and reformist. Manto's writings, on the other hand, were loud and emphatic. He offered a realistic and lucid exposition of the psychology of the characters whose personalities had been influenced by the adversities of an unjust social order. He explained that there was no equipment for beautification in his parlour. But he was highly sensitive and humanistic in his own way while writing on the Partition or on women who had experienced the ravages of a patriarchal and exploitative social order. While delineating the damaged psychology of women victims and in exploring the centrality of female consciousness, Manto's feminism was present implicitly. On social problems, Bedi's portrayal of women also remained feminist. Ismat Chughtai will be remembered as a pioneer of the feminist movement in India even before it started in the West.

While writing on various social themes, the progressive writers did not neglect the craft of fiction. They maintained a high level of craftsmanship while dealing with varied themes. Manto's stories 'Khol Do', 'Thanda Gosht', 'Kali Salwar', and 'Boo', Rajinder Singh Bedi's

'Kalyani', and 'Lajwanti', Krishan Chander's 'The Peshawar Express' and Ismat Chughtai's 'Lihaf', 'Do Hath', and 'Roots' are perfect examples of their craftsmanship.

After 1936, the Urdu short story branched off into two major streams; sociological stories were the preserve of Rajinder Singh Bedi, Krishan Chander, and Ahmad Nadim Qasmi, and psychological stories dealing with the themes of sex and human psychology were the preserve of Manto, Ismat Chughtai, and Mumtaz Mufti.

Although the PWA was born in 1936 and ended around 1950, its contribution during this short period to Indian literature that focuses on social problems has been most valuable. The new trend initiated by the PWA continued to impress writers even after it had lost its original impetus. Qurratulain Haidar, Mohinder Nath, Shaukat Siddiqi, Joginder Pal, Ehsan Faruqi, Kashmiri Lal Zakir, and many others kept the flame lit after Independence. Although the progressive writers were charged with obscenity and were tried in court for writing on entirely private issues, their impact on society was tremendous. Social thinking was revolutionized. The PWM gave a new direction to the examination of gender issues and widened the sphere of social history. In this changed social milieu, social historians started focusing on crucial aspects by exploring various source materials. This openness is evident in recent studies.

Hence, it would not be incorrect to say that the PWM motivated a number of intellectuals to work for combating gender discrimination and oppression. In this context, Ismat Chughtai's observation is apt. She wrote, 'The Progressive Movement's foundation stone was laid when the first man in the history of mankind groaned under oppression experienced through injustice, the usurpation of his rights, exploitation, inequality and tyranny. As long as there is the possibility of progress on this planet, progressivism will live.'[8] A study of the writings of those who spearheaded the PWM between the 1930s and the 1950s shows clearly that this literary movement had an everlasting impact on social thinking in India. The boldness of the progressive writers in portraying society realistically, in order to make it congenial for a dignified and meaningful life for all especially women, made the PWM a socially radical movement.

8. Kumar, op. cit., p. 129.

Interviews

WITH BHISHM SAHNI, RENOWNED
NOVELIST ON 12.12.1999

Q. Sir, what do you understand by radicalism in Urdu literature?

Ans. Stirring literature is called radical literature, which stirred society in many ways.

Q. In your view which factors were responsible for the origin and organization of the Progressive Writers' Movement?

Ans. When British imperialism accelerated its policy of exploitation of Indians, some intellectuals started thinking and writing against the avarice and exploitation of imperialism. Side by side, they also started thinking and writing about the evils that prevailed in Indian society at that time. The extent of exploitation of the peasantry, the position of women, and village life were pitiable. The intellectuals who were extremists regarding social reforms were called radical or progressive writers.

It [the movement] started with the inception of British exploitation, but it took organized shape in the 1930s. Many writers started writing against the British policy of oppression and exploitation and also about the social evils prevailing in Indian society from the beginning of the twentieth century. After 1930, it grew very fast. Some intellectuals and writers oriented themselves towards socialism and [the fight against] social evils.

Q. Were they influenced by communism or foreign education?

Ans. Yes, there was a tremendous effect of Western education on them. Munshi Premchand translated some works of the English writer, Eliot, into Urdu during the last days of his illness. Munshi Premchand said that he wanted to write a last book regarding the independence or freedom of India, but he passed away in 1936. There were tremendous effects of English education and culture on intellectuals. The world wars also influenced the ideology of these radical writers. Ancient Indian culture for which they had a high esteem also influenced them.

Q. What was the basic ideology of the Progressive Writers' Association regarding our system or culture?

Ans. When Eastern and Western cultures collided, the spark, that arose gave impetus to social radicalism. First of all, these writers wanted to liberate the country from the foreign yoke. Secondly, they dreamt about an independent India, which would be free of political, social, and economic and cultural exploitation and social evils. This independent society would be free from casteism and communalism, in which there would be no child marriage. Women would get a better status and esteem in society. Indian society would be free from every kind of slavery. After getting freedom, Indian society would be free from social and economic evils.

Most of the writers attached to the Progressive Writers' Association were from middle-class families. Naturally, they were influenced by the national and international environment and events.

WITH KASHMIRI LAL ZAKIR,
NOTED WRITER, ON 9 DECEMBER 2002

Q. Sir, the PWA was the outcome of *Angare*. Do you agree with this?

Ans. Yes. *Angare* was the foundation stone of PWM, because the stories in *Angare* challenged the continuing trend in literature. Though I consider Ghalib and Hali as progressives in their own times, they could not start an organized movement. Rashid Jahan, one of the co-writers of *Angare*, challenged the prevalent taboos in Muslim society.

Q. Sir, the PWA emerged as a forceful movement like a storm but ended silently. Why?

Ans. The progressive writers started this movement with some objectives, such as [the desire] to liberate the country from foreign rule, to abolish the zamindari system, to provide equality and justice to all by narrowing the gap between rich and poor and removing poverty, etc. These objectives influenced the common man. Though the movement was started by staunch communists and they were official members of the Communist Party, due to its strong and deep appeal people from all walks of life supported it and the movement gained momentum. After 1947, India got freedom and a new constitution came into existence; the major objectives got fulfilled. The new constitution promised to give equal rights to all men and women, rich and poor. Then there remained no slogan to lead the movement. The movement thus started weakening. But one thing I want to stress upon is that though PWM was weakened after 1947, the trend of progressivism was there. Progressive philosophy and progressive thought have always been inspiring creative writers, progressivism is never dead.

Q. Rajinder Singh Bedi portrayed social issues in a mild tone. What do you say about this?

Ans. Rajinder Singh Bedi was an employee in a post office. He closely realized [*sic*] each aspect of society. But his tone was mild, though his craftsmanship was perfect. He did not openly favour communism. Sometimes the official members of the party, for example, the progressive writers at the initial stage hesitated to call R.S. Bedi, Manto, K.L. Zakir, and Upendra Nath Ashk progressive because they had not become members of that party by paying the required subscription.

Q. How do you see the social aspects in Krishan Chander's writings?

Ans. Krishan Chander was a most prolific writer, the most widely read, and was admired due to his specific romantic flair, but it was his bad luck that he got no significant official recognition and great awards.

Q. How far did the progressive writers succeeded in their goal?

Ans. The progressive writers awakened the masses to a great extent. These writers made people aware of their rights, about injustice towards them, and provoked them to think about the causes of backwardness. They disfavoured useless customs like *purdah* and dowry. They were against foreign rule, which was responsible for the pitiable condition of the masses, and wanted to liberate the country. Ultimately, India got freedom and their dream came true and the new Constitution of India guaranteed to safeguard the rights of the people.

Q. Why was the PWA criticized?

Ans. Actually, the chief critics were anti-leftist because this movement was much under the influence of communism. The critics called them mere propagandists and declared their literature was forged. These critics did not have an organized movement. They themselves were confused.

Q. Sir, why did you write your novel *Karmanwali* more than two decades after Partition?

Ans. Wordsworth said that there were two stages of creative process, the first immediately after the event, and the second long after the event. The first process is an emotional outburst, while in the second the various thoughts, impressions, and effects of the particular event get accumulated in the mind. They are deeply probed in tranquillity. When you sit to write, a more balanced and realistic picture comes to the mind. This is what happened in the case of *Karmanwali*. It depicts some uncovered and untouched aspects of Partition. I was myself a victim of Partition. I wrote some stories like 'Teen Chithde', 'Yeh Khandhar Mere Hain', in 1948. I wrote 'Ek Dari Hui Ladki' several years after Partition. It was about a girl who had [to deal with] the cruel psychological impact of the sexual violence faced by her mother in a refugee camp. The impact went on from one generation to the other.

I agree with [the existence of] the second creative process as mentioned by Wordsworth. This process imparts a more universal and human appeal to a creative piece. The literature so created is more lasting.

Bibliography

PRIMARY SOURCES

1. PUBLIC RECORDS
   - (i) *Home Political, 1934–40*, New Delhi: National Archives of India (NAI).
   - (ii) *Home, Police*, 1932–40, New Delhi: NAI.
   - (iii) *Home, Medical*, New Delhi: NAI.
   - (iv) Records relating to PWA, New Delhi: NAI.
   - (v) Records relating to infanticide, Panchkula: Haryana State Archives (HSA).

2. WORKS OF PROGRESSIVE WRITERS
   1. Sajjad Zaheer
      - (i) *London Ki Ek Raat* (novel), n.p., 1937.
      - (ii) *Naqush-i-Zindan*: A collection of letters written to his wife from jail, n.p., 1942.
      - (iii) *Roshnai*, Delhi: Seema Publishers, 1985.
      - (iv) *Sajjad Zaheer: Roshni Ka Safar*, ed. Naresh Nadim, New Delhi: Saransh Publications, 1994.
   2. Dr Rashid Jahan
      - (i) *Aurat*: A collection of seven dramas, n.p., 1937.
      - (ii) *Shola Jwala*: A collection of short stories, n.p., n.d.
   3. Saadat Hasan Manto
      - (i) *Aatish Pare*, n.p., 1936.
      - (ii) *Manto Ke Afsane*, n.p., 1940.
      - (iii) *Dhuan*, n.p., 1941.
      - (iv) *Syah Hashiye*, n.p., 1948.

      These are all collections of short stories.
   4. Krishan Chander
      - (i) *Anna Data*, n.p., n.d.
      - (ii) *Tilisma-e-Khayal*, n.p., n.d.
      - (iii) *Zindagi Ke Morh Par*, n.p., n.d.
      - (iv) *Tute Huye Tare*, n.p., n.d.

(v) *Shikshat*, n.p., n.d.
(vi) *Dadarpur Ke Bache*, n.p., n.d.
(vii) *Ak Aurat Hajar Diwane*, n.p., n.d.
(viii) *Jab Khet Jage*, n.p., n.d.

5. Ismat Chughtai
(i) *Ziddi, Masooma, Dil Ki Duniya, Ajib Aadmi, Jungli Kabootar* (all novels) and *Bandi* (novelette).
(ii) *Kaliyan, Chotein* (1942), *Ek Bat, Do Hath, Badan Ki Khushbu*. These are all collections of short stories published between 1940 and 1960.

6. Rajinder Singh Bedi
(i) *Dana-o-Dam*, n.p., 1936.
(ii) *Grahan*, n.p., 1942.
(iii) *Kokh Jali*, n.p., 1949.
(iv) *Apne Dukh Mujhe De Do*, n.p., 1965.
(v) *Ek Chadar Maili Si* (novelette), n.p., 1962.

3. Reports
(i) *Census of India, N.W. Provinces of Agra and Oudh, 1901*, vol. XVI, Allahabad.
(ii) *Census of India, Punjab, 1911*, vol. XIV, part II, Lahore.
(iii) *Census of India, United Provinces of Agra and Oudh, 1931*, vol. XVIII, part 1, Allahabad.
(iv) *Census of India, Punjab, 1931*, vol. XVII, part 1, Lahore.
(v) *Confidential, District and Miscellaneous Reports on the Punjab Disturbances*, April 1919, Lahore.
(vi) *Directory of Educational, Scientific, Literary and Cultural Organizations in India*, Calcutta, 1948.
(vii) *A Glossary of the Tribes and Castes of the Punjab and N.W. Frontier Province* compiled by H.A. Rose, vol. 1, 1919, Lahore.

4. Gazetteers and Manuals
(i) *Imperial Gazetteer of India, Punjab*, vol. 1, Calcutta, 1908.
(ii) *District Gazetteer, Amritsar*, vol. XXA, Lahore, 1914.
(iii) *District Gazetteer, Gurgaon*, vol. IVA, Lahore, 1910.
(iv) *District Gazetteer*, Rohtak, vol. IIIA, Lahore, 1914.
(v) *Gazetteer of India, Country and People*, vol. 1 (rpt.), Faridabad, 1973.
(vi) *Gazetteer of India, History and Culture*, vol. 2 (rpt.), Faridabad: Ministry of Education and Social Welfare, 1973.
(vii) *Gazettcer of India*, Ministry of Information and Broadcasting, Faridabad, vol. I, 1964.

(viii) *Land Resettlement Manual for Punjab and Pepsu*, by Trilok Singh, Simla, 1952.

5. UNPUBLISHED THESES
   (i) 'Ismat Chughtai Ke Afsano Ka Fanny Wa Fikri Zaiza', by Renu Behl, Department of Urdu, Panjab University, Chandigarh, 1998.
   (ii) 'Urdu Novel Mein Mutavasit Tabqe Ke Masail', by Farzana Nasim, Deptartment of Urdu, Panjab University, Chandigarh, 1993.

6. INSTITUTIONAL PAPERS
   - Taraqui Pasand Tehreek Papers, Anjuman-i-Taraqui, Delhi
   - Taraqui Pasand Adab, Ghalib Akademi, Delhi
   - Taraqui Pasand Mussanfin, Urdu Ghar, Delhi
   - Communist Party Papers, Ajoy Bhawan, Delhi
   - Contemporary Newspapers, Nehru Mamorial Museum & Library (NMML), New Delhi
   - Works of Progressive Writers, Indian Institute of Advanced Study (IIAS), Simla.

7. JOURNALS, PROCEEDINGS, AND NEWPAPERS

Journals

English:

Annual of Urdu Studies
Alternatives Journal
Bengal, Past and Future
Calcutta Historical Journal
Indian Journal of Gender Studies
Indian Economic and Social History Review
Indian Journal of Social Work
Indian Literature
Journal of South Asian Literature
Modern Asian Studies
Twentieth Century Literature
Secular Perspective

Urdu:

Ismat
Fun Aur Shakhsiat
Guftgoo

Proceedings

Indian History Congress

Newspapers
English:
The Leader
Hindustan Times
The Tribune
Urdu:
Madina
Such
Sidq

SECONDARY SOURCES

BOOKS: ENGLISH

Acton, William, *Prostitution*, London: Macgibon & Kee, 1968.

Agnew, Vijay, *Elite Women in Indian Politics*, New Delhi: Vikas, 1979.

Ahmad, Aziz, *An Intellectual History of Islam in India*, Edinburgh: University Press, 1969.

Anand, Mulk Raj, *Between Tears and Laughter*, Delhi: Sterling, 1992.

Asaduddin, M. (tr.), *Ismat Chughtai: Lifting the Veil: Selected Writings of Ismat Chughtai*, New Delhi: Penguin, 2001.

Bailey, T. Graham, *History of Urdu Literature*, Calcutta: Association Press, 1932.

Ballhatchet, Kenneth, *Race, Sex and Class Under the Raj*, New Delhi: Vikas, 1980.

Banga, Indu and Jaidev (eds.), *Cultural Reorientation in Modern India*, Shimla: Indian Institute of Advanced Study, 1996.

Banu, Shaista Akhtar, *The Development of Urdu Novels and Short Stories*, London: Longman, 1986.

Basu, Aparna and Anup Taneja (eds.), *Breaking Out of Invisibility: Women in Indian History*, New Delhi: Indian Council of Historical Research, 2002.

Bedi, Mohinder Singh, *Protection of Women in Moral Danger*, Udaipur: Himanshu, 1992.

Begum, Nawab Sultan Jahan, *Al Hijab (Why Purdah is Necessary)*, Calcutta: Thacker Spink & Co., 1922.

Bhalla, Alok (ed.), *Life and Works of Saadat Hasan Manto*, Shimla: Indian Institute of Advanced Study, 1997.

Bhat, Yashodhara (ed.), *The Image of Women in Indian Literature, New World Literature Series*, Delhi: B.R. Publishers, 1993.

Bhattacharya, Narendra Nath, *History of Indian Erotic Literature*, New Delhi: Munshiram Manoharlal, 1975.

Blimberg, Rhoda Lois and Leela Dwaraki, *India's Educated Women: Options and Constraints*, Delhi: Hindustan Pub. Corporation, 1980.

Brijbhushan, Jamila, *Muslim Women: In Purdah and Out of It*, New Delhi: Vikas, 1980.

Butalia, Urvashi, *The Other Side of Silence: Voices from the Partition of India*, New Delhi: Viking, 1998.

Caudwell, Christopher, *Illusion and Reality*, New Delhi: People's Publishing House, 1956.

Carr, E.H., *What is History?*, London: Penguin, 1961.

Chakravarti, Renu, *Communists in India's Women's Movement 1940–1950*, New Delhi: People's Publishing House, 1980.

Chakravarti, Uma and Preeti Gill (eds.), *Shadow Lines: Writings on Widowhood*, New Delhi: Kali for Women, 2001.

Chandra, Sudhir (ed.), *Enslaved Daughters: Colonialism, Law and Women's Rights*, New Delhi: Oxford University Press, 1998.

———, *Literature and Colonial Connection*, New Delhi: NMML, 1998.

Chandra, Sudhir, *Social Transformation and the Creative Imagination*, New Delhi: Allied Publishers, 1984.

Chetwynd, Jane and Oonagh Harnett (eds.), *The Sex Role System: Psychological and Sociological Perspectives*, London: Routledge, 1978.

Chowdhry, Prem, *The Veiled Women. Shifting Gender Equations in Rural Haryana, 1880–1990*, New Delhi: Oxford University Press, 1994.

Collins, Harry and Dominique Lapierre, *Feedom at Midnight*, New Delhi: Vikas, 1976.

Craig, David (ed.), *Marxists on Literature: An Anthology*, New Delhi: Penguin, 1986.

Dandvate, Pramila, Ranjana Kumar and Jamila Verghese (eds.), *Widows, Abandoned and Destitute Women in India*, New Delhi: Radiant, 1989.

Das, Manmath, *Partition and Independence of India*, New Delhi: Vision, 1982.

Das, Sisir Kumar, *A History of Indian Literature, 1911–1956: Struggle for Freedom: Triumph and Tragedy*, New Delhi: Sahitya Akademi, 1995.

Davis, Nira Yoval, *Gender and Nation*, London: Sage, 1998.

Desai, A.R., *Social Background of Indian Nationalism*, Bombay: Popular Prakashan, 1975.

Dharmarajan, Geeta (ed.), *Separate Journeys*, Bombay: Indian Book Distributors, 1993.

Divakar, V.D. (ed.), *Social Reform Movement in India: A Historical Perspective*, Bombay: Popular Prakashan, 1991.

Datta, V.N. (ed.), *New Light on the Punjab Disturbances in 1919*, vols. I and II, Shimla: IIAS, 1975.

Engels, Dagmar, *Beyond Purdah? Women in Bengal 1890–1939*, New Delhi: Oxford University Press, 1996.

Engineer, Asghar Ali, *Communalism in India: A Historical and Empirical Study*, Delhi: Vikas, 1995.

———, *Status of Women in Islam*, Delhi: Ajanta, 1987.

Everett, Jana Matson, *Women and Social Change in India*, Delhi: Heritage, 1979.

Faruqi, Shamsher Rahman, *Early Urdu Literary Culture and History*, New Delhi: Oxford University Press, 2000.

Ford, Madox Ford, *The March of Literature*, London: George Allen & Unwin, 1947.

Frechtman, Bernard (tr.), *What is Literature?*, London: Methuen, 1950.

Gathorne, Hardy, *Love, Sex, Marriage and Divorce*, London: Jonathan Cape, 1981.

George, K.M. (ed.), *Modern Indian Literature: An Anthology*, vol. II, New Delhi: Sahitya Akademi, 1993.

Gopal, Madan, *Munshi Premchand: A Literary Biography*, New Delhi: Asia Publishing House, 1964.

Gorekar, N.S., *Glimpses of Urdu Literature*, Bombay: Jaico, 1961.

Gupta, Madan, *Origin and Development of Hindi/Urdu Literature*, New Delhi: Deep & Deep, 1996.

———(tr.), *Saadat Hasan Manto: Selected Stories*, New Delhi: Cosmo, 1997.

Gupta, Manmath Das, *Pragatiwad Ki Rooprekha* (Hindi), Delhi: Atma Ram & Sons, 1952.

Hameed, Syeda and Sughra Mehdi (eds.), *Parwaaz: Urdu Short Stories by Women*, New Delhi: Kali for Women, 1996.

Hamid, Shahid, *Disastrous Twilights: A Personal Record of the Partition of India*, London: Secker & Warburg, 1986.

Hansen, Anders Bjorn, *Partition and Genocide: Manifestation of Violence in Punjab 1937–1947*, New Delhi: India Research Press, 2002.

Harlen, Lindsey and Paul B. Courtright (eds.), *From the Margins of Hindu Marriage: Essays on Gender, Religion and Culture*, New York: Oxford University Press, 1995.

Hasan, Khalid (ed.), *The Unicorn and the Dancing Girls: Poems of Faiz Ahmad Faiz with Original Text*, New Delhi: Allied Publishers, 1988.

———(tr.), *Saadat Hasan Manto: Mottled Dawn: Fifty Sketches and Stories of Partition*, New Delhi: Penguin, 1997.

———(tr.), *Saadat Hasan Manto: Kingdom's End and Other Stories*, Calcutta: Penguin, 1987.

Hasan, Mushirul and M. Asaduddin (eds.), *Image and Representation: Stories of Muslim Lives in India*, New Delhi: Oxford University Press, 2000.

Hasan, Mushirul (ed.), *India Partitioned: The Other Face of Freedom*, New Delhi: Roli Books, 1995.

———(ed.), *India Partitioned: Process, Strategy and Mobilization*, New Delhi: Oxford University Press, 1993.

———(ed.), *Inventing Boundaries: Gender, Politics and the Partition of India*, New Delhi: Oxford University Press, 2000.

Jaidev (ed.), *On Literature*, New Delhi: Allied Publishers, 1990.

Jain, Devaki (ed.), *Indian Women*, New Delhi: Ministry of Information and Broadcasting, 1996.

Jain, Pratibha and Raman Mohan (eds.), *Women Images*, Jaipur: Rawat, 1996.

Jain, S.P., *The Social Structure of Hindu-Muslim Communities*, New Delhi: National Publishing House, 1975.

Jalil, Rakhshanda (tr.), *The Gift of a Cow, by Premchand*, London: George Allen & Unwin, 1968.

———(tr.) *Urdu Stories*, New Delhi: Srishti, 2002.

Jeffery, Patricia, *Frogs in a Well: Indian Women in Purdah*, New Delhi: Manohar, 2000.

Joardar, Biswa Nath, *Prostitution in Historical and Modern Perpectives*, New Delhi: Inter-India, 1984.

Joshi, Varsha, *Polygamy and Purdah: Women and Society Among Rajputs*, New Delhi: Rawat, 1980.

Kakar, Sudhir, *The Colour of Violence*, New Delhi: Viking, 1995.

———(ed.), *Indian Love Stories*, New Delhi: Roli Books, 1999.

Kamal, Daud (tr.) and Khalid Hasan (ed.), *The Unicorn and The Dancing Girls, Poems of Faiz Ahmad Faiz with Original Text*, New Delhi: Allied, 1988.

Kasl, Charlotte Davis, *Women, Sex and Addiction: A Search for Love and Power*, New York: Ticknow & Fields, 1989.

Kaul, R.K. and Jaidev, *Social Awareness in Modern Indian Literature*, Shimla: IIAS, 1993.

Kaul, Suvir (ed.), *The Partitions of Memory: The Afterlife of the Division of India*, New Delhi: Permanent Black, 2001.

Khan, Mazhar-ul-Haq, *Purdah and Polygamy*, New Delhi: Amar, 1982.

Khosla, Gopal Das, *Stern Reckoning: A Survey of the Events Leading up to and Following the Partition*, New Delhi: Oxford University Press, 1999.

Kiernan V.G., *Poems by Faiz Ahmad Faiz*, New Delhi: Oxford University Press, 2000.

Klein, Holger (ed.), *The First World War in Fiction: A Collection of Critical Essays*, London: MacMillan, 1976.

Kumar, Sukrita Paul, *The New Story: A Scrutiny of Modernity in Hindi and Urdu Short Fiction*, Shimla: IIAS, 1990.

———(ed.), *Breakthrough: Modern Hindi and Urdu Short Stories*, Shimla: IIAS, 1993.

———(ed.), *Ismat: Her Life, Her Times*, New Delhi: Katha, 2000.

Legous, Emile, *History of English Literature*, n.p., n.d., 1966.

Lucas, F.C., *Literature and Psychology*, London: Casell, 1951.

Manra, Balraj and Sharad Dutt, *Saadat Hasan Manto: Dastavez*, parts I-II (Hindi), New Delhi: Rajkamal, 1993.

Mathur, Ramesh and Mahendra Kulsreshtha (ed.), *Writings on India's Partition*, Delhi: Simant, 1976.

Mehta, Hansa, *Indian Women*, Delhi: Butala & Co., 1981.

Menon, Muhammad Umar (ed. & tr.), *An Epic Unwritten*, New Delhi: Penguin, 1998.

Menon, Ritu and Kamla Bhasin, *Borders & Boundaries: Women in India's Partition*, New Delhi: Kali for Women, 1998.

Miller, Barbara, *The Endangered Sex: Neglect of Female Children in Rural India*, New Delhi: Oxford University Press, 1997.

Millet, Fred B., *A History of English Literature*, New York: Charles, 1956.

Minault, Gail, *Secluded Scholars: Women's Education and Muslim Social Reform in Colonial India*, New Delhi: Oxford University Press, 1998.

Misra, Shiv Kumar (ed.), *Premchand: Our Contemporary*, New Delhi: National, 1986.

Mohan, Kamlesh, *Militant Nationalism in Punjab 1919-1935*, New Delhi: Manohar, 1985.

———, *Towards Gender History: Images, Roles and Identities*, Delhi, Patiala: Vision Venture, 2003.

Mowry, George E., *The Progressive Movement 1900-1920: Recent Ideas and New Literature*, American Historical Association, n.p., 1958.

Mukherji, Santosh Kumar, *Prostitution in India*, New Delhi: Inter-India, 1986.

Nadim, Naresh (ed.), *Sajjad Zaheer, Roshni Ka Safar* (Hindi), New Delhi: Saransh, 1994.

Nainar, Vahida, *Muslim Women's View on Personal Laws*, Bombay: Women Research and Action Group, 2000.

Nanda, B.R. (ed.), *Indian Women: From Purdah to Modenity*, New Delhi: Vikas, 1976.

Naqvi, Tahira (tr.), *Ismat Chughtai: The Crooked Line*, New Delhi: Kali for Women, 1995.

———(tr.), *Ismat Chughtai: My Friend, My Enemy*, New Delhi: Kali for Women, 2001.

Naqvi, Tahira and Syeda S. Hameed (trs.), *Ismat Chughtai: The Quilt and Other Stories*, New Delhi: Kali for Women, 1990.

Narain, Iqbal and Luther Lutze (eds.), *Literature, Social Consciousness and Polity*, New Delhi: Manohar, 1987.

Narang, Gopi Chand, *Urdu Language and Literature: Critical Perspectives*, New Delhi: Sterling, 1991.

Nopany, Nandini (tr.), *Twenty-Four Stories by Premchand*, New Delhi: Vikas, 1980.

Ong, Walter J., *Fighting for Life: Contest, Sexuality and Consciousness*, London: Carnell, 1981.

Orther, Sherry B. and Harriet Whitehead (eds.), *Sexual Meanings: The Cultural Construction of Gender and Sexuality*, Cambridge: Cambridge University Press, 1984.

Pandey, Geetanjali, *An Intellectual Biography of Premchand*, New Delhi: Manohar, 1989.

Pandey, Gyanendra, *Remembering Partition*, Cambridge: Cambridge Univeristy Press, 2001.

Pandey, Indu Prakash, *Romantic Feminism in Hindi Novels Written by Women*, New Delhi: House of Letters, 1989.

Pannikar, K.N. (ed.), *National and Left Movements in India*, New Delhi: Vikas, 1980.

Pollard, A.R., *Factors in Modern History*, 3rd edn., n.p., 1948.

Priestly, J.B., *Literature and Western Men*, London: Reader's Union, 1962.

Rab, Syed Fazle, *Sociology of Literature: A Study of Urdu Novels*, New Delhi: Commonwealth, 1992.

Raghav, Sulochana Rangeya, *Sociology of Indian Literature: A Sociological Study of Hindi Novels*, Jaipur: Rawat, 1987.

Rai, Alok (tr.), *Nirmala: Premchand*, New Delhi: Oxford University Press, 1999.

Rai, Satya M., *Partition of Punjab: A Study of Its Effects on Politics and Administration, 1947–1956*, New Delhi: Asia Publishing House, 1965.

Ratan, Jai (ed. & tr.), *Modern Urdu Short Stories*, New Delhi: Allied, 1987.

———(tr.), *Krishan Chander: Selected Short Stories*, New Delhi: Sahitya Akademi, 1989.

———(ed. & tr.), *The Best of Manto: A Collection of His Short Stories*, New Delhi: Sterling, 1989.

———(tr.), *Rajinder Singh Bedi: Selected Short Stories*, New Delhi: Sahitya Akademi, 1989.

Raychoudhary, Tapan, *Europe Reconsidered*, New Delhi: Oxford University Press, 1988.

Rickett, Arthur Compton, *A History of English Literature: From Earlier Times to 1916*, Toronto: Thomas Nelson & Sons Ltd., 1958.

Roadarmel, Gordon C. (tr.), *The Gift of a Cow by Premchand*, London: George Allen & Unwin Ltd., 1968.

Rubin, David (tr.), *Premchand: Deliverance and Other Stories*, New Delhi: Penguin, 1988.

———(tr.), *The World of Premchand: Selected Short Stories*, New Delhi: Oxford University Press, 2001.

———(tr.), *Widows, Wives and Other Heroines: Twelve Stories by Premchand*, New Delhi: Oxford University Press, 2000.

Russell, Ralph, *The Pursuit of Urdu Literature: A Select History*, New Delhi: Oxford University Press, 1992.

———, *How Not to Write the History of Urdu Literature and Other Essays on Urdu and Islam*, New Delhi: Oxford University Press, 1999.

———, *Hidden in the Lute: An Anthology of Two Centuries of Urdu Literature*, New Delhi: Viking, 1995.

Sadiq, Mohammad, *A History of Urdu Literature*, New Delhi: Oxford University Press, 1964, 2nd edn., 1984.

Sangari, Kumkum and Uma Chakravarti (eds.), *From Myth to Markets: Essays on Gender*, New Delhi: Manohar, 1999.

Sangari, Kumkum and Sudesh Vaid (eds.), *Recasting Women: Essays in Colonial History*, New Delhi: Kali for Women, 1989.

Sarkar, Susobhan, *Marxian Glimpses of History*, New Delhi: People's Publishing House, 1975.

Saxena, Ram Babu, *A History of Urdu Literature*, Lucknow: Newal Kishore Press, 1952.

Settar, S. and Indira B. Gupta (eds.), *Pangs of Partition: The Human Dimension*, vols. 1–2, New Delhi: Manohar and ICHR, 2002.

Shah, A.M., B.S. Baviskar and E.R. Ramaswamy (eds.), *Social Structure and Change: Women in Indian Society*, vols. 1–2, New Delhi: Sage, 1996.

Shah, Ghanshyam, *Social Movements in India: A Review of Literature*, New Delhi: Sage, 1990.

Sharma, Gobind Narain, *Premchand: Novelist and Thinker*, Delhi: Pragati, 1999.

Singer, Jane, *Androgyny: Towards a New Theory of Sexuality*, London: Routledge, 1973.

Smellie, K.B., *Why We Read History?* London: Paul Elek, 1947.

Smith, Willfred Cantwell, *Modern Islam in India: A Social Analysis*, Lahore: Anarkali, 1943.

Srinivas M.N., *Village, Caste, Gender and Method: Essays in Social Anthropology*, New Delhi: Oxford University Press, 1998.

———(ed.), *Caste: Its Twentieth-Century Avatar*, New Delhi: Viking, 1996.

Suroor, A.A., *Aligarh History of Urdu Literature*, Bombay: Asia Publishing House, 1964.

Tarkunde, V.M., *Radical Humanism: The Philosophy of Freedom and Democracy*, Delhi: Ajanta, 1983.

Thadani, Giti Sakhiyani, *Lesbian Desire in Ancient and Modern India*, London: Casell, 1996.

Tharu, Susie and K. Lalita (eds.), *Women's Writings in India: 600 B.C. to the Present*, New Delhi: Oxford University Press, 1995.

———*Truth Tales: Contemporary Writings by Indian Women*, New Delhi: Kali for Women, 1986.

Uberoi, Patricia (ed.), *Social Reform: Sexuality and the State*, New Delhi: Sage, 1996.

Vanaik, Achin, *Communalism Contested: Religion, Modernity and Secularization*, New Delhi: Vistar, 1997.

Vikram, Nand Kishore, *Urdu Kahanikar: Ismat Chughtai* (Hindi), Delhi: Indraprasth Prakashan, 1996.

Wadhawan, Jagdish Chander (tr.), *Manto Nama: Life of Saadat Hasan Manto*, New Delhi: Lotus, 1998.

Warrior, N.V. Krishna, *Contribution of Writers to Indian Freedom Movement*, Kottayam: Indian Writers Union, 1988.

Weeks, Jeffrey, *Sex, Politics and Society: The Regulation of Sexuality Since 1800*, London: Longman, 1981.

Wellek, Rene and Austin Warren, *Theory of Literature: A Seminal Study of the Nature and Functions of Literature in All Its Contexts*, n.p.: Penguin, 1948.

Zaidi, Ali Jawad, *A History of Urdu Literature*, New Delhi: Sahitya Akademi, 1993.

BOOKS: URDU

Abidi, Khurshid Zehra, *Taraqui Pasand Afsane Mein Aurat Ka Tassavur*, Delhi: J.R. Offset Printers, 1987.

Ahmad, Shakeel, *Urdu Afsane Mein Samaji Masail Ki Akkasi*, Gorakhpur: Offset Press, 1984.

Akhtar, Ansari, *Afadi Adab*, Delhi: Hali Publishing House, 1946.

Alvi, Varis, *Manto, Ek Mutalia*, New Delhi: Vijay, .1998.

Azmi, Khalil-ur-Rehman, *Taraqui Pasand Tehreek*, Aligarh: Education Books House, 1984.

Aziz, Ahmad, *Taraqui Pasand Adab*, Delhi: Chanan Book Depot.

Banu, Shahida, *Dr. Rashid Jahan: Hyat Aur Karname*, Lucknow: Nusrat Publishers, 1990.

Jafri, Ali Sardar, *Taraqui Pasand Tehreek Ki Nisf Sadi*, New Delhi: Educational Publishing House, 1991.

Mittal, Gopal, *Adab Mein Taraqui Pasand: Ak Adabi Tehreek Ya Sajish*, Delhi: National Academy, 1985.

Rais, Qamar and Ashoor Kazmi (eds.), *Taraqui Pasand Adab: Pachas Sala Safar*, New Delhi: Educational Publishing House, 1987.

Sadiq, Mohammad, *Taraqui Pasand Tehreek Aur Urdu Afsane*, New Delhi: Urdu Majis, 1981.

Zakir, K.L., *Karmanwali*, Delhi: Modern Publishing House, 1982.

MAGAZINES AND NEWSPAPERS

1. *Comma*, International Council on Archives, Paris
2. *First National Conference of Sex Workers*, Durbar Mahila Samanwaya Samiti, Calcutta
3. *Tamir-e-Haryana*, Chandigarh
4. *Tribune* (English), Chandigarh
5. *National Herald* (English), Delhi
6. *Indian Express* (English), Chandigarh
7. *Punjab Kesari* (Hindi), Chandigarh

Index